ISBN 978-1-331-98554-9
PIBN 10116307

English
Français
Deutsche
Italiano
Español
Português

www.forgottenbooks.com

Mythology Photography **Fiction**
Fishing Christianity **Art** Cooking
Essays Buddhism Freemasonry
Medicine **Biology** Music **Ancient**
Egypt Evolution Carpentry Physics
Dance Geology **Mathematics** Fitness
Shakespeare **Folklore** Yoga Marketing
Confidence Immortality Biographies
Poetry **Psychology** Witchcraft
Electronics Chemistry History **Law**
Accounting **Philosophy** Anthropology
Alchemy Drama Quantum Mechanics
Atheism Sexual Health **Ancient History**
Entrepreneurship Languages Sport
Paleontology Needlework Islam
Metaphysics Investment Archaeology
Parenting Statistics Criminology
Motivational

THE

IONIAN ISLANDS

IN THE YEAR 1863.

BY

PROFESSOR D. T. ANSTED, M.A., F.R.S.,

ETC., ETC., ETC.

"The isles of Greece!   The isles of Greece!·
Where burning Sappho loved and sung—
Where grew the arts of war and peace."—BYRON.

LONDON:

WM. H. ALLEN & CO., 13, WATERLOO PLACE, S.W.

1863.

LEWIS AND SON, PRINTERS, SWAN BUILDINGS, MOORGATE STREET.

PREFACE.

WHEN it became probable that the islands forming the Septinsular Republic of Ionia after having remained under the protection of the British Crown since the Peace of 1815, were likely soon to become a part of Greece, I felt that it would be interesting, in every way, to visit them before so great a change should take place. The presence of my fellow-countrymen could not fail to render the task of investigation comparatively easy. I should see a country preparing for a peaceful revolution. I should be able to judge in some measure what England had done, how far she had fulfilled the responsible office she had undertaken, and what was the probability of her plans being carried out. I should be able at a turning point in their history to observe and study

the physical geography and geology of the islands
and the customs of the people; and, although a
mere looker on, I might perhaps see as from without, and judge more fairly than those mingled in
the strife how far there was reason for the unpopu-
larity of British government in the National Assembly that had been so long notorious.

The results of my visit will be found in the
following pages. They represent the islands and
people as they are, and as I saw them, and I hope
they will reflect a part of that satisfaction and pleasure I experienced whilst making my observations.

I owe the warmest acknowledgments to all my
numerous and kind friends in all the islands. From
the Lord High Commissioner, the Residents, the
Secretary to the Government, and the other officers
of State, through every rank to the poorest boat-
man, mule driver, policeman, and servant, both from
my fellow-countrymen and from natives of the
islands, I have everywhere met with the most
friendly hospitality, and the most ready attention to
all my wants.

Hospitality is, indeed, now no less than in classical times a sacred duty in these islands, and it is
a duty most conscientiously performed. Where all
have exhibited such kindness, I dare not particu-

larize; but I confess I have been as frequently touched at the evident pain with which the refusal to accept some act of simple kindness has been received as with the expression of satisfaction when some small service has been rendered.

That a people with so many good qualities as these islanders, should possess at the same time a share of the weaknesses and vices so common on the shores of the Levant, is not surprising. But their good qualities exist, and must not be forgotten.

No one who has visited the Ionian Islands can, I think, doubt that a change from the present mode of government to that which will succeed it under a Greek king must involve a period of great trial. The enthusiasm with which union of Greece will be welcomed must soon cool down under the influence of reality, and a very difficult task will then be commenced, that, namely, of adapting the old method under which the people have grown up —always in leading-strings—to any new method consistent with the management of a kingdom under a constitutional government.

That the ultimate result may be satisfactory, that England may see the kingdom of Greece flourish and become great under the Prince who has now been selected to guide her destinies, and that the East may once more possess a powerful, independent, and well-governed Christian kingdom, would be a result worthy of the nineteenth century, remarkable already for the revival and restoration of Italy.

And let not an apparent failure or early troubles discourage those who wish well to Greece. The way to freedom is not smooth and flowery. Freedom loves to dwell on rocky shores and in almost inaccessible haunts; but Greece has already been her home, and she does not easily forget the spots once made sacred by her presence.

IMPINGTON HALL,
    Cambridge, August, 1863.

CONTENTS.

CORFU.

CHAPTER I.

CHAPTER II.

CHAPTER III.

SANTA MAURA.

ITHACA.

CONTENTS.

CEPHALONIA.

CHAPTER X.

CHAPTER XI.

CHAPTER XII.

ZANTE.

CHAPTER XIII.

CHAPTER XIV.

CHAPTER XV.

CHAPTER XVI.

LIST OF ILLUSTRATIONS.

CORFU.

———◆———

                  " I will lead
Thy steps toward my royal father's house
Where all Phæacia's nobles thou shalt see.
There, on the summit of the hill, is built
Our city, with proud bulwarks fenced around,
And laved on both sides by its pleasant port
Of narrow entrance, where our gallant barks
Line all the road, each station'd in her place,
And where, adjoining close the splendid fane
Of Neptune, stands the forum with huge stones
From quarries thither drawn, constructed strong."

                        ODYSS. vi., 308 *et seq.*

CHAPTER I.

A JOURNEY from London to the Ionian Islands, at the
present time, is too easy and matter-of-course an event
to require much description.   For the benefit of those
who may not be accustomed to trips of this kind, or
who are interested in the route, I may mention that,
by travelling day and night, Vienna is reached by
several lines of railway in about three days from
London, and that Trieste is about twenty-two hours
distant from Vienna by ordinary, and fifteen hours by
express trains.   As the latter, in winter, run only

twice a week, and start at a quarter to seven o'clock
in the morning, special arrangement must be made to
take advantage of them.*   The travelling from Vienna
is comfortable; but the contrast is great between the
easy-going style here considered sufficient and the
rapid movements to which English people are accustomed.   Except the occasional express, there are only
two trains daily each way.   Near Vienna, stoppages
occur about every five minutes.   Afterwards, the
intervals are longer, as the country is more thinly
inhabited; but wherever they take place, there is time
enough allowed for anything that may be needed; and
wherever there is a *buffet*, it may safely be taken advantage of.   To those who have not previously travelled
over the road, in the old time, by schnell-post, the rail-
road between Vienna and Trieste is not without interest,
but nothing is seen of the towns.   Occasional views of
the Eastern Alps,—not, of course, of the highest tops
of that mighty chain, but peaks for many months snow-
capped—are fine, and break the monotony of the scenery.
A large part of the road near Trieste is over singular
limestone plains, amongst which almost the only objects
of interest seen by tourists are the vast caverns near
Adelsberg.   To the geologist, the scene is especially
interesting, especially if he has not before become
familiar with great limestone plateaux elsewhere.   The
karst, as the limestone plateau is here called, resembles
some parts of the south of Spain; and the singular,
cold, bluish grey colour of the limestone—the occa-

* At present, Monday and Thursday are the days in Winter, and
Tuesday, Thursday, and Saturday, in Summer.

sional softer rocks—the curious rounded forms, and
the cracked appearance of the mass—the deep, narrow
gorges, always dry, because the water that falls on them
passes rapidly out of sight—these are features which
deserve more than passing notice, and suggest important
lessons.

Among the peculiarities of this great flat, barren,
lofty tract of limestone, the fierce north wind that
rushes over it is by no means one of the smallest, or
the least disagreeable. Travelling southwards from
Vienna, it is only when the train is stopping, or is
exposed sideways by a turn of the road, that the full
force is appreciated. The wind then rushes into the
carriage, through all the crevices, with such force as
to make one doubt whether the windows can be closed.
It roars and blusters so loud that one can scarcely hear
oneself speak; and its dry piercing nature is very soon
appreciated through the thickest wraps. But when it
is necessary to meet this terrible tempest, the traveller
is to be pitied indeed. He must be well provided
with furs, and must use them all to keep life and soul
together; and there seems some reason to fear that
the train must certainly be checked, if not stopped,
should the wind continue. Still, this fearful blast
steadily and incessantly rushes on, for it is the cold
dry air of the north making its way as best it can to
the south to fill up the vacuum formed in the Mediterranean when the warm rays of the sun expand the
air, and tend to lift it to the upper regions of the
atmosphere. The great storm-wind will never cease
to blow across this low pass of the Eastern Alps so

long as Europe and Asia retain their present form and
character, and so long as the countries south of the
Alps are warmer and more pleasant than those to the
north.

Trieste is a bright, lively, bustling town, with excellent hotels, and with a fair amount of shipping in the
offing and port.   It is said to be now decreasing in
importance, though, for many years, it has been rapidly
increasing.   Ancona, the port of the newly-born kingdom of Italy, is beginning to claim its share of Adriatic
traffic; and being already connected by railway with
the principal Italian cities, it will probably increase
with greater rapidity, and at the expense of Trieste.
The continuation of the Italian railway from Ancona
to Otranto will also affect Trieste very seriously; and
as soon as the tunnel under the Mont Cenis is completed, and quick trains are organised on the chief
Italian railroads, there is no reason why the Indian
mail and the great traffic of the East should not find
its way at a much quicker rate than at present to the
southern ports of Italy within a very short distance of
Alexandria.

The streets of Trieste are, for the most part, narrow,
and the houses rather lofty.   The quay is wide and
fine.   All the streets are paved with large flat stones,
well adapted to the peculiar, low, small-wheeled ox-carts,
which are here chiefly used for heavy traffic.   Horses
are not very much used for draught in Trieste, and,
indeed, the extreme care with which it is necessary to
clothe them in winter makes it evident that the sharp
winds from the karst are not at all less felt by the brutes

than by the human race. It would be inconvenient in other ways to replace the ox by the horse, for even the narrowest of the many narrow streets and lanes are generally passable by these ox-carts; and although, occasionally, there is a dead lock, the convenience is great, for the narrowness of the streets ensures shade in summer.

The lower classes of the inhabitants of Trieste are picturesque, and their occupations are not less so. Most of the wares sold are exposed in the open air; and one passes pleasantly from yellow, picturesque crockery, of ancient form and the most primitive style of ornament, to shawls and calicoes that speak of Paisley and Manchester; and so again by curious old Venetian and mediæval goldsmith's work, back to the wooden tools and implements where style is, perhaps, the oldest of all. Everybody screaming, and everybody, apparently, very happy, though doing very little,—the contrast to an English seaport town, even at its busiest time, is exceedingly striking. The common food, too, is peculiar. A variety of beans, of colours and sizes almost incredible, is everywhere exposed, and seems the first necessary of existence; grain, of many sorts, dried herrings and oranges, apples and lemons, figs, dates, olives and potatoes, are all huddled together in the same baskets; close by are combs, knives, buttons, and small haberdashery, then a little very coarse glass, then more handkerchiefs and shawls, and so on in every narrow street and open square throughout the lower part of the town. A little above are detached houses and villas, some very fine, and many of them pic-

turesquely placed, but not pleasant to reach in the
terrible wind that meets one at every turn. Hot sun
and biting wind do their work in Trieste. I noticed
in the "Diavoletto," a local journal of very exceptional
name, but well conducted, a sanitary report of the past
week. Among the various diseases named as the cause
of death, a marked preponderance were those involving,
or resulting from, disorders of the respiratory organs.
Consumption, bronchial attacks, and pleurisy, often
recurred. In the streets, I was struck with the
appearance of a young girl, who had manufactured
for herself an imperfect respirator by a little bit of rag,
not too clean, which she kept hanging out of her mouth.
It is to be hoped that it was more efficacious than it
was ornamental, but it told a tale. I doubt whether
Trieste can be healthy, for many reasons; but, at any
rate, it is certain that the causes of consumption and
pulmonary disorder which are so strongly indicated
there, exist, though in a smaller degree, throughout
the north of Italy, and extend to Tuscany. They are,
also, very decidedly present in the north of Spain. It
is true that we all must die of some disease, and, perhaps, this is better than typhus and malaria fever,
common in many warmer climates on the shores of
the Mediterranean. It is to be hoped that the thin
dry air and constant north wind at Trieste preserve it
from malaria; and, at any rate, there should be no
difficulty about the drainage of the suburbs, for they
slope so steeply that nothing but a free course to the
sea can be needed.

One sees, in Trieste, a considerable admixture of

costumes and physiognomy, although hardly more than might be expected from its position,—with Italy on one side, the Sclave population of Istria and Dalmatia on the other, Germany to the north, and Greece and Turkey not far off. There is much trade between Trieste and Greece, extending to Constantinople and Alexandria, the steamers touching at all the principal ports of the Levant.

There is little tide in the Adriatic, and thus it is easy to construct a length of quay, with occasional moles and jetties, to which steamers of all sizes can, at all times, be moored. Small boats are thus not much needed. It is worth while, however, to put off to some distance from the town, in order to see the glorious panorama there presented. Immediately behind the houses are the villas, on the steep hill-side; above them, the hills continue to rise rapidly to a considerable elevation, and, apparently, without break. As the distance from the shore is increased, still higher hills succeed those near the town; and soon the long and picturesque line of the Alps rises, and occupies a prominent place in the landscape. One after another, the snowy tops are recognised, until they also are lost in the light grey mist which defines the horizon.

The steamer by which I travelled from Trieste to Corfu was more remarkable for its comfortable arrangements than for speed. The number of first-class passengers was very small, and the society not lively, but the *cuisine* was fair, and everything clean and well ordered. Italian was the language almost exclusively spoken, though German was understood. Italian po-

litics, also, were altogether in the ascendant.   One of
the party at table (the doctor) was an Austrian Pole,—
a little, weazen old man, whose chief occupation seemed
to be to lament and maunder, *sotto voce*, in German, on
some matter that had been the subject of conversation
half an hour before.   Long after the two or three persons who remained in the cabin after dinner had left
the table and were amusing themselves with reading,
this poor gentleman would be heard muttering to himself, or addressing one of his companions without the
smallest chance or expectation of being replied to.
The purser who, like the doctor, was out of uniform,
was the chief talker.   The captain appeared generally
in light kid gloves, and was accompanied by his wife
and children.   He was, evidently, far too fine a gentleman to do anything but please himself.

The voyage from Trieste to Corfu direct, without
stopping at Ancona, occupies about forty-eight hours,
but, in bad weather, may take three or four hours
more.   On the present occasion, the weather was perfectly favourable; and I was informed by the purser,
that had we been provided with English coal only, we
should have gained some hours.   But there was nothing
to regret.   Coasting, during the first evening, close to
the eastern shores of the Adriatic, we passed next
morning near several islands, the largest of which,
Lyssa, is an Austrian settlement of about 8,000 Dalmatians, and a war harbour of some little importance.
We also passed in sight of several smaller and unin-
habited islands and rocks.   During the rest of the
second day, there was nothing worthy of notice.   On

the third morning, the high ground of the north of Corfu was visible in the distance, and the grand Acroceraunian cliffs of Albania, rising abruptly from the water in a steep slope, almost amounting to a vertical wall, were seen streaked with snow where they cut the blue sky. Behind them, at intervals, could be seen, from time to time, the far loftier ridges of the Albanian mountains. These were so completely and densely covered with snow that no break, or shadow, was discernible in the flat expanse they presented; and their whiteness contrasted with the thin greyish outline of the nearer and more thinly-clad summits.

Very soon the hills of Corfu become more distinct; the little light-house of Trogonos is shot past; the low hills that separate the great sheet of water behind Butrinto from the open channel, are lost sight of; and, presently, the deep, open bay and sheltered roads of Corfu are seen, graced by several large ships of war and numerous smaller craft, and protected by the little bristling island of Vido, and the loftier citadel and castle close to the town.

The first aspect of Corfu, and most of the views that can afterwards be obtained of the island and of the opposite Albanian coast, are extremely grand. The channel of Corfu is so narrow at the upper or northern extremity, and the ground is so high in that direction, that the appearance of the channel from the middle of the island is that of a bay or inlet of the sea. Towards the south, the island curves round to the south east, and the main land curves to meet it, so that the southern outlet of the channel is also narrowed, though less so

than the north, and thus from some points, the whole
resembles a vast lake. Few islands can be seen except
Vido and the Lazzaretto, and no well supplied river of
the smallest importance breaks the long line of coast.
There is, too, a certain monotony in the general effect
that will be understood by those who are in the habit
of noticing the causes of picturesque beauty, for all the
rocks are of the same material—limestone,—and most
of them are in the same state. Still, that traveller
must be very fastidious in scenery, who would not be
both delighted and surprised at the first sight of Corfu.

The landing at Corfu is not unlike that at Gibraltar.
The same low, narrow, dirty entrance, and total
absence of decent accommodation. The same crowd
of bipeds and quadrupeds, the same mixture of fish
and oranges. There is, however, an apparent difference,
the empty form of a Custom House having to be passed.
This, as far as my experience goes, was not more terrible than the same institution elsewhere; a simple
question and answer settling the whole matter. True
my luggage was not excessive, which may have helped
the transit.

The crowd, seen at the water gate of the city, does
not diminish as we advance further into the great
thoroughfares. We at first pass through a kind of
market, a bazaar always so full of human beings, and
stalls of fruit and vegetables, that it is really difficult
to get on. And if, as is the case, picturesque effect is
produced by an admixture of every conceivable style
of all kinds of objects, natural and artificial, living and
dead, very few places in the world are superior to

Corfu. The narrow streets of this part of the town combine all that is most striking in Gibraltar, Genoa, Algiers, Bologna, Turin and Marseilles. Arcades, under whose shelter all classes meet; gloomy recesses, open, indeed, towards the street, but so black in their own darkness, that the Greek or Jew seated within is as invisible as the spider in its web; houses of rich Greeks, where the rooms are luxuriously furnished, but which can be visited only by entering dirty, shabby doors, and climbing dirtier and shabbier staircases; adjoining houses tumbling down, and not affording shelter enough for an English pig; churches, only differing from stables by bells placed above them; such are among the first things seen. As we proceed, the streets are less crowded, and the houses wider apart and better built, and, at length, we emerge upon a fine terrace or piazza, at one extremity of which, is the handsome residence of the principal dignitary of the place, known only in the island as the " Lord High," but who, in England, is called by his full title of Lord High Commissioner of the Ionian Islands. In the middle of the side opposite the terrace, the citadel is seen, occupying a curious promontory, rising into two lofty cliffs, crowned with forts and a telegraph. From the palace and citadel the views are charming, and exhibit that lake-like character of the channel of Corfu, to which allusion has already been made.

Other parts of the town are regular, and somewhat better built than the streets near the entrance, but as it is often the case elsewhere, in proportion as they are regular and comfortable, in exactly the same proportion do they lose all that is characteristic and interesting as well as beautiful. Strange that the practical and economical styles introduced by the western Europeans, should so invariably oppose and clash with the older architectural forms, whether Gothic or classical. There seems no reason why the house architecture of the eighteenth and nineteenth centuries, should be so ugly, and still less reason, if possible, why the specimens in which most care and money were expended, should be the most hopelessly and incorrigibly bad. It is so, however, and in this little town of Corfu, where there have been no architects, and no idea of taste, the result is more striking than if every effort had been exerted to produce effect. Certainly, no artist could fail to enjoy, and take advantage of the innumerable morsels of combined form, colour, and grouping, presented at every turn in the lower and poorer parts of this mixed Venetian, Greek, and Turkish town.

Of the inhabitants of the town and suburbs, it may be said that they form three very distinct groups. One third consists of Jews, who resemble their brethren elsewhere, but are a superior class with fewer distinguishing marks. Another third is an admixture of Turks, Maltese, Italians, Albanians, Dalmatians, and many other races; all, indeed, of that mongrel class, for which the shores of the Mediterranean have been notorious from time immemorial; these are, as it were, the camp followers of the English garrison. They live largely upon them, and are a pestiferous race that cannot be got rid of. They do no credit to anybody.

Only the remaining third can pretend to be Greeks: but even these are not Greeks of pure descent, being greatly mixed up with the remains of the old Venetians. On the whole, they form a tolerably respectable and not unimportant body. They are intensely national; often without or against apparent reason. But who shall say that national feeling is other than a most admirable and praiseworthy instinct? Or, what Englishman who would scout the idea that by any combination of circumstances he should lose the right of calling himself by that name, can venture to blame the Greek for desiring to be once more a member of the Greek nation, while he supports the claim of the Italian to Italy, and even recognises and honours the poor Pole in his hopeless struggles against the tyrants who would crush out his very name.

The more respectable of the middle classes consist of those Ionians, and others, who are occupied in trading. Of these a large number are English, and a few are Germans, many of whom have been long settled in the island, doing business as merchants and bankers. Most of them are well off, and are naturally well satisfied with the steady and firm hand which has repressed political yearnings, and ensured for the people an amount of material good which would assuredly have been lost to them, had they unfortunately been enabled to throw off the mild protectorate of the Queen of England—that excellent mother in Israel—for the miserable mismanagement and real tyranny of an Otho. Most of them know and feel this, and are ready enough to admit it; but if Greece can be governed steadily

and prudently under a constitutional monarch, it is no
discredit to the Ionians to desire that they may once more
form part of their mother country. It may be, that
as sons who have grown rich and strong under the
guardianship of wise and wealthy strangers, they will
expect and claim a large share of the general government, when united to Greece; but, after all, this is an
affair for themselves and the inhabitants of the main
land; and if both agree, we have no right to complain.
Although, then, only a third of the effective population of the town of Corfu and its suburbs might honestly
desire and be proud of a return to Greece, while another
third should be indifferent, and the rest opposed to
such a change; it is evident that the voices must be
weighed, and not estimated merely by their loudness
and numbers. This is, perhaps, much more difficult
than it may at first seem; and it must not be forgotten
that, although noisy and demonstrative, the town of
Corfu contains only a small part of the Greek population of the island; and Corfu is but one of the islands
of the septinsular republic.

There is a Ghetto, or Jew's quarter, in the town.
It is neither dirtier, nor more noisy, nor more crowded,
than the other narrow streets. Though there is little
remarkable in their personal appearance, the Jews are
easily distinguished by their blue dresses, if not by
their physiognomy. The latter is unusually pleasing.
There are none, or at least I saw none, of those highly
characteristic and almost caricatured features, one sees
in many towns. I am inclined to attribute this not
a little to the fact, that these poor people have not

been so long or so terribly persecuted here as else-where.

A principal employment of the Corfiot Jews seems to be moving furniture and goods, and they act as porters, to the exclusion of furniture vans. Thus, one is constantly liable, in passing along the narrow streets of the town, to meet a procession of good-natured sons of Israel,—one, entirely buried under a huge chest of drawers—another, fantastically covered with a chair—a third, yawning under a bedstead—and a fourth, decorated with pots, pans, glass and crockery.

While the Jews serve as porters, the Istrians and Dalmatians, as well as the Albanians, seem to wander about for the sake of meeting and chatting, and airing their curious cloaks or togas of sheepskin. The wool of these sheepskins is generally turned outside, and is considered to afford such excellent cover for fleas, that I found my friends carefully making a small circuit to avoid a near approximation, and not venturing to pass through the gates where the owners of these cloaks sleep, but rather walking outside them. There is, however, another reason why it is prudent to avoid gloomy thoroughfares, and it is curious as indicating peculiarities, for which Corcyra is celebrated in classical poetry. Fortunately for me, the time of year of my visit was such as to diminish greatly the chance of being devoured by parasites; and I was the less troubled by unsavoury odours, inasmuch as the peculiar wind of Corfu kept me in a state of perpetual catarrh during the whole time of my visit.

The churches of Corfu are not without interest.

The principal church, dedicated to St. Spiridion, contains the relics of that saint enshrined in a chest with a silver case. It is a fine and richly-decorated construction, not very large, but well proportioned and lofty; and the ceiling, which is in compartments, is covered with paintings, tolerably executed, drawn in good perspective, and much adorned with bold gilding. The ceiling is flat, and richly decorated. No Roman Catholic cathedral could be more completely covered with works of pictorial art. The length of the building is divided into three parts, as is usual in Greek churches; but all the people, women as well as men, seemed to have free access to two parts, which are alone seen. The high altar is completely concealed by a screen reaching the ceiling. At the time of my visit a priest was reading from a desk. A large number of other priests were present, all with their hats on, but they were loitering about, and did not seem to take any part in the proceedings, except that every now and then they joined in some response. As soon as the reading was over, they began to amuse themselves, talking apparently on indifferent subjects, either amongst themselves or with their acquaintances. There was no appearance of any sacred character either belonging to them or the building. Some, probably the acolytes, near the entrance to the high altar, were incessantly crossing themselves, in the complicated Greek fashion. Others were simply idling; but the number of those belonging to the priesthood was so large as to form a marked proportion of the congregation.

The relics of the saint are in a little chapel, or

recess, at the further end of the church, at the side of
the altar. The only light in this dark corner was from
a few lamps burning so dimly, that nothing but the
reflection from the silver casing of the shrine could be
perceived. Endeavouring to feel my way round, I
came in contact with the head of some votary, either
male or female, and was obliged to beat a retreat.
The very small space left round the shrine was nearly
filled by two or three worshippers, and the darkness
was too great to make anything out. The shrine was
covered with plates of silver extremely thin, and
beaten out into a very high relief. The body of the
saint is preserved inside, and is said to be embalmed.

Others of the churches, though not so highly ornamented, possess considerable interest, owing to the
pictures they contain. These, like those in the church
of St. Spiridion, are by no means always in Chinese
perspective. Some are really well designed and well
painted. There are generally some small pictures
ranged in frames at a convenient height against the
great screen, and it is amusing to watch the people of
all ages making the round of all these, kissing the pictures as they pass, with more or less reverence. They
hardly seem to cross themselves in doing this, though
many of them go through the complicated formalities
of the Greek crossing so incessantly, while engaged in
their acts of worship, that it is difficult to find an
interval. They do not select any particular part of
the picture, none of them, indeed, kissing the face, but
making for hands, sleeves, body, or feet, indifferently.

The priests in Corfu are easily known by their

dress, the style of which is always the same, though
the material and state of cleanliness differs exceedingly.
There are two classes; the celibates, among whom are
the monastic priests, and from whom the bishops and
archbishops must be selected, and the parochial clergy,
who must be married.   In the event of the latter becoming widowers, they cannot marry again, and are
obliged to enter the monastic orders.   The dress of
all the priests and of the deacons is nearly the same.
It consists of a loose flowing oriental robe, with wide
sleeves, made of some dark-coloured material, but
whether dark brown, dark purple, or dark green, does
not seem to be of much consequence, nor is the material very important.   Cylindrical hats of the same
material, but without rims, are worn in the towns.   .
In the ease of the celibates, or monastic monks, the flat
top of the hat is larger than would fit the cylinder, so
that the effect is rather that of an ordinary hat put on
upside down.   The parish priests, and others who are
married, are known at once by the top of the hat not
projecting beyond the cylinder.   The hat of the archbishop has a veil attached.   The archbishop wears the
same kind of dress as the other priests, but there is a
violet lining to it, and he is also distinguished by a
large gold cross worn on the breast.   All the priests
wear the hair, both of the head and the beard, long,
and many of them have long flowing curls hanging
down behind, resembling those corkscrew curls that it
was the fashion for English ladies to exhibit suspended
at the side of the head some years ago.
     The priests in the town are, on the whole, respect-

able. In the country, they are often so wretchedly provided for, that they scarcely rise above the lowest classes. I was ferried by a priest across the Lake of Calichiopulo, who was so exceedingly filthy and stank so abominably, that it was necessary to get to windward of him, to avoid a positive nuisance. The poor man was endeavouring to earn a few pence in the absence of his friend the ferryman.

The Greek church in the Ionian Islands, derives its highest orders from the Patriarch of Constantinople; and, in this respect, differs from Greece, which, since the recovery of freedom from the Turks, is nearly, if not quite, independent. There is, however, no supremacy acknowledged to the Patriarch, or anything approaching to the claim of papal jurisdiction in any country where the religion of the eastern, or, as they delight to call themselves, the Orthodox Church, flourishes.

The education of the clergy is carried on in their own establishments, and is understood to be very imperfect. The university of Corfu is only for the education of students in medicine and law, and is not numerously attended. Probably, as the method of competitive examinations has recently been introduced, the youth of the islands would have found it necessary to attend more carefully to the acquisition of sound knowledge, if the English rule were likely to be perpetuated.* Many of the professors of the university,

---

* The system of examination adopted has been modelled entirely upon the Cambridge University method. A number of questions are set, and a limited time allowed for each paper. A certain minimum of marks must be obtained in every subject of examination, and unless

and some of the more intelligent islanders, have been
educated in Italy, and others have even proceeded to
Paris.

The University is a large house at the extremity of
the Parade, not ill adapted for the purpose for which
it is required, but altogether without order or arrangement. On the ground floor are some antiquities,
almost entirely collected from the remains of ancient
Corcyra. They include two or three inscriptions of
extreme antiquity; some vases and fragments of pottery, and a few other articles, probably of the second
Greek city, and a large number of miscellaneous antiquities of the later Roman period. Some of the latter
are in good condition, and of interest. There are
sepulchral vases of large size, containing bones, many
amphoræ, and a few large jars, of the kind formerly
buried in the earth for storing corn. There are also
many squares of flooring in a coarse mosaic, representing. the bustard in various attitudes. Besides
these, are terminal stones, and some fragments of
busts and statues. Much more valuable results might
probably be obtained by systematic exploration.

On the upper floor of the university building are
class rooms, a laboratory, and a museum. The latter
is only worth notice as containing the commencement

that minimum is reached, no excellence in other subjects counts.
Spelling and grammar are closely attended to—a matter rather hard
on the Greeks, who rarely trouble themselves about such matters in
in the modern Romaic form of the language. The examination is held
in both the Greek and Italian languages, both being equally essential
in the Islands.

of a local ornithological collection. The other collections are from Paris or Italy, and are both poor and unarranged. The number of students is not large, and rarely exceeds twenty in each faculty.

With the exception of the palace of the Lord High Commissioner, called the Palace of St. Michael and St. George, and the house of the President of the Septinsular Republic immediately adjacent, there are no public buildings in Corfu that can attract attention, or delay the traveller even for a few moments. The palace is large, well contrived, and well placed. It faces the esplanade, looking out upon a small but well-kept garden, planted with palms and other trees, and evergreen shrubs. At the back, is a private garden. From the windows at the back of the palace, there is a superb view of the harbour of the Channel of Corfu, and of the Albanian mountains, on the opposite shore. The elevation of the building is handsome, and it has a neat colonnade in front, with two gates, one on each side. That to the left, connects the palace with the garrison, library and reading rooms, which forms one wing; and to the right, there is a corresponding structure, which forms another wing.

The length of frontage is very considerable. On the ground floor, are the offices of the Senate on one side, and of the Chief Secretary and the Director of Police on the other. There is a very noble hall of entrance, a fine double staircase, and a second upper hall. The reception rooms are large, well proportioned, and handsomely furnished; and the whole does no discredit to the British nation. Two statues, an obelisk, and a quaint little circular temple, serve to adorn the esplanade.

The stranger looks in vain in Corfu for any special industry. A little goldsmiths' work may be seen in some of the shops in the lower town, but it is chiefly the remains of a Venetian craft. Most of the shops are loaded with the most heterogeneous articles; even those in the principal streets and in the esplanade not being free from this odd peculiarity. Old books, old crockery and millinery; mirrors, photographs and soda water; jewellery of the modern kind, canes, hats, umbrellas and night caps. These all elbow each other in the stores, which more resemble what is seen in America than shops in an English town.

In the streets of the lower town, near the landing-place, and in the back streets throughout the town, the shops are for the most part mere stalls, and the greater number of them are confined to the sale of articles of food. At this season of Lent, all kinds of meat, and indeed everything that can in any sense be connected with animal food, is strictly forbidden, not only to the priests, but to the orthodox of all ages and both sexes. Even oil is not permitted, though the olives are allowed to be eaten; and this state of things lasts for the whole of the first and last week of Lent, and on every Wednesday and Friday. I knew an instance in which a poor boy refused bread offered to him, because he did not know that eggs had not been used in making it. The food, therefore, during Lent is adapted to the time. It includes abundance of dried fruit of all kinds; and, among the rest, a peculiar kind of almond paste, made up with sugar, is very common. It is sold in large cakes that can be cut with a knife. It is not unpalatable, and, being very oily, is no doubt nourishing. There is also caviare in large quantities consumed at this time, but this is brought from the Black Sea. I presume it is not animal food. The days that are not kept with such absolute strictness, are still parts of the great fast of Lent, but as far as I could learn, the highly orthodox are chiefly met with among women, and in the lower classes, although the pretence of fasting is kept up in all Greek houses, and no society is invited.

In the villages by the sea, there is a species of *echinus*, or sea-urchin, that seems a great favourite; and oysters are allowed to be eaten except on the strict days; but the supply of crustaceans and molluscs in this part of the Mediterranean is not very large. Cuttle fish (*sepia* and *octopus*) are excellent, but they are not to be had every day, and are regarded as flesh. Among other articles of food, not quite familiar to those coming from England, may be mentioned melon seeds, which are sold in a dried state, and eaten by the children in the streets.

The fishes of the Eastern Mediterranean are not generally very excellent, and the variety is small. Red and grey mullet are, perhaps, the best kinds. A fish like the bream is common, but woolly. Sardines and anchovies are caught, and are delicious. The tunny is abundant, but is not pleasant food. A smaller fish, between the tunny and the mackerel, is better. The john-dory, sole and other flat fish are common enough. Of fish not used as food, the sharks are, perhaps, the most remarkable. They are not very numerous; but, from time to time, very large and fierce individuals make their way to these waters, following, probably, the large ships. On one occasion, a sailor swimming out a short distance from his ship was bitten in half before he could be saved by his companions, who saw the fish coming, and had thrown a rope over, too late for the poor victim to be lifted in time. On another occasion, a woman was washing clothes at the water's edge, and a large shark threw himself so far towards the shore as to be caught between two rocks and retained a prisoner, unable to retreat. Such accounts seem to show that these animals wander, occasionally, out of their natural beat rather than that they are permanent residents on these shores. Whales of considerable size have sometimes come into the waters round the islands of Corfu, and have generally been shoaled and brought to shore. Such events afford a great harvest to the natives of the neighbouring villages, who combine their forces to secure the prey.

The beef and mutton consumed at Corfu in ordinary seasons are the meat of a small kind of ox and a small kind of sheep from Albania. Young lamb and young kid are eaten in the early spring, and are excellent; but the mutton is apt to be tough, and the beef is not first-rate. The Albanian sheep is a pretty animal, with wool almost approaching to hair, and somewhat silky. The ox is not remarkable. Meat sells in the market at the rate of about fivepence per pound; but on the other side of the channel, in Albania, the price is said to be much lower.

The principal suburbs of Corfu are Castrades, to the south, between the town and the peninsula, and near the old city of Corcyra, Manduchio, to the west, and San Rocco between them. Castrades contained, in 1860, upwards of 2,000 persons, including those in the Penitentiary. It is occupied by a very poor and sickly population, exposed to malaria from the un-drained lake of Calichiopulo. Several fragments of the old Greek and Roman city exist in it, built into walls and houses, but they hardly tell any story. One interesting fragment is built into a modern church and forms its western entrance.

Pottery is manufactured in this suburb of a clay obtained from the spot. It is light, but fine, and makes a neat, though not strong, material. The same place has probably been occupied in the same way from time immemorial, and it is curious to compare the modern with the ancient production. Not only are the forms identical, but even the strange waved lines on the necks of the vessels, scratched with a stick as a kind of rough ornamentation, are unchanged. Compare these with the marks made by the Greeks more than two thousand years ago, on similar vases, and you cannot distinguish between them. The total absence of any change in such absolute trifles as the size of the various kinds, the form of the lip and the handle, and the width of the neck; the retention of forms perfect of their kind, and many of them exceedingly elegant, with markings in

the highest degree inartistic and unmeaning; the fact
that all these articles are, and were, made by hand,
but never vary in the slightest degree from one generation to another, is a subject of intense interest to any
one who cares to consider what good taste is, how it
has happened that a people once struck out a few
shapes which have never been surpassed, and how it
is that the descendants of these people retain the
power of reproducing these without the smallest
power of improving them.   Nothing better has since
been done; and, for scores of generations, all that is
left of the intelligence of the old Greek potter is first
to copy and admire, and then to continue to copy, but
forget.   Perhaps, after all, Chinese nature is not so
much unlike human nature elsewhere as we sometimes
fancy, in the incessant repetition, without improvement,
of so many of their inventions.

Manduchio is much larger than Castrades, its population amounting to 4,000.   There is nothing very
noticeable about it, beyond the fact that it looks less
squalid and unhealthy than its neighbour.   It is chiefly
occupied by the lower classes, but among them is a
colony of Parguinotes, the former Christian inhabitants
of Parga, a small territory opposite the island of Paxo,
given up to the Porte after the settlement of the Ionian
Islands under British protection.   The inhabitants of
Parga, bitterly hated by Ali Pasha, the tyrant of Joannina, preferred selling their property, and leaving
their country, to being delivered up to his tender
mercies, and some of them removed to Corfu when
their little province was surrendered, establishing

themselves in a curious wide street of small houses in the middle of Manduchio. There they remain to this day, industrious, hardy, and respectable.

San Rocco is the third principal suburb of Corfu. It contains about 800 inhabitants, and is a very busy, bustling place, both by day and night. It is passed through on going northwards or westwards from the town, and always seems crowded. By day, it is a continual horse and cattle fair,—horses, mules, donkeys, pigs, goats, and other animals, herding in the road, and pushed about by every comer. Here, also, are the blacksmiths; and here, at night, every stall is open, and brilliantly illuminated, for the sale of meats and drinks, and an infinite variety of sundries. The houses begin close to the gates of the town, and extend along two roads, on either side of which numerous sheds and low huts are built. There is a fourth suburb, called Molino a Vento, also tolerably populous. The lunatic asylum is in San Rocco.

The whole population of Corfu, in 1860, was 17,699, of whom 4,453 were foreigners. There had been an increase of about 1,000 souls since the census of 1848. The suburbs during that time had only increased by 300; and Manduchio was the only one that exhibited any marked difference.

The town of Corfu is at present lighted with oil; but gas works are in progress. The streets are generally well paved, and kept in tolerable order; but as I did not see it in a trying season, I cannot tell how far it may be pleasant in rain, or during great heats. There are some large, new, convenient houses in a terrace in the upper part of the town, but, with these exceptions, the decent houses are so mixed up with those of very inferior construction, that it is not easy to discover them. Almost all the larger houses are built so as to be inhabited by several families, one on each floor.

Corfu is indifferently supplied with hotels. There are several inns, about equally good, but the rooms are inconveniently arranged, and the accommodation very deficient. The entrances, also, are miserably poor, shabby, and dirty; and the attendance is indifferent. It is somewhat singular that, in a place so much visited, and visited by persons who require, and would willingly pay for, the comforts and luxuries of home, no one has yet established a good hotel. It is probably too late now, or there would be a good opening for a company.

I found, at Turnock's Royal Hotel, all the comforts that seemed to exist elsewhere, and met with good food, civility, and moderate charges. Carter's, the Hotel de l'Orient and the Hotel de l'Europe, are the names of the others. All seemed to be on about the same scale.

The habits of the English at Corfu are somewhat monotonous; and our countrymen do not mix much with the natives. There is, of necessity, a considerable amount of official and formal division into sets,— the civil and military departments keeping, in some measure, apart. Few of the residents or officers take interest in anything beyond the ordinary occupations of their respective professions.

I observed, on one occasion, an amusement of the common people of rather a curious kind. It took place in a small open space, or piazza, close to the main street, much to the satisfaction of a crowd of men and boys, of various nationalities, and a little to the obstruction of the traffic. It was a hurdle race by dogs. The owner of a dog took his stand, holding his dog at one end of the square, while several men held up cloths, and other obstructions, in a straight line. The dog had been taught, when let loose, to leap madly over all these at a great pace, and so reach the opposite side without escaping a hurdle. There was a fair amount of excitement, but not so much as there would have been in Italy. No doubt, there was also some betting. While I was looking on, the race commenced. The dog, without a false start, cleared the first and second hurdles very cleverly, but refused the third. He was a good deal excited, and probably another time might do better.

Hunts of another kind, called here paper-hunts, are common among the officers of the garrison and their friends. Ladies often join. Some one is selected who is a bold rider; and he goes on a-head, across country, dropping, at intervals, pieces of paper prepared for the occasion. The field then follows; and it becomes a kind of steeple-chase, every one endeavouring to take the leaps and ride over the difficult ground that the leader has marked out. As the whole country is unenclosed, and there are plenty of small difficulties, the sport is often very exciting; but, not unnaturally, the cultivators complain that their crops are injured, and their land cut up, by this wild romp. It is not easy to appreciate this kind of amusement without some knowledge of the country round Corfu.

In the absence of these exciting pursuits, all the *beau monde* of the town are to be seen, every afternoon, performing a pilgrimage on the road from the parade to the little convent at the end of the promontory on which old Corcyra was built. This walk is technically called the walk to the one-gun, because it is said that there was formerly a small battery there, no remains of which now exist. The promontory is very pictu-resque; and the upper road, among the olive trees, past the village of Ascension, is charming and soli-tary. A few romantic lovers may occasionally wander through the groves, and gaze with reflected tenderness on the lake of Calichiopulo, extended at their feet; but of the Corfu polite world, there is seldom anybody to be seen beyond the gateway leading to the grounds of Sir Patrick Colquhoun's pleasant villa. The stranger in Corfu should enter these gates and stroll through the park, which is always open, for there may be seen in it some of the noblest cypresses and one of the most remarkable olive trees of the island. The latter tree is twenty-seven feet in girth, and must be of extreme age. It still, however, bears excellent fruit.

The citadel occupies a rocky promontory, jutting out into the channel of Corfu, and rising into two rather lofty peaks, on one of which is a telegraph and signal station. It is detached from the land by a ditch, and connected by a bridge, which opens into the middle of the east side of the esplanade. An excellent view of the town and suburbs is obtained from the signal-station. The *enceinte* includes the residence of the general in command and of some of the officers, extensive barracks, the military hospital, the ordnance stores, and the powder magazines. The garrison church is also there; and it is a handsome building of white stone, the model of a heathen temple, very classical at any rate, if not exactly adapted to its present use. A great deal of the ramparts of the citadel consists of old work, but the most essential parts have been put in repair.

Opposite the citadel, outside the town on the west side towards the suburb of Manduchio, is another fort of considerable extent, and there are others round the town of greater or less importance. Some are in good condition, but others are so rotten that the firing of a heavy gun from them would shake their foundations. These forts were, most of them, constructed by the Venetians, and are utterly unfit to cope with modern artillery. Large sums have been expended since the English occupation, to put them in repair; but the work seems to have been rather unwisely undertaken, owing to the loose state of the material.

There are a few islands in the bay, enclosed between the high mountain chain of the north of Corfu and the tongue of land terminating with the citadel. Of these, Vido is, beyond comparison, the most important, as it is only a short distance either from the citadel or from another of the principal forts, and entirely protects the harbour both from bad weather and hostile attacks. It is a low island, fortified very strongly, and mounting heavy guns towards the channel, but comparatively open, and commanded by the citadel and fort, towards the land. There is generally smooth water between Vido and the town, and always an open passage both ways. Vido is more remarkable for its military value than for its picturesque beauty. It presents nothing interesting in the latter respect. Little of the enormous outlay that has been expended to strengthen this island can be recognised by the passing traveller, although it has been said that every stone in it has cost a dollar. Almost all the heavy guns and the principal batteries are masked, and except a low tower and a still lower fort, there is nothing to mark the nature of the works. The whole place is casemated. It has been much reduced in extent of late years.

The Lazaretto occupies another island in this bay. The building is large and convenient; but few would desire to avail themselves of its advantages, whatever they may be. Corfu has, in former times, suffered so fearfully from the plague—nearly half the island having been depopulated—that it is not wonderful if the people are still nervously anxious about contagion. The seeds of the pestilence fell into good ground when, by some unhappy accident, they were conveyed to Lefkimo. The island has never recovered its population; and whether it has become permanently unhealthy, owing to any change in the climate, or whether it is due to other causes, certain it is that the people do not increase with due rapidity, and there is a languor and listlessness amongst them which prevents their availing themselves fully of their great natural advantages.

CHAPTER II.

IF we may believe the account of Homer, describing
to us the beautiful country of the Phæacians and the
gardens of Alcinöus, the charms of ancient Corcyra,
the softness of its climate, and its wealth of oil, wine,
corn, pears, figs, pomegranates, apples, and other fruits,
we shall feel, in visiting the Corfu of to-day, that modern civilisation has not even approached the perfection
of former times.   And if, too, we read the accounts of
its inhabitants—their women industriously spinning

and weaving fine cloth—their men working in metals, building ships, trading and manufacturing—we shall be still more disappointed at the contrast now presented to us. It is true that one traffic spoken of by Homer—that in slaves—is no longer a source of profit, and that the want of hospitality and the roughness that then characterised the people has disappeared with their commercial habits, but the habits of luxury and the taste for art, the poetry and the music, the dance and the games, have also disappeared, and no modern Demodocus replaces him who once sung the loves of Mars and Venus, and first gave to his countrymen and the world a taste for dramatic representation.*

The picture of domestic institutions presented by Homer, and supposed to refer especially to the earliest history of Corfu, is well known, but can bear repetition. The queen, or mistress, seated amongst her women, weaves rich crimson cloths, while her daughter, the Nausicaa of poetry, looks after the household affairs, or sees to the washing of the family linen.

ἵνα κλυτὰ ειματ᾽ ἄγωμαι
ἐς ποταμον πλυνεουσα.

And here, as in Greece, the fountains remain little changed—the gnarled olive tree still overhangs the path—the little walls of stone, roughly built up to enable the women to beat the linen without stooping,

* Plutarch speaks of Demodocus of Corcyra as having given the first notions of the drama.—*See* Πλυταρχ ἐν τῳ πιρι μουσικῆς.

are still used for the same purpose—the hanging gardens of Alcinöus are visible from the spring still connected with the name of Cressida—the vine flourishes—the apple and the pear ripen—the fig yields its luscious sweetness, and the pomegranate its delicious juice, but the people have become listless, idle, and bad cultivators—they are little capable of self-government—they distrust each other, and all that belongs to them; and while they yield implicit confidence to the stranger in some matters, they are equally and foolishly inclined to suspect him of interested or political motives whenever he endeavours to introduce improvements into the old, complicated, and badly-working methods to which they are accustomed.

It is impossible to remain in Corfu a short time—it is difficult even to pay the island a cursory visit without one's mind and memory being carried back to those classic days when its history was first written, and to the many important events in the progress of civilisation with which it has been connected. Its excellent and roomy harbour was the rendezvous of some of the largest fleets of ancient times. The great collection of ships that afterwards perished at Syracuse was passed in review here. Not far from here was fought the battle of Actium, and here, long afterwards, were collected the ships that destroyed the Turkish navy off Lepanto. From time to time, this noble and well-sheltered roadstead has seen all varieties of naval construction, from the earliest Phæacian galley to the heaviest modern three-decker, with its screw propeller, its steam power, and its Armstrong guns.

Corfu is the ancient Corcyra, described by Herodotus, alluded to by Homer, described in its high day
of wealth and prosperity by Xenophon, absorbed into
the great Roman Empire about two centuries before
Christ, visited by Nero, seized by the Crusaders, long
in the possession of pirates, and taken under the protection of the Venetians when their republic was in
its prime. It was attacked in vain by the Turks at
the beginning of the last century, when the Ottoman
power made, and failed in, its last great effort at sub-
jugating Europe. It was successively in the hands of
Russians and French, and has now, for half a century,
remained under English care.

The old town of Corcyra did not occupy the site
selected for the modern town, but seems to have been
built on, and near, the eastern shore of the lake Calichiopulo, once an important arm of the sea, though
now a mere swamp. Twenty centuries ago, it seems
to have been used as the principal shelter for small
vessels, and was then called the Hyllaic Harbour; but,
at that time, it was doubtless both deeper and more
healthy than it is now. All the harbours and recesses
of the coast of this part of the Mediterranean are
rapidly silting up, and the effect is very visible in the
diminished salubrity of the islands and adjacent coasts
wherever the process is going on rapidly.*

---

* It has been by no fault, or neglect, of the Lord High Commissioners,
either formerly or lately, that the nuisance of Lake Calichiopulo has
been perpetuated. I am informed, that Sir Frederick Adam took
all necessary measures to drain it, and was on the point of commencing work, when it appeared that the lake was private property,

It has, indeed, been assumed that the land is up-heaved, and that this upheaval has some reference to the numerous slight earthquake undulations with which the islands have been affected; but there is little ground for this assumption, and it is not necessary to have re-course to it to account for the alterations of level observable.

The promontory extends from outside the walls of the modern town of Corfu, towards the south, for a distance of about two miles from the suburb of Cas-trades. The ground rises into a range of hills, whose extreme height is about 250 feet. The slope is chiefly towards the east, the ground falling precipitately to the west, where it presents a low cliff towards the channel. It was on the eastern slopes, and chiefly on the lower ground, that the old city seems to have been built, although there are remains of more than one ancient temple on the brow of the hill overhanging the western cliffs. This projecting land parallel to the coast has formed an arm of the sea and the old " Hyllaic Harbour," of which all that remains is the modern lake of Calichiopulo.

There is no high ground near the neck of this pro-montory, the isthmus which connects it being low and

and could not be touched. Rather than give up a fishery of some small present value, the owners would sacrifice the certainty of a great increase in the value of the property by the recovered lands, and they were quite willing that the health of the town should suffer into the bargain. Certainly, a little wholesome tyranny in such cases would not be misplaced; but Lord High Commissioners have enemies enough when acting strictly within their powers, to permit them to risk illegal interference for the public good.

flat, and used as the race-course. At some pre-historic period, the high ground must have formed an island, for all the land around is low, and nearly level, and has been below the sea. The old town was probably large, but it may have somewhat shifted its position in successive ages, and certainly underwent many changes as time went on,—the fragments of antiquity found in the ground all around, whenever it is turned up, indicating the existence of the various peoples who successively built, modified, or occupied it. Most of the larger remains are naturally those of its more recent masters, the Romans; and after they had left, it would seem that the present town was planted still nearer the present citadel. After this removal, the neglect and destruction of the old town inevitably followed.

The whole of the promontory is interesting, and its position immediately adjacent to the town, traversed by convenient roads, together with its villages, chapels and olive groves, which afford pleasant shelter from the sun, would ensure frequent visits, even if it were not almost the only available easy walk out of the town. It also has the advantage of being in fashion. In no other direction can one find such convenient walking ground for ladies, and it has long been the general resort of all classes, both for walking and driving. Many of the inhabitants rarely get much beyond it. It contains two or three country houses, a village, and some rich and well cultivated gardens. In most parts of it, whenever houses are built, or fields turned up, numerous copper coins, a few silver coins, frag-

ments of squared stones, and other curiosities, belonging to the latest occupants, are found, but not
many of them are perfect enough to possess any value.
A walk to the principal points of view over the olive-
covered hill, which forms the central and terminating
point of this tongue of land, I found sufficient to
remove almost entirely the troublesome sense of new-
ness and town manners that pervades Corfu. After
all, this is merely a thin varnish of modern civilisation,
that will pass away with our rule, and, in a few years
after our departure, there will be no trace of it. On
the hills, there are only two country houses, one (not
generally occupied) belongs to the Lord High Commissioner, and the other to Sir Patrick Colquhoun,
the present Chief Justice of the Islands. These,
though placed so as to command exquisite points of
view, do not at all interfere with the effect of the
natural scenery of the spot.

After passing the second of the country houses, two
or three paths are seen, one of which winds about
among the olive groves, and brings us to the group of
cottages forming the picturesque valley of the Ascension. Passing on, and making one's way to the summit
of the low hills of marl and calcareous sand, a view is
obtained across the Hyllaic Harbour—the modern
Lake Calichiopulo—already alluded to. The Channel
of Corfu is also in sight from one end to the other.
The Citadel, and the Island of Vido, jut out midway
between the two bays, and the lofty spars of the ships
of war indicate the position of the roads. It is impossible to have a more magnificent back ground for

these objects, than that afforded by the mountains of
Albania. They are, indeed, equally grand from every
point of view, and from every principal height, throughout the Island, and they strengthen and extend in all
the landscape. The near views from the village of
Ascension are hardly less charming than those including the opposite mountains.

Immediately below, at our feet, a fine spring bursts
forth, close to the foundations and some of the columns
of an ancient temple of Neptune, which occupied a site
on the cliff midway between the two ancient harbours
and beyond the old town, but looking across the
channel, and not within sight of the Hyllaic Harbour.
From the top, where is an old chapel, the view across
to the ancient harbour is even more beautiful than that
just alluded to, and extends far back into the interior
of Corfu. The worst feature it presents, is the half
swamp-like state of the greater portion of the lake,
which is now reduced to a small, shallow pool; and it
is impossible that this should be other than mischievous,
for, with a summer sun, it must serve as a hot bed for
malaria, and, even in winter and spring, it is not without danger.

The little village of Ascension I found more interesting than the greater part of the modern town of
Corfu. It is almost entirely peopled by families of
Suliots, some of whom settled here when driven from
their hearths and homes by Ali Pasha, the tyrant of
Joannina. They were Christians; and, at one time,
are said to have numbered 4,000 families, who lived in
practical independence in their mountain homes in

Albania. At length, almost destroyed by incessant persecution, they became scattered over the islands of the Ionian group, and a few are comfortably settled in Corfu. Their modest, but picturesque huts, by no means dirty looking, and their peculiar physiognomy and costume, distinguish them from their neighbours. They are an interesting people, and more industrious than the Corfiots.

The main road through the promontory leaves Ascension to the left, and terminates in a bluff marly cliff. At the foot of this, a narrow causeway stretches out into the lake nearly a third of the way across, and at its extremity there is a monastery on the very smallest scale. On a lumpy mass of limestone, near the middle of the opening of the harbour, is another equally small conventual building, picturesquely rising out of the rock, and overtopped by a few cypresses. It is not unlike, either in size or shape, one of the very ancient Greek galleys. It is called the ship of Ulysses; and, we are told, that after landing the hero in the harbour, the Phæacian galley that had conducted him hither, preparing to return, was suddenly arrested by Neptune, who, angry that it had so far contravened his wishes, suddenly converted it into the rock we now see. This legend is alluded to in the thirteenth book of the Odyssey:—

"Swift as the swallow sweeps the liquid way,
The winged pinnace shot along the sea;
The god arrests her with a sudden stroke,
And roots her down an everlasting rock."

Another rock, near the north coast, competes with this

for the honour of being the petrified ship. The visitor
to the pass of Pantaleone, whence the rival is seen, may
exercise his judgment as to the probability of one or
the other having thus originated.

There is a ferry across the lake of Calichiopulo, from
the monastery at the end of the causeway to the other
side, and a beautiful walk through the olive groves
leads on among the hills towards Gasturi, or back
to Corfu past the fountain of Cressida, where there
is a perpetual source of delicious water. The sparkling element here bursts forth from the rock in a full
stream, among a variety of bright green water-plants,
which greatly increase the effect. The water is cool,
and said to be very uniform in quantity and temperature. Tradition points to this as the spot where the
daughter of Alcinöus* and her maidens were appealed
to by Ulysses; and, certainly, there is nothing either
in the position of the fountain or the circumstances of
the narrative to render it improbable, though, on the
other hand, there is certainly a wonderfully small
amount of evidence in favour of the assumption.
The adjoining plains are now covered with olive
trees, or are under cultivation for wine and corn;
but when the lake was a harbour, it is not unlikely
that these fields may have formed part of its bed, and

* The groves on the steep hill-side of the promontory overlooking
the Hyllaic Harbour are considered to represent the ancient hanging-
gardens of Alcinous, whose palace may, in that case, have occupied the
part of the hill beyond the village of Ascension. A charming glade
exists there, in which a house might be built with great advantage but
for the present state of the lake below.

that the harbour approached the fountain much nearer than it does at present. The statement in the Odyssey would seem to point to a more distant fountain than this from the palace at Corcyra.

A range of low hills to the north seems to afford a natural boundary to the ancient harbour; and as the soil up to the foot of these hills is clearly alluvial, it is the more probable that they anciently formed its limit. At present, although the lake is several hundred yards distant, the smallest ditch dug in the soil shows that water is very close to the surface.

It seems strange that the water of the springs of Cressida, which is close at hand and abundant, should not have been made use of rather than that of Benizze to supply Corfu. Doubtless, the fall of the water from the latter place, which is considerable, is a great advantage, but it can hardly counterbalance the expense of conveying a stream through seven or eight miles of closed conduit over a difficult country. It seems, also, that the natural choking up of long pipes by limestone water was not anticipated, though it has already taken place to some extent.

There are not many excursions in Corfu that are within the limits of an easy walk from the town; and except to the promontory and the path towards Cressida's fountain, it is necessary to go, and return, two or three miles over a dull, flat, and uninteresting country, to reach much that is striking. All the roads are, however, carriageable; and the traveller has only to select that excursion which his time will best enable him to complete without inconvenience.

For the convenience of description, I have preferred
giving an account of what I saw in the island, in
separate chapters, one referring to the middle part of
the island, another to the south, and a third to the
north. In the present chapter, I shall confine myself
to the circle of comparatively low, cultivable land, extending around the town, and from the town to the
cliffs in the west, or the hills in the north and south.
In this way, the reader may, if he please, familiarise
himself first with the nearer, and then with the more
distant trips.

In a general way, the island of Corfu may be said
to be divided into three parts:—a northern mountain
district,—a southern tract, much of which is comparatively low but not flat,—and a central district of
broken ground, surrounded by mountains and hills.
The northern and southern districts are connected by
the high ground of the west coast. The northern and
central districts thus belong to each other, and the
southern is distinct. The latter is, in fact, the unhealthy and narrow tail of the island, about fifteen
miles in length, and from two to three miles wide, thinly
peopled, and rarely visited. There is in it some fine
scenery, and a line of cliff, rising into hill, extends on
the west side to Cape Bianca, which terminates the
island, but it nowhere approaches the rest of the island
in variety of outline or in elevation.

Of the northern and central parts, the mountain districts in the north, of which San Salvador is the highest
point, and the mountains of Santa Deca (or rather
Santi Deca—*ten saints*,—to be hereafter alluded to)

and San Mathias in the south, afford distinct points of
interest. The cliffs of the west, with many isolated
but noble hills, terminating in steep and nearly vertical
precipices towards the west, require special notice.
On the whole, the country may be said to slope from
the north, the west, and the south of this principal district, towards a large semi-circular area, forming a half
basin, in the centre of which is the town of Corfu.
This is the part of the island best known, and most
easily visited, being all within convenient distance of
the capital. The vicinity to the town is a great advantage, as notwithstanding the large size, and, especially, the great length of the island, there is, really, no
second town or village to be found within it, in which
a night's lodging and food can be obtained by the
traveller without making previous special arrangements, and obtaining introductions from the police
authorities, or letters from the owners of decent
houses who occasionally visit their country estates.

To obtain an idea of the aspect of the interior of
Corfu and its peculiarities, which are many and very
interesting, the central basin, as I shall call this semi-
circular area, must be crossed in many directions, and
the mountains to the north and south, as well as the
hills and cliffs to the west, must be ascended. This is
neither troublesome nor tedious, and the best plan to
adopt, is to cross the island, first of all, in its narrowest
part, towards Pelleka, which will be described in the
next chapter. This course was suggested to me by
Mr. Lear, an artist, whose accurate and conscientious
pictures of Corfu are well known, and who, fortunately

for me, very kindly undertook to accompany me in my first drive. I am satisfied that the same route may safely be recommended to future visitors.

Leaving Corfu, we soon come in sight of the low, marshy shores of Lake Calichiopulo, and continue to pass through a cultivated plain, till we reach the little hill and village of Alepu. From this point the scenery begins to improve, and we at once enter one of those remarkable and magnificent olive groves, which are the glory and wealth of the Ionian Islands, but more especially of Corfu.

Growing freely and naturally all over Greece, the Greek Islands, and the shores of Asia Minor, cultivated for its fruit, and valuable for the oil obtained from the fruit by the most simple contrivances of crushing and squeezing, the olive is one of those trees which may be regarded as almost essential for the existence of the people in these countries. It abounds in all the Ionian Islands, but the Venetians, in their day, anxious to take full advantage of the profit to be hence derived, long encouraged the planting of olives by a bounty of a sequin for every tree. The Corfiots desired to take the benefit of this chance, and seem to have covered every available part of their island with a young olive tree. The effect is now seen in the wide spread of groves of old trees in every direction. Once planted and grafted, the tree has been left to its own devices, and has availed itself of this perfect liberty.

It is not the custom of the Corfiot to work when he can remain idle, and he has, therefore, left his tree to the accidents of time and weather, and as it is not the fashion in the island to construct hedges or walls, or ditches or any other limits of property, the whole place has become one unbroken olive forest for miles and miles together.

The total absence of pruning and training after once grafting, and the habit of only collecting the fruit when quite ripe, and never gathering it as in Italy, have combined to induce the inhabitants to leave the tree to adapt itself to circumstances; and so far as picturesque beauty is concerned, no lover of fine trees can regret that such a course has been pursued.

The olive tree of Greece and Corfu has a very different growth from the cultivated trees of Italy and Provence. It appears to grow spirally, with a number of small stems interlocking and embracing in a singular manner, and this growth continues indefinitely at all ages of the tree. The trunks thus present a honey-combed and latticed appearance, and attain dimensions almost incredible. I have seen (in the island of Santa Maura) three large trees, each seven or eight feet in girth, all growing within the compass of one living bark, so that the girth of the whole group, which is, to all intents and purposes, a single tree, is nearly forty feet. There is a fine tree in the grounds of Sir Patrick Colquhoun, close to Corfu, which is also, to all appearance, a single individual, whose girth is twenty-seven feet. Not unfrequently, in the complicated trunk of one tree, there will be apertures—not arising from accident, but clearly the result of natural growth—large enough, and open enough, for a boy to

E

climb completely through; and the great majority of
the trees are so deeply furrowed on the outside by the
twisted and contorted condition of the trunk, that they
present, in every part, deep recesses, into which one
might thrust an arm. These, it will be understood,
are not the result of decay.

The trees, thus attaining a most unusual bulk, grow
also to a very great height; and their foliage is very
thick, the branches being long and pendulous, and
exceedingly graceful. Young trees seem to grow
from the roots of the old, and old trees obtain fresh
vigour from the embraces of the young, the whole of
a gigantic tree being, apparently, a family of many
generations rather than the mere development of a
single trunk from one root.

The olive in this part of the world does not fruit
generally more than once in two years, although, on
the coast of Greece, there are trees that fruit annually.
These latter are somewhat different, in their growth
and appearance, from the others, and are not considered to be, on the whole, more profitable. In
Corfu, the tree is rarely touched, even the dead wood
not being removed, nor are the roots ever attended to.
In the other islands, and by careful proprietors in
Corfu, the tree is trimmed every spring; the roots
are laid bare every year, and some slow manure is
dug in with them. The result is very manifest. In
Corfu and Santa Maura, the trees are never pollarded.

The number of trees in a given area in Corfu is not
easily estimated, owing to the extreme irregularity
with which they are planted. As a rough calculation,

I believe about fifty to the acre will not be found very far wrong; and as, perhaps, nearly a hundred square miles of the surface of Corfu may be thus occupied, the total number must exceed a quarter of a million. As there are no statistics of the agriculture and cultivation of the island, and as the properties are so much mixed and so much subdivided as to render it almost impossible that there should ever be any under the existing laws, all calculation of the crop is exceedingly vague. It is certain, however, that only one crop in two years is expected, and that only one good crop out of five (once in ten years) can be calculated on. It is evident, too, that the crop is extremely speculative,—the yield of a tree varying from almost nothing to about five gallons of oil, and occasionally much exceeding that. I was told, in Corfu, that, one year with another and one tree with another for an average of twenty years, a return of oil to the value of sixpence per tree per annum is all that can be calculated on. I am inclined, however, to think that this estimate is greatly below the mark; and, in some of the other islands, it is certainly very greatly exceeded.

The olive suffers from an insect that attacks it occasionally, and entirely destroys the crop. It is also affected by unfavourable seasons, especially by bad weather near the time of ripening, and again when the fruit is falling.

Unlike the custom in France and Italy, where the finest oil is made, the Corfiots allow the fruit to ripen on the tree and fall to the ground, or, when quite ripe, the tree is sometimes beaten. The fruit is small and

pointed; it is of a deep purple colour, and the juice is
also of a deep purple. It is inevitably bruised by
falling. Women and children are employed to lift
the fallen fruit, which they put first into their aprons,
or into bags, and then tumble into baskets. It then
becomes more bruised. When collected, the fruit is
left in heaps till the mill is ready to receive it; and,
during that time, it is subject to heat. The oil is
obtained by grinding the fruit and stone between an
upright cylindrical roller and a horizontal stone table;
but the stone is very roughly broken. When thus
crushed, the whole result is put into round baskets
made for the purpose, and a number of these being
placed together, one above another, are squeezed under
a screw press. The oil that runs out is thick, and very
highly coloured; but after being kept in jars, it clears
itself. It is highly valued for exportation to the East
and the Mediterranean shores.

The quantity of oil that pays the export duty from
Corfu is from 150,000 to 200,000 barrels, of sixteen
gallons each, equivalent to about three millions of gallons. Probably as much is retained for home use;
and a very large but unknown quantity is smuggled
out of the country.

Growing with the olive tree, and equally characteristic of the scenery of Corfu, is the cypress.
Gloomy and forbidding, but wonderfully majestic,
this noble tree—its foliage almost becoming black
with advancing age—stands out in the landscape,
overtopping the olive, and rarely rivalled by any
other form of vegetation. The cypress has often,

perhaps generally, planted itself, and has known how
to select good and telling positions. In some places,
it appears in groups amongst rocky ground, where
olives would not be convenient; often it is seen by
the road side, or by the side of some ancient path,
now obliterated, but wherever it appears, it is generally in lines nearly, or quite, straight, and several
in number. It seems to designate the form of the
country, and is suggestive of ancient limits of property which do not now exist, but whether this is a
mere accident, I am unable to say. I think if it were
not for the cypress, the vast extension of the olive
would be tame and monotonous; but, on the other
hand, if it were not for the olive, the cypress would
be too melancholy in its stately individuality. Even
when several trees are together, each full-grown cypress
is an individual, and stands apart from its neighbours
as an object in the landscape; and one may study every
one with advantage, whether in the wooded plains of
the middle of the island, the pleasant and sunny cliffs
of the west coast, or the dark hill sides of the northern
range.

But it is not only when full-grown that the cypress
claims attention. For every one such well-grown king
of the trees, there are thousands of younger and fresher,
but less prominent offspring, dotted everywhere about
the country. Some of these, half grown, are already
assuming the family stateliness, but the rest, the baby
trees, by far the most numerous, are so prim and so
pretty in their primness, that one laughs at the absurdity of their pretence. To see scores of these young

plants, from six inches to three feet in height, ranged
in straight lines, or in lines that will suggest straight-
ness, whether they are straight or not, contrasting with
the wild luxuriance of the myrtle and thorn, and other
brushwood with which they are associated, is almost
ludicrous. But it is impossible to help noticing them
wherever they are; and they are so abundant as to be
characteristic of the island.

The cause of the great luxuriance of the cypress in
Corfu is doubtless the existence of so calcareous a
soil, and the favourable state of the rock for the
growth of the plant. As in England, the chalk
favours the yew, so in Corfu, the limestone favours
the cypress. There are many other parts of the world
where trees of this kind are common enough, but I
have been tempted to record my impressions of the
peculiar effect they have on the scenery of Corfu,
because I have nowhere seen them take a more
prominent place in the landscape.

There are neither olives nor cypresses, neither
vines nor fig-trees in the numerous undrained valleys
of Corfu. It is in the dry hollows and on the slopes
looking towards the East that they are chiefly abundant. Olives are admirable resources for an idle
people, and they tend to encourage speculation, but
they are a valuable crop. The possessor of a few
acres of olive trees and orange trees might bid
defiance to fortune, if he were to look forward and
make provision for the alternate years of famine, without being obliged always to borrow when the evil day
comes, and thus remain hopelessly and permanently in

debt. But this is too much to expect of mortal Greek. He might as well not live as not speculate, and thus the olive is well suited to his nature and also encourages his small vices. We may easily study the phases of Greek character without introducing agricultural statistics. On arriving at one of the little villages commonly resorted to by the residents of the island, who, in summer, spend much time and money in picnics, a crowd of young villagers collects around the party. All are idle, noisy, and useless in an equal degree. All claim with equal urgency to be employed, and all enjoy equal and supreme ignorance and indifference to the object the traveller has in view. Every one desires to be allowed to act as guide. No guide at all is wanted, for one has only to follow any of the little paths at hand, and observe the clue of broken bottles and oyster shells, to reach the usual point of view, whatever it be. To save this trouble, however, and, as we vainly hope, to rid ourselves of the other pests, some Themistocles, or Aristides or Miltiades, is selected. He carries your cloak, if you desire it, and marches on; but the others, with perfect civility and with extreme volubility, have no idea of parting with you, and all follow in train. You cannot move a step without having half-a-dozen on each side and a dozen at your heels; and as the consumption of garlic has been carried on amongst the islanders generally for many generations, you are at once fully immersed in all its fragrant perfume. You cannot speak to your friend on any subject, however indifferent, or in any language, without a volley of modern Greek being thrown at you, *à propos des bottes*, liberally seasoned with the favourite condiment. These boys of all ages, from five to fifteen, or more, not only form a circle round you as you go, but if you stand still to make a note or a sketch, they squat round in a small circle in a dozen different attitudes, any one of which would be a fortune to an artist or photographer. They are imperturbably good-natured, but very tiresome; and when you finally take leave, and present sixpence to the selected lad, the others, though quite aware that they have earned nothing, are all clamorous for some reminiscence. It is not difficult, indeed, to satisfy them, for a few coins, each worth the tenth of a penny, thrown amongst them, occupy them all long enough to enable you to escape; but the true oriental clamour for *bakshish*, or payment for annoyance, is invariably heard.*

After all, these children and their parents are acute, shrewd, and good-natured. They are as quick at repartee as the Irish; and not unfrequently give hard hits and good answers to those who meet them on their own ground. At the same time, they are respectful, and never encroach. Nor are they disagreeable and hardy beggars like those too often seen in many parts of Ireland. They do not continue to persecute you by asking for money, although they

---

* It must be acknowledged that our country people have brought this upon themselves. Nothing of the kind is observable in country villages out of the way of tourists and pic-nic parties; nor do the people in the other islands make the same demand. Experience has taught the natives of the frequented spots what they may expect as the reward of clamour.

follow your footsteps closely. In fact, they follow the visitor partly out of vague curiosity; partly out of utter idleness; and partly, no doubt, with the hope of making something out of him. But they do not actually beg till the moment of departure, and are then easily and cheaply stopped.

One sees but few of the women in the villages near Corfu, and these seldom wear any other part of their ancient costume than the handkerchief—the Turkish *yash-mak*—which, when coquettishly put on by young and pretty girls, add as much piquant effect as it renders more hideous the features of the old and ugly crones who also adopt it. The children of both sexes are generally very pretty, and the growing girls not less so; but they fade early, and pass at once into old women. It is then much better that they should not show themselves. In the cases where I observed the women with their children, the latter were rather put forward and invited to address the stranger than held back, and kept out of sight in the manner so common in Italy. There seems, in Corfu, no dread of the *evil eye*, though, when first under the protection of England, the case was very different. Even now, there is no want of belief in various matters of the grossest and most pagan superstition.

The usual dress of the women in the middle of Corfu presents little that is remarkable, and nothing that is pleasing. Only on the great festivals of the church do they put on their ancient costumes; and these, as they gradually wear out, are not very conscientiously replaced.

When working in the fields, or walking along the roads, it is not always easy, at a little distance, to tell whether the miserable figure before us, clad in a scanty blue skirt, with the legs muffled up in a thick wrapper, and an exceedingly dirty handkerchief hanging over the head, can really be a woman. No doubt, there are many exceptions; but, on the whole, it is to be feared that the gentler sex is still very orientally handled in these fair islands. When young and good-looking, they are shut up; when married, their husbands are at first foolishly jealous, and then cruelly indifferent. They have to take a full share of all house and field work, and enjoy few or no indulgences, except it may be on the rare occasions when there are great festivals. No wonder, then, that they soon look faded and miserable. I have seen, notwithstanding, even in Corfu, sufficient bright eyes and pretty features among the very young girls to feel sure that beauty is not wanting, and that, with time, should the people become more educated, their condition in this respect will improve.

There are not wanting a few pretty villages around Corfu, both in the plain country and among the low hills covered with olive trees and vines. Potamó is one of these. It is chiefly remarkable for the *campanile*, or bell tower, belonging to its church. This is a prominent object from the coast road, and is much more lofty and of better proportions than is usual. It is, no doubt, one of the results of Venetian rule.

The houses of Potamó, some of them with large and cultivated gardens, are prettily grouped round the church, which, though not of greater architectural pretence than is usual with village churches, looks well in its position. This town, as its name imports, is built on the banks of the river that runs down and enters the sea a few miles below, after passing under a stone bridge, perhaps the only one in the island.

Corfu is singularly without running water. Numerous springs arise out of the limestone at the foot of the hills, and some of these are very abundant; but, with very few exceptions, hardly any water reaches the sea during those seasons when heavy rain is not falling. Two or three of the streams are called Potamos; but the one we are now alluding to is the chief. The name is simply the Greek word ποταμος, a river. The little stream under consideration, takes its rise at some distance from the sea, runs down through a narrow choked-up passage for a few miles, receives here and there a few small drains as tributaries, and, when it enters the plains, is hardly more than a respectable brook, not running with any rapidity. A wide space has, however, to be left for it to expand, for it occasionally becomes a torrent; though, judging by the small size and paucity in number of the blocks of stone brought down by it, there can never be the stream that, in so large an island, might be expected. The water no doubt disappears in the crevices of the limestone, and the whole drainage is explained by the nature of the rock of which the island is formed; but I must not detain the reader here with physical dissertations on scientific subjects.

Among the smallest of the feeders of the Potamos,

is a rivulet, derived partly from a ferruginous spring,
bursting out in the hills near the villa residence of Sir
Demetrio Curcumelli, the present Regent or Préfet of
Corfu, a gentleman who takes a great interest in de-
veloping the resources of his island.   The spring in
question rises through a vein of gypsum, containing
iron pyrites, and tastes warm in winter and cool in summer, having always, it would appear, the mean temperature of the locality.   No use has yet been made of
it.   Other mineral springs are known in various parts
of the island, but they also are neglected.

The village of Alepu is another of those little groups
of houses also on the course of the Potamos, but much
smaller, and less important than Potamó.   Including
a suburb, called Triclino, it only musters 200 inhabitants, whereas Potamó boasts of 1,500.   Alepu is
prettily placed on a low sand hill cut through by the
road leading to Pelleka, and takes its name from the
foxes that doubtless were formerly common enough
in the brushwood, at that time thickly covering the
ground.   Foxes, however, have left Corfu; and, though
wolves and jackals still hold their own in some of the
islands, most of these wild animals are rare.   There is
nothing remarkable in the village of Alepu, beyond its
position; and one would pass it by without notice,
were it not for the view obtained of the country to the
west, on first emerging from the little cutting alluded to.

Passing a number of small properties, and through
extensive olive groves, we approach Afra and the village of Curcumelli, near which is the country house of

the gentleman of that name, picturesquely placed on a low hill. Sir Demetrio Curcumelli is the present Regent of Corfu, that being the title of the chief officer of the municipality, rather corresponding to the French Préfet than the English Mayor. He has interested himself greatly in the material progress of the island, and has improved the cultivation of the land in his own neighbourhood.

The peasantry in this part of Corfu seem to obtain fair wages and plenty of work during the busy time of the year. Their condition, however, if judged of by English eyes, and with English ideas of comfort, and cottage neatness, is very inferior to that of the corresponding class in England, with even smaller wages. I visited the house of a working man who had a large family, including several young children. The wages of the family were said to amount to about 14s. 6d. per week, and the house consisted only of two dark rooms on the ground floor. A large part of one was taken up with an oven, while the corners appeared to serve as general receptacles for odds and ends. Adjoining was a room with a very small opening in the wall to let in light and air. In this, slept the women and young children. There was, besides these two rooms, only a kind of loft, with a floor of loose reeds on the beams of the sleeping room, and reached by a ladder. It is usual for the men to sleep wrapped up in their cloaks in any corner they find convenient. The floors of all the rooms consisted of dried beaten earth, and the furniture was limited to the very smallest amount of movables. The whole food of such a family was stated to consist of a very coarse bread, made of Indian corn. This bread was sweet, and good of its kind, and is sold at the rate of about a halfpenny a pound; but, being made at home, could not cost so much. Beyond this bread, nothing in the way of food was expected, beyond a little oil, the value of which was about tenpence per week,* and an occasional fowl, on very special occasions. For their hovel, a rent of a dollar a year was paid; and fuel costs nothing but time, the women picking up stray branches and brushwood sufficient for the oven, which is all that the climate requires. For clothes, the expenditure must be wonderfully small, if one may guess from the bundles of rags covering the women and children. Certainly, a family receiving such wages in England would enjoy many more comforts; and, it is a curious instance of extravagance in the midst of this penury in Corfu, that most of the families possess a dog, who eats nearly as much bread as a man. The average consumption is estimated at three pounds per diem for each member of the family, and two for the dog; but I imagine this must be somewhat in excess.

It must not be supposed that all the country people are thus poor. There are some whose houses though apparently little different in the exterior, are really much more commodious, and are far better furnished. As a contrast to the hovel just described, I was taken into the house of a respectable small farmer, one who farmed a certain tract of olive grove, vineyard and

---

* The present price of oil (1863) is about 2s. per gallon in Corfu.

arable land, partly his own, partly paying a rent, either
in money or kind. The entry of this house also was
the cellar and general store. At least, a score of large
casks for wine or oil were ranged in order on each side.
Besides these, there were various implements and some
miscellaneous property. A decent. stair conducted
into two upper rooms. We only entered one of them,
and it happened to be the apartment of the women.
It was of large size and good proportion. There was
a very large high bed, nearly seven feet square, in one
corner. On it were two mattrasses, one of maize
straw, and another of wool. In the room, were three
large old Venetian linen chests, in which were, no
doubt, the household linen and the costumes, worn
only on feast days. These chests were ornamented
with a quaint kind of carving. Hanging on the wall,
was one of those good old fashioned looking glasses,
with large wooden frames, that one sees now and then
in farm-houses in England, and a smaller one below.
On some shelves, were a number of square glass
bottles, like liqueur bottles. Several pictures of Greek
saints were there, and the wedding-wreath of the house-
mother was carefully suspended on the wall, covered
with a cloth. It was much faded. There were tables,
good, strong and sound, some benches, and some chairs.
The whole was comfortable and substantial.

This house was the habitation of five men, four
women or grown-up girls, and three children, all
young. No doubt, the people were sufficiently well
off to be well fed and comfortably provided; but they
could not live much in the house. There seemed no

special apartment for eating; and it is most likely that the bedroom we visited answered all purposes.

With regard to the field labour in such a family as that we were now visiting, it would be managed by the joint effort of two or three neighbours. True it is that the labour is very small. The vines are pruned and the earth turned up around the roots in spring, and the olives shaken off the trees, and picked up when they fall in autumn. The loose, open soil is prepared for planting maize, and perhaps beans, and then all is over. The people are industrious only by fits and starts; but certainly, when they do work, they seem to get over the ground quickly. I saw a considerable patch of vines, at which three boys of about thirteen were digging, and one old man pruning. The work they had got through since the morning was much more than could have been expected from the tools they use. The soil, however, was very light.

My companions were curious about the age of the people, and other matters; but so suspicious are most of the villagers and so much more accustomed to ask questions than answer them, that we feared we had seriously offended one family, whose house we had entered, by our minute enquiries. A young and pretty girl, who certainly had no sufficient reason for concealing her age, for she could not have emerged from her teens, bridled up, and replied that she did not remember being born. Another older one looked daggers, and altogether declined replying. As the party of whom I formed one was in company with the Regent, who, moreover, was a near neighbour, and took an interest in his neighbours, it might have been thought that an apology would be sufficient to put things right; but Sir D. Curcumelli informed us, next day, that he had great difficulty in explaining why a party of English gentlemen should come and look into their houses and ask their ages. They certainly did not accept as true the real reason; but connected the enquiry with some deep political stratagem.

In the open country, away from the village, it is not unusual to find houses of some size consisting chiefly of one large chamber, and one much smaller out of sight. These houses are not raised above the ground-floor; they are built with stone walls, and roofed with tiles, the roof projecting three feet or more beyond the walls. Such houses are wayside taverns, and in them may be obtained wine, raki (the common spirit of the country), and generally, at a few minutes' notice, an excellent cup of coffee. On all the chief roads out of Corfu these houses exist, and they seem to do a good business. Carts, each loaded with half-a-dozen people, drive up at a hand-gallop, and immediately the whole party jump out singing and shouting in a truly oriental and tho-roughly unmusical manner, and turn in to one of these taverns. Sometimes they seem to come out of their way to patronise a favourite establishment, for, after they have enjoyed themselves, they return by the road whence they came. No women join in these revels.

Such houses are often picturesquely placed far away

from a village, and with a back ground of olive-trees and oranges, that is very pleasing. Occasionally, they occupy prominent positions on a hill side, and they always add to the effect of the landscape. If not on the road side, such establishments will be found at the entrance of the villages; but the traveller must not suppose that he would obtain food or a night's lodging at them; they are mere drinking booths, with one wretched dark chamber behind.

Of the better class of country houses, and of villas belonging to the higher classes, there are very few. That built and occupied by Sir D. Curcumelli, is an exception, for it is large, roomy, handsomely furnished, and charmingly placed. A large court-yard is enclosed by buildings, which include stables, stores, offices, and convenient sheds for making wine and obtaining oil. Over this court yard is a trellis-work covered with vines, which, in the heat of summer, must afford a delicious shade. Smaller villas there are, but they are few, and not connected with property; they are mere summer resorts.

Govino is another village of the plains, not very far from Curcumelli, and as it is one that has a history of some interest, it deserves a brief notice.

In 1848, Govino numbered 162 inhabitants. In 1860, the number had dwindled to 118. It is one of those unfortunate localities where nature has granted beauty, but denied health. It looks inviting and pleasant, but residence in it involves an attack of malaria and fever. During the time when the Venetians occupied Corfu, they selected the natural harbour of

Govino as one of their chief places of resort. Here they constructed an arsenal, store-houses, and other public buildings; and here, no doubt, they planted a town which they believed would be permanent. It is not unlikely that, at that time, the harbour was deeper than it now is, and the neighbourhood less unhealthy, but at any rate, after a time, the town was abandoned, and even the few straggling sickly families, who now call themselves its inhabitants, live at some distance from the harbour. It is a silent and rarely visited spot, for there is poison in the air around.

And yet to look at Govino from a little distance, one would be inclined to select it as the site, of all others, for a town; a fine harbour, with an entrance both north and south, an island and promontory stationed as if to fend off all troublesome winds and keep the sea calm, and rich vegetation clothing the ground everywhere, all look tempting. The stagnant waters on the swampy plains around, and the rapid evaporation from the calm waters of the harbour, which receive all kinds of dying and dead matter, and are too little disturbed ever to get rid of them by any other method than allowing them to decompose, fully explain the state of the case. The want of tide is a fearful want in the Mediterranean, and the farther we go east the more is this great want felt. It was necessary, perhaps, that some drawback should exist on these beautiful shores, that man should not find a paradise too complete, and that he should be taught caution, and made to tremble where he would otherwise have been inclined to lie down in the careless enjoyment of too much terrestrial happiness. Certain it is that the absence of regular and considerable movement of the sea is the great cause of all the fever that is so rife on the shores of the eastern Mediterranean.

It is not necessary to describe at length the other villages and places of interest within the area of comparatively low ground encircling the town of Corfu. All partake of the same general character, and consist of picturesque but small and irregular groups of houses half buried in groves of fine olive-trees, and varied by low hills or projecting rocks of limestone. There are few or no regular valleys, no rivers, and no commanding points of view, but all is pleasing and cheerful. The people, too, are civil and well-disposed, but are thinly spread over the country, there being few detached houses. The population of the villages is rarely above 600, and there are nowhere any marks of growth as exemplified by new buildings.

CHAPTER III.

I HAVE already said that the first visit of the stranger in Corfu, desirous of seeing the country and knowing the island, should be to Pelleka. It is not far, the distance from the town being only about eight miles. It is rapidly reached in a carriage, over a good road, and the way to it crosses much beautiful and characteristic scenery: wild-looking, though valuable, olive groves, noble cypresses, isolated pinnacles and cliffs of limestone, the bed of a small stream with sometimes—not always—a little water; handsome pines,

trees not too common in the island, but always beautiful and well-grown when they are found; swelling
plains, and at last a long rise up a picturesque and
well-wooded hill side: these varied beauties succeed
each other till at length we reach the modest little
village with its 725 inhabitants perched high up on
the side of the hill, within a few hundred yards of the
summit. Quitting the carriage at this point, a steep,
narrow path conducts towards a chapel, small, but
more picturesque than chapels of the Greek Church
usually are, placed at the edge of a steep and lofty
cliff overhanging the sea, and presenting to view a
few miles of that most beautiful part of Corfu, its
west coast. Very grand is the contrast of the lofty
cliffs and picturesque hills terminating the mountain
chain of San Salvador towards the west, with the
valley clothed with rich vegetation spread out to the
east, and equally interesting the view of the town and
citadel of Corfu, apparently not very distant; the
channel of Corfu looking like a great lake, and the
noble Albanian mountains with their caps of snow
closing the view in that direction.

A continuous path along the edge of the cliff deve-
lops every minute a fresh point of view: the mountains in the south, Santi Deca and San Mathias, connect themselves with the northern range of San Salvador by means of the high ground on which we
stand, and the whole forms a noble amphitheatre,
having a radius of at least ten miles.

The beautiful ridge near Pelleka is greatly visited
from Corfu, being among the places resorted to for

celebrating that singularly British institution the picnic. Large deposits of oyster shells and broken champagne bottles will clearly indicate to future generations the important uses and sacred character of the place, and long after Great Britain has ceased to act as the Protecting Power of the Ionian Islands, long after even our roads—the most durable mark of England's empire—have become obliterated, future travellers will discover in their search after the remains of a former people, these unmistakable proofs of the taste and habits of the western rulers of the world.

Pelleka, though small, is flourishing; at least this is the conclusion forced upon one by the rush of children, of all ages, who greet the arrival of every carriage, and the persistent devotion with which every stray traveller is pursued from the moment he leaves the carriage till the last instant of his stay in the neighbourhood. The children, too, look healthy and free, and contrast strongly with the pallid and haggard appearance of the inhabitants of Castrades and the lower part of the town of Corfu. Still more favourably do they contrast with the inhabitants of the villages below, either on the shores of the marine swamps, or of the fresh-water marshes. Referring to the census tables, I find that since 1848 the increase of population from 1848 to 1860 is as much as 134, or at the rate of nearly two per cent. per annum; not very fast it is true, but better than the average of the island. The villages on the plains, on the other hand, many of them show an actual decrease, or, at the best, stagnation.

Passing along the cliff from the south towards the north we find another little chapel also prettily situated, and not far from it a very bold, jagged, projecting rock, suddenly ending in a precipitous fall towards the east and north. From this point there is a view, not without great beauty, but even more interesting than that already alluded to as involving considerations in reference to the singularly small and slowly-increasing population and sanitary condition of the island. Immediately beneath the eye, in two directions, are extensive plains; one running to the west of north towards the foot of the great transverse mountain-chain of the island, and the other towards the east, smaller, but of the same nature. The former is the Val di Roppa, a place well known to sportsmen from the garrison, for the enormous supply of water-fowl to be shot there in the winter. It is one of the most singular and most mischievous of several similar valleys in the island of Corfu, and deserves special attention.

From the picturesque extremity of the rocky cliff of Pelleka—the beautiful hill of San Georgio rising, with its double-rounded summit, to the left, and a continuous coast range beyond, as far as the eye can reach—with the high mountain range terminating in San Salvador immediately before us, and with lower picturesque hills to the right, let us contemplate for a moment the level space at our feet, extending for about six miles without interruption.

This level bottom is the Val di Roppa. No river enters it; none emerges from it; none runs through it. It is the bottom of a basin, or long trough, receiving all the water that falls on the slopes of the surrounding hills and mountains, allowing the water to soak into the interior as long as it can do so, and then allowing the rest to remain on its surface till it has been slowly evaporated off by the hot sun. So long is this process going on, that when I saw it, during the month of February, after two month's drought, the whole of the part nearest the mountains —which appears to be the highest, but must really be the lowest, part—was still under water, and the rest was like a half-drained marsh.

The angel of death hovers over this wide plain,— death in the terrible form of a wasting and poisonous fever. Here are always at hand the seeds of malaria ready to attack every victim who comes within their influence; and in the miserable villages on the plains and low hill-sides around, we may read the effects of a badly-chosen locality.

In order to estimate this fairly, I have taken from the census the details of the population of six villages surrounding the valley, comparing their state at the two periods, 1848 and 1860. I find that in these six villages, the total population in the former year was 1,750, and in the latter, 1,754; that of three of the villages the population had sensibly decreased, and in the other three had slightly increased. With a single exception, none of these villages have a population of 500 inhabitants; and one of them is now reduced to 64. I think it is impossible to show more clearly that something seriously and radically bad must exist in the air around.

There would be little practical difficulty in draining the whole of this large tract, and bringing it into permanent and profitable cultivation; and it is much to be desired that a work so important should .be taken in hand while the island yet remains under British protection.

Besides the Val di Roppa, another smaller tract of marsh land is below our feet when standing on the edge of the cliff at Pelleka. Without being so much exposed to evil influences and receiving less water than the larger valley, there can be little doubt that, in its way and in its proportion, this, also, is injurious.

A little chapel, dedicated to St. John the Evangelist, stands near the extremity of the precipice, overlooking the plains below. Very small, with no window, and only one door—a mere shed roofed in— this chapel is a great attraction, and the object of many a weary pilgrimage when the proper day arrives. The picturesque costumes and striking groups that then cover this beautiful cliff, and, perhaps, some interesting pagan customs, traceable in the worship and amusements of the day, would render a visit at that time very pleasant.

A more distant excursion than that to Pelleka conducts the traveller past the village of Potamó (leaving it to the left), and not far from the village of Curcumelli, to the north of the Pelleka road, and so through olive groves, and pines, and cypresses, past many picturesque rocky precipices to the foot of the San Salvador chain, and so up a long, steep zigzag, round the shoulder of the hill to the summit of another lofty cliff, whence the eye looks down with delight on a nearer and equally beautiful glimpse of the western shores of Corfu. Down this cliff, along a steep, but well-made road, we rapidly descend, and soon come in sight of a multitude of little bays, each with its lovely white sands and clear blue water— each with some fantastic rock jutting out of the water or terminating the bay, and every one brilliant and sparkling in the sunshine and almost touching the foot of the cliff, on which alternate vines and cypresses, myrtles and olives, are growing and flourishing. About two-thirds of the way down, the cliff and hill are entirely formed of beautiful sparkling gypsum, quite crystalline and pure. The rest of the hill is of the ordinary limestone of the country.

At the foot of the cliff, on a little hillock forming a kind of promontory, connected by a hilly isthmus separating two symmetrical little bays, are the monastery and convent of Paleocastrizza,—the object of many a charming pic-nic, and the occasional habitation, during summer, of some of the English residents of Corfu, who are able to offer a sufficient inducement to the regular proprietors to justify them in accommodating themselves elsewhere. The consideration is not very serious.

The distance of Paleocastrizza from the town is about seventeen miles, and the road is good; but it takes three hours to drive there, owing to the hilly nature of the way. The situation is charming; very retired, but far from dull; and it well deserves' to be, as it is, one of the most frequented and favourite resorts of those who visit, or reside in, the island.

Nothing can be imagined more exquisite than the broken and indented coast here presented. The steep cliff rises behind to a height of from 800 to 1,000 feet; but, both in approaching it by the road and from the sea, a great multitude of rocks of all shapes and sizes are observed lying about in wild confusion. All are covered with a rich vegetation. At our feet are at least a dozen tiny little bays, the horns of which stretch far out into the bright blue water, while little crescents of the most delicate white shingle, as fine as sand, tempt the foot of the bather. A few caverns are seen at intervals, but they are only accessible by boats. The last but one of the small bays is separated from the last by the promontory, on the top of which is the monastery. It is so calm, so clean-looking, and so comfortable in its accommodation that I greatly admired the taste, not only of the original monks, but of my friends and companions, who had, last summer, taken possession of the place, under arrangement with the monks, and occupied it themselves. A more delightful retreat cannot be imagined; and during the intense heats of summer, far removed from all danger of malaria, and with the beautiful sea, and rocks, and sky all around, it would be hard to select a spot where life could be more enjoyable.

Both monks and nuns are attached to this establishment. The latter, indeed, are more like the *sœurs de charité* than nuns of the Romish church, and are usually old women. We saw, however, two, and neither of them was very old. One was spinning flax with a distaff, and the other was embroidering a kind of girdle, or belt, with gold and red, in a style of which there were some examples in the Ionian Court of the International Exhibition. One of the ladies of our party purchased a belt just completed; but the price paid (nearly nine shillings) seemed to me very high. There are, however, too many English visitors; and there is too much demand for wares of the kind, even among the villagers, to let the prices fall. The embroideress was good-looking, and scarcely middle aged. She wore a serge dress, plain and becoming, rather different in style from the dress of the peasants, but not remarkable in any way. I observed that, although she spoke chiefly, and by preference, the Greek language, she understood, and could speak, Italian.

There is a fair amount of cultivation on the hill sides near the convent; but in order to keep up the soil, there are numerous terraces. These must have been built at an enormous expense of time and trouble, even if they did not cost actual money. The vine is one of the trees here planted, and, it seemed to me, the chief one; but, no doubt, there are grain and root crops in due season. The sides of the slope appear to be too steep to admit of any other kind of cultivation with a chance of success. The ground that is at all level is occupied with olive trees.

A ruined castle is seen on the summit of the high

cliff nearly adjacent, but a long and rough road must
be travelled to reach it. It dates from the Venetian
period, like most of the mediæval ruins of the island,
and is called the Castel St. Angelo. The position is
strong and fine, but the remains are not very extensive. Beyond it is a fine bay.

Paleocastrizza seems to be almost the only accessible
part of the coast of Corfu at which genuine cliff scenery
can be found; and what is here seen is, beyond question, extremely bold and fine, contrasting powerfully
with the other limestone scenery of the island. A
large and valuable mass of gypsum is cut through by
the road a little before arriving at the foot of the cliff,
but it has not been worked. With this exception, the
cliffs are entirely calcareous. Many pleasant walks
and excursions might be made from the monastery;
but the wandering about in the little bays—climbing
the low cliffs near the sea—reaching the numerous
headlands by land, or paddling about in a little boat
that peeps invitingly out of a small recess in the rock
under the convent—would, perhaps, suffice to occupy
most of those who come here to escape the intense
heat of the summer sun, which burns up everything
in Corfu. The clearness of the water is extraordinary
as it ripples over the delicate bed of shingles and
minute shells,—the shingles being, as I have said, so
small as to deserve being called sand. There is here
none of that muddy appearance seen on the shore in
the channel of Corfu; and as a healthy summer resort,
there is, probably, nothing in any part of the island to
compare with it.

The establishment at the convent is small compared with the size of the building and the large church accommodation. Without the slightest architectural pretension, the chapel is large, lofty, and well proportioned. It is ornamented with a few pictures, probably by native artists,—one series representing, in a very incomprehensible way, the creation of the world. Each picture was divided into compartments representing some one event. The creation of the fowls of the air was pretty clearly indicated by the simplest of all contrivances. It was a poultry-yard in an uproar. The expulsion of Adam and Eve from Paradise was neatly executed by an angel in a brown great coat and scarlet waistcoat, with small golden wings. The flames of the sword were also golden. Some of the image pictures were curious. The painted part, consisting of the face and breast, seemed well done, and was recessed deeply behind the silver plate which so usually covers the dress of pictures of this class in the Greek church. A box for alms, thinly plated with silver, was placed within sight.

I cannot refrain from inserting here, for its own sake and as an instance of the style of the Baron Theotoki, the native historian of Corfu, the brief notice he gives of this gem of the island. It is at once illustrative of the Greek character and amusing in itself. I give it in his own French, which is no less characteristic than the matter and treatment. It would be easy to find passages far more inflated, for every place in turn comes in for its share of description, and language evidently fails to convey the intensity of his patriotism.

" *Paleocastriti.*—Si quelqu'un aime à chercher le vrai pour le connôitre, non pas pour s'en glorifier, si quelqu'un aime à se concentrer, purifier son cœur, et retrancher tout ce qu'il peut y avoir de contraire à la droiture, qu'il aille se réfugier dans cet asyle. Sur des bords glissans et ignorés d'une mer sans bornes, il lui parôitra n'appartenir plus à la terre, si ce n'est pour craindre les embuches des avares qui l'habitent.* D'un côté un ancien chateau bâti par le frère du dernier Souverain de Byzance, comme un colosse foudroyè, sort des eaux pour deposer contre les fastes de la grandeur humaine; de l'autre, le mont Hercule fend le ciel d'un sommet nu, couvre le pays, et ajoute à l'illusion de ce site solitaire, un sentiment profond et sublime."—*Details sur Corfu*, 1826; p. 25.

Beyond the exquisite coast scenery and the simple but quiet residence, there is really nothing in Paleocastrizza that admits of description; but no one having any love for nature could spend a few weeks in its cahn seclusion without benefit to mental as well as physical health. It is the perfection of its peculiar, but charming, style.

Not very far from Paleocastrizza, a road branches off, and traversing one of the little hollow valleys so common in the islands, rises gradually to the village of Scriperó, on the shoulder of a portion of the mag-

---

* Je dis des avares, car je suis persuadé que sur cent calamités qui affligent la terre, les 99 sont le résultat de l'avarice (dans une acception très étendue).

nificent escarpment of limestone that continues at
various heights all across the north of the island.
From Scriperó, the road continues to ascend in a
zigzag to the pass of Pantaleone, one of the favourite
points of view. Scriperó itself is a pretty and very
picturesque group of whitewashed houses, placed irregularly, and offering no special peculiarities, but
embosomed in gardens whose walls, at the time of
my visit, were covered with rose trees in full blossom,
with a few almond trees also in full bloom, to break
the monotony. I do not remember to have seen,
anywhere, more beautiful children than those of this
village. They were, however, all boys; and, indeed,
young girls are rarely seen anywhere. The women
in this neighbourhood wear yellow or pink flowered
handkerchiefs across the bosom; and the head-dress is
a large piece of cloth turned over in a curious way,
making a square bandeau over the forehead. They
thus show more of costume than is usual, though the
plain ugly blue skirt remains, and the legs are swathed
in thick bandages. The feet are generally covered with
thick shoes, turned up at the toe.

From the top of the pass, the view across the island
to the south is very fine; and the better to enjoy the
prospect, I mounted a hill about 250 feet above the
termination of the range towards the sea. The pass
itself I estimated at about 1,090 feet. From the
pass, looking northwards, and from the higher land
above, a noble view is obtained of the north-west
corner of the island, and also of the group of small
islands beyond. Among the latter is one that divides,

G

with the island at the mouth of Lake Calichiopulo, the honour of being the petrified ship of Ulysses. Few things in the island are grander than the scenery from this point, and no one ought to omit seeing it. But still more interesting and even finer than the view from the pass are those obtained on descending towards the north, and passing under the lofty and precipitous cliffs between Pantaleone and the little village of Spagus. The whole country is broken and wild; and it is evident that large and frequent falls take place from these cliffs, which, in some places, actually overhang the road. Going on in this direction, and leaving one or two villages behind, we at length reach a point where a stream of water gushes forth in the strangest and wildest manner, through a large hole in a projecting wall of rock, and leaping down a great height, forms at once a small river. Near here, there is an additional interest for the geologist,—the rocks being greatly disturbed, and a singular deposit of gypsum, loaded with sulphur, and of native sulphur, in large quantity, occupies the valley. Up to this point, the rock in sight has been chiefly a tufaceous and brecciated limestone. Here it suddenly changes to a black clay, and soon flat beds of gypsum are seen, alternating with rotten clay. Among these, the sulphur is found in great abundance. I was shown a little quarry, a few feet square, whence a vast quantity of sulphur had been taken to dress the vines. As much as 10,000 lbs. weight—no doubt of gypsum and sulphur together—was said to have been extracted, and the result was described as very efficacious. The mixture of gypsum would help the good effect of the sulphur.

I was much amused at the scene presented while I was examining this quarry. I counted seventeen men and boys who had followed in my train when I left the village of Spagus, but who had hitherto been straggling. Here they all collected and grouped themselves in a semi-circle, some sitting, some leaning, some standing. Most of them were in true island costume, but one fellow looked supremely ridiculous, having obtained a sailor's glazed straw hat, quite new and very much too small; this he set jauntily on his head in utter disregard to the contrast it presented to his baggy blue trowsers and dirty white stockings. Every one of my audience, however, was seriously intent on the case under consideration, and many of them were looking for specimens, which, indeed, were not difficult to find. At the head of the party was the chief officer of the village—the Primate—a stout, respectable-looking person, not unlike a Turk, who afterwards regaled me with coffee and bread. The whole party would have accompanied me for miles had I had time to continue the investigation, but I was obliged soon to return. Sulphur springs issue at no great distance, and the whole rock is deeply impregnated with sulphur for miles around.

The country people in this part of Corfu, where visitors seldom come, are very different from, and decidedly superior to, the peasants near the great roads. There was no asking for money, no attempt at pressing upon one's footsteps, no word said, except when any one was addressed.   Great interest was evidently felt in the matter, and I obtained easily every information I desired in the most intelligent manner. The primate quite understood my map, and could even point out the supposed boundary of the sulphur district.   I do not think so much interest or curiosity would have been expressed in a country village of England, and the intelligence of the people was shown in many ways.

The range of San Salvador stretches across from the mountains behind Spagus to the east at a high level, and is generally precipitous towards the south, forming a table-land in the middle part, behind and to the north of the country between Scriperó and the highest summit.   There are several villages on the north side, but Spartilla is almost the only one besides Scriperó placed high up on the south flank of the chain, and indeed there is not place for a village along most part of the range.. Spartilla is best reached from Ipso, a place on the coast in the angle of the bay, formed by the low land of the middle of the island to the south and the almost vertical wall of rock that cuts across it towards the east.   The name Ipso is derived from the extensive deposits of gypsum on the level ground close by.   The distance of Ipso from Corfu is about eight miles.

Ipso is hardly a village, but it is a name on the map.   There are one or two houses and a boat on the beach, but that is all.   The name does not appear in the census returns.   Such as it is, it is prettily situated at the foot of the mountain chain, and close to it there are some curious strong springs of fresh water bubbling up through the salt water in the bay and among the fallen rocks. A rough beach, covered with large boulders not yet broken up, extends for some distance, and then the cliff terminates beneath the water. It .is possible, however, .to climb round for some distance, and reach one or two small caverns that offer nothing remarkable beyond the view of the bay looking outwards. A larger cavern is described as being at no great distance, but to enter this a boat is necessary.

From Ipso a road has been traced and partly made in the direction of Spartilla. This place is a pretty village of about 600 inhabitants, half-way up the mountain side, in a position which seems very inconvenient. Below the village, and near the road, is a naked face of the mountain covered with a considerable accumulation of a kind of stalagmitic marble mixed with alabaster, some slabs of which had been sent to the International Exhibition of 1863, and which it was hoped might be worked to profit. The quantity obtainable is, no doubt, large; but of the quality and cost, no sufficient trial had been made to justify an opinion. It is a pretty, variegated marble with pink concentric markings. White gypsum might, no doubt, be obtained in abundance, and perhaps, also, alabaster fit for ornamental purposes.

This visit having in view the examination of the marble quarries, I was accompanied by the primate of the village and some friends from Corfu. After visiting the mines, and on our way back to Ipso, the primate, who seemed a very sensible man, informed an influential member of our party that the union with Greece was a thing very much to be desired, but . that, on the whole, he would prefer having the road completed to his village.

The inhabitants of this part of the island, I observed to be particularly handsome, and the primate, who accompanied us with several others in the rear, were noble specimens of their race. Among the common people there seemed, to me, a little of the Turkish character and cast of countenance, and indeed it is very rare to be able to trace any of those true Greek peculiarities one would like to see. What with the Albanians on the one hand, the Venetians on the other, and the Turks over-riding both, there is little chance of finding, even among the mountaineers, much ancient blood of the island. Corcyra must be very poorly represented in the modern Corfu, and the Corcyrian still less so in the Corfiot.

Spartilla is built on the steep slope, about a third of the way up to the imperfect plateau, or table-land, from which rise the two pyramidal peaks of San Salvador and Mavrona. The whole of this plateau is lofty and rocky, and its effect fine from all points. San Salvador is the highest peak. It is considered to be the Mount Istone of the ancients, where, in the Peloponnesian war, the remains of the aristocratic party of the Corcyrians made a last stand. "After various alternations of fortune and unheard-of cruelties, committed by the democrats and aristocrats reciprocally, five hundred of the latter, having escaped the massacre committed by the democrats, under the protection of the Athenian fleet, commanded by Eurymedon, fled to the continent. From thence they returned secretly, and disembarking on the island, lest they should ever be again induced to quit it, they burnt their boats. They then fortified themselves on this commanding height, whence they were only dislodged with the assistance of the Athenian fleet."*

The whole of the San Salvador range is fine and bold, rising well from the sea at the south, sufficiently detached from the high valley on the north, and disconnected also from the hills to the east. It is certainly well adapted for defence, but there are no such remains of Cyclopean walls, crowned with an Acropolis, as we see in the islands of Leucadia (Santa Maura), Ithaca and Cephalonia. Indeed, the north of Corfu seems almost without marks of ancient occupation. It is not unlikely that in the best time of the Greeks, it was, like so many others of the Greek mountains, thickly covered with wood, and not very accessible. The removal of the wood has certainly not been for the advantage of the islands, except, indeed, that it has probably cleared away the shelter from many tribes of robbers, who would be troublesome neighbours to the inhabitants of the villages below.

From the village of Spartilla, which is one of those

---

* According to another account, the real Mount Istone was on the other side of the island, near the present village of Vistona, below the Castle of St. Angelo, and not far from Paleocastrizza. Like many classical localities, there are reasonable doubts as to the modern representative rights.

that would have suffered from the forests as much, perhaps, as they would have been benefited, it would certainly be possible, and probably not difficult, to ascend the peak of Mavrona, and thence proceed along the table-land to San Salvador. I was not able to accomplish this, and was obliged to make the ascent of the mountain the subject of a special excursion. About the time of my visit (the end of February), the weather already showed symptoms of breaking up, and was not to be trusted from day to day. I decided, however, to make the experiment, and, acting under good advice, I determined to ascend through a ravine from Glypho, a small port, which could only be reached by a boat from Corfu. Thanks to the kindness of my excellent friend, Sir Patrick Colquhoun, the Chief Justice of Corfu, I was provided with all needful appliances, and was also enabled to take with me an aneroid barometer, as I desired to check the various statements that had been made as to the height of San Salvador. I had also been fortunate enough to secure a pleasant and congenial companion. The trip and the ascent are, however, by no means arduous, and, in case of fine weather, the whole may be very easily completed without fatigue between breakfast and dinner. Ladies can very well make the ascent on horseback.

The pull across the Bay is one succession of charming and interesting incidents. The little port alluded to, is about eight miles distant from the starting point in Corfu, the boat passing close under a corner of Vido, and leaving the Lazzaretto and Govino far to the left. Immediately in front, the whole mass of the mountain rises directly out of the sea, and is so steep, that the little monastery on the summit almost appears to overhang the Bay. This is indeed by no means the case, as it is situated probably two miles within the line of the shore, but the effect from a small boat is very fine. The remaining part of the chain to the east is also well seen, as it falls back towards the north, and gradually lowers.

Glypho is the name of our little port; but in what way, if at all, its name or history is connected with glyptic art, I am unable to say. The port is created by a vast block of limestone rock, that has fallen into the sea from the mountain side at some distant period, and has thus formed a little rocky promontory and a small bay, in which boats can take shelter. It is a beautiful object, this little promontory of rock, covered with vegetation. Its form is picturesque, and it is as useful as it is beautiful. A house is built on the slope of the hill, close to the landing-place, but there seems no other house adjacent, and only two or three straggling huts around. There was, however, a fair population of men and boys to welcome our arrival.

Like many other monasteries similarly situated on lofty heights and mountain tops, that of San Salvador is the object of a pilgrimage at a certain season of the year; and, although not regularly inhabited, there is always sufficient communication to keep the well-made path to the summit in order. The top may indeed be reached from more than one point, and there is a village about half way up. No difficulty, therefore, could exist in finding one's way, but it was quite im-

possible to avoid taking with us one of the little crowd
of human beings who had evidently quite made up
their minds on the subject. Either we must fasten
upon one, or the whole number would fasten themselves upon us, and accompany us all the way. As
the smallest evil, we selected a very little, dark-eyed,
olive-complexioned youth, by no means Greek looking,
and probably about ten years old. Slinging on his
back a loaf, an over-coat, and a small cask of water, as
symbols of office, he started on his way in great
glee, disappearing in an instant in a small olive grove,
growing down almost to the sea, and followed by my
companion and myself, at a quick pace. But we were
not to get rid of our following quite so easily. Half-
a-dozen of the other lads followed for a time, but one
by one they left us. One only, a half-witted strip of
a youth, miserable looking, and of the most unnatural
leanness, his very face not being much thicker than a
walking stick, but odoriferous beyond all endurance
with the fumes of garlic, would insist on dogging our
footsteps, now passing before, then dropping close behind, and sometimes sidling up to one of us, apparently
arranging that we should always be reminded of his
presence in the most disagreeable way. In vain did
I exercise my Italian phrases; in vain did my companion anathematise in modern Greek. He would
not, or could not, understand how or why he offended,
and we were fairly obliged at last to use threats, and
drive him back. After all, we found that a few
decided remarks in very plain English delivered *ore
rotundo*, answered the purpose much better than good

natured remonstrances. The poor wretch held out his hand for an *obolus* (halfpenny), and finally disappeared.

About two hours and a-half were occupied by us in the ascent. The path proceeds along the 'side of a narrow gorge opposite the mountain of San Salvador, and rounds the head of this ravine after a slight descent; it then continues steadily ascending until, about half way up from the sea, we come to the utterly desolate-looking village of Signes. At first it resembles a city of the dead: a church unroofed; houses looking as if their inhabitants were all locked up asleep, or imprisoned within them; ground unenclosed, and apparently uncultivated; and not even the barking of a hound to break the utter monotony of the scene.

Signes is, however, a real living village, which, in the last census, is stated to have had 1,218 inhabitants. Where they stow themselves, or what becomes of them, it would certainly puzzle any one passing through the place to discover. We did not see a single child; the houses were closed, and the only appearance of life anywhere traceable over the landscape before us, consisted of three people at a distance digging in a small walled garden that had at first escaped notice.

After this village the road continues wide and paved to the top of the mountain; but the rock is naked, except where covered by wild herbs and flowers. The views of the surrounding country to the east and south are fine, looking down upon the lake of Butrinto and the plains of Vrana, and presenting a charming outline of the lofty mountains of Albania in the back ground. The view across the bay to Corfu, and the back ground of lower mountains in that direction, is also fine and interesting.

Unfortunately the weather, which had long been threatening, determined to pour forth its wrath upon us just at the time we reached the summit. We took shelter in the monastery; but there were only bare walls and a roof to protect us, and terrible cutting draughts which were worse than the rain. After refreshing ourselves with a morsel of bread, and a draught of water, which I drew up in a broken jar from the well on the summit, we made a hasty tour of the little territory, looked at the rough ground that forms the plateau on the south side of the range, and endeavoured to think how beautiful it would have been had the weather been favourable. We then decided to commence our descent, and this we safely accomplished in very much less time than it had taken us to get to the top. I estimated the mountain to be about 3,300 feet. It is well placed for commanding a prospect to the east and north, but in other respects cannot, I think, be regarded as a first-rate point of view. No fineness of weather could give an extensive or instructive view from the top towards the south, and it is impossible to see beyond the very near and almost equally lofty summits to the north-east and south-west. I am quite aware, however, that a rainy day affords but a poor opportunity of judging of the extent and beauty of a landscape from a great elevation, and will therefore say no more.

At Glypho, which we reached in a constantly increasing rain, we found our boatmen ready with a meal which was not unwelcome, and which we ate seated on a bench at a round stone table in front of the little house by the landing-place. Never did Albanian mutton taste more tender, or the excellent country wine provided for us by our friend more acceptable. At least a dozen men and children were ranged round in all sorts of picturesque attitudes calmly staring at us; but we paid them no attention, and, wrapped in our warm cloaks, despised the weather and them. On leaving, we distributed a few small coins among the children in return for the use of the stone table, and even two or three well-dressed men did not object to receive their share. The children were very pretty. One of them I noticed particularly, a little thing about five years old, dressed like a girl, and with a girl's face; but I was told by the brother, who was in charge, that this, too, was a boy. No girls were seen; and we saw no women but two or three, who were washing clothes at a trough among the olive-trees, and these carefully turned aside as we approached. They were probably neither young nor good-looking.

It is a curious habit of the Greeks, that almost all the common people, men as well as women, ride sideways on the saddle. It is true that the women are rarely indulged with a ride at all. One may see group after group of peasants, each group consisting perhaps of three or four men of various ages and two or three women, all probably members of one family, and a loaded mule, or donkey. Each of the women will have on her head a load of wood large enough to conceal her features. One of the men will shoulder his hoe, another will have some light load, another will ride the beast of burden, and another will lead him. It is evident that even now woman occupies but a low place in the scale of humanity in these countries bordering on the east. In Corfu this remark chiefly applies to the women of the lower classes, but is there very marked.

As is usual in eastern countries, the women marry young, the match being arranged by the seniors of the family, and objection is said to be rarely made by the girl.

The wedding portion of a bride consists of the family jewels, or at least of such a proportion of personal ornaments as can be collected together for the occasion. These are really valuable, including much gold and silver, and embroidery, and the costumes themselves are expensive. Afterwards, when children and hard times come, when the oil crop falls short, and the maize fails to yield its accustomed return, when the rain destroys some things, or, which is more common, the drought and sun prevent the due growth of others, these resources become available. They are savings banks at which no interest is given. The husband borrows the dower, and raises money upon it by pawning; and as the *mont de piété* is under government superintendence, and a definite proportion of the estimated value is always lent on fair terms, there is no great harm done. After a while, a good olive year, which is pretty sure to return perennially, enables the pledge to be redeemed, and it goes back among the other little valuables into the family chest. But by degrees these valuables come into the market, and are finally disposed of. In this way beautiful specimens of silver manufacture, used formerly for ladies' belts, are sometimes to be purchased for the value of the metal.

CHAPTER IV.

THE country to the south of Corfu rises almost immediately into low hills, and includes broken ground,
abounding with picturesque points of view. In this
direction, also, after the Lake of Calichiopulo is past,
there are cliffs on the east coast of the island, which
continue for some distance, and render the view from
the sea extremely fine.

A charming excursion, whether by sea or land, is
that from Corfu to Benizze, a little village of only
250 inhabitants, occupying the narrow space between
these eastern cliffs and the sea. The distance by
water is only between five and six miles, passing the
mouth of the old Hyllaic Harbour, and the ship of
Ulysses. The land journey is much greater, owing

to the detour made to avoid the lake and the winding of the road on the side of the hills, both in the ascent to Gasturi and the subsequent descent to Benizze.

The road out of Corfu passes the head of Calichio-pulo, and soon enters the olive groves. Before long, we begin to rise. One or two small villages are seen, and more than one road branches off—one to the pass of Garuna, another to Santi Deca, and a third to the village of Gasturi, all points well worth visiting. Two of the roads conduct to the south of the island, a district rarely visited, little peopled, and, in summer time, very unhealthy. This part of Corfu is compara-tively level, and a large tract of flat land projects out into the channel at one point for several miles. Ex-tensive salinas have formerly existed there, but they are not carried on at present. Beyond these, and at the furthest extremity, but on the west coast, there is a considerable tract of high ground presenting a steep face towards the sea, and terminating in Cape Bianco, the southernmost extremity of Corfu.

There is another place in Corfu, and several in other islands of the Ionian group, where salinas have been established. They are always marine marshes, but they do not seem to be necessarily unhealthy. This depends, no doubt, partly on the amount of decompo-sing organic matter drifting into their neighbourhood, but chiefly on the facility of access of the sea. In Corfu, both are unhealthy, and the villages of Lefkimo are eminently so.

The population of this group of five villages, which almost join each other, was, in 1848, 3,850, and in

1860 had only increased to 4,008, a difference of four
per cent. in twelve years   This stagnation is most
probably due to the insalubrity of the district.

On the road to Benizze, in the early morning, one
meets numerous groups of villagers, bringing market
produce into Corfu. Some carry their burdens on
their heads, others on the backs of mules or donkeys.
Most of the groups consist of men and boys, but occasionally both women and young girls are seen. All
the peasants struck me as being cleaner, more healthy,
better looking, and better grown, than the same classes
in the villages near the town to the west. The younger
women were somewhat better dressed, though always
with the same plain skirt of blue, the same kind of
high chemisette, cut square under the breasts, and a
handkerchief over the head, partly covering the face,
but every now and then so arranged as to set off to
advantage the features that were thought best worth
presenting.

The country in this direction is well cultivated, and
abounds in fruit and vegetables. The villages are
small, but prettily placed, and look clean at a distance,
though they hardly bear close inspection. This is
especially the case with Gasturi. It is built on a somewhat steep hill side, the houses being at different levels.
Immediately behind the village, rises a pyramidal mass
of rock, overlooking the whole, and itself crowned
with a small, but picturesque, country house, the seat
of Sir Peter Braila, a well informed and intelligent
gentleman, occupying a high position in the government. This villa is not inhabited except during the

summer months, when the heat at Corfu is excessive. The view from it across the Channel of Corfu to the Albanian Mountains, and the fresh cool breeze coming from their summits, which are only free from snow for a very short season, contrasted with the rich vegetation of Corfu, and especially of the central plains immediately below, is extremely fine. The closely adjacent village of Gasturi and the mountain of Santi Deca are also extremely picturesque. Gasturi itself has more than a thousand inhabitants, and contains several good houses.

From the house of Sir P. Braila commences the descent to Benizze, by a road cut in a long succession of zigzags, down an almost vertical cliff. This is really one of the wonders of the island; not so much for the construction of the road, which involves no greater difficulties than have been overcome elsewhere in similar positions, but because of the exquisite and constantly varied beauty of the scenery which changes at every turn, and alternates the most romantic, with the softest and most lovely views. It is also remarkable, that so good and costly a road should have been constructed to accommodate so very small a population, for it does not lead beyond the village, and there seems nothing there in the style of the houses, as there certainly is nothing in the number of the people to require so much accommodation. All the villagers, whether on foot, or with beasts of burden, carefully avoid the high road, for the Corfiot seems to object very strongly to zigzags on a mountain side, and greatly prefers toiling·laboriously up a nearly vertical stony path to walking at his ease and conducting his animal along the easy ascent of a good but longer road.

Benizze is prettily placed, but it is chiefly interesting from the springs of pure water that burst out of the rock in a ravine behind the village, about a third of the way up the steep cliff. This water has been conducted to a reservoir, and is thence passed along a conduit, carefully constructed along the cliff and across the country, to supply the town of Corfu. Enough remains, after filling the reservoir, to keep a multitude of small mills at work, whose cheerful noise is never lost, and which are seen in succession, as we rise rapidly on the hill side, and up the ravine to the source. Beyond Benizze, a beautiful and romantic walk of a few miles leads to a small stream, up which towards the source is the mediæval ruin of Paleocastra, another fine spring of water gushes out of the rock, originating the little river, which, like that in the north of the island, is known by no other name than Potamos.

Without being very remarkable, the ravine up which one ascends to the place where the water bursts forth from the rock above Benizze, is picturesque, and well worth a visit. Wild limestone rocks shut in the view on each side, and, if we turn back, the blue water of the sea, and the noble mountains beyond, form the usual admirable contrast. The water issues from a natural cleft in the limestone in a considerable stream, and is increased by two or three small springs adjacent. It falls almost immediately about twelve feet over a shelf of rock into a pool, whence it enters a narrow, rocky, and in parts, an artificial channel, till it reaches the first mill. A variety of trees grow thickly around, taking advantage of the perennial moisture, and the ravine behind and above closes in rapidly.

A steep climb conducts past a house perched on the hill side to a road which leads to the village of Stavró, or the Cross, one of the wildest of those in this part of the island, built high up on a narrow ridge just facing Santi Deca on the one side, and looking down on Gasturi on another, while far below at one's feet are the pretty white houses of Benizze. The village has, like many others, a sad, deserted look during the day, not a soul being visible, and not a sound heard. The houses are so close together, that it would often be difficult for two stout men to pass each other in the interval left, and so irregularly placed that the narrow streets or lanes between them appear to end suddenly every half dozen yards. The houses are almost without windows looking outwards, and have a very oriental look.

Most of the houses are mere hovels, and I was rather suprised to come suddenly on a handsome gateway, evidently once the entrance of a building of some pretence. A semicircular arch of good proportions, and, with a quaint face sculptured out of the keystone, was surmounted by a square and ornamented entablature, and this again by a small and exceedingly quaint full-length figure enclosed between scrolls. Within this gate there were a few fragmentary remains of a house, apparently larger and better than the others, but with no architectural features remaining. In a small court-yard was a round siliceous stone, placed like a table, but used as a sharpener of knives, tools, and swords.

The church of Stavró is large and much superior in external appearance to the ordinary village churches of the island. It is situated quite at the extremity of the ridge on which the village is built, some distance from the houses, and on the highest and most exposed point. The view from it is superb. Benizze lies below, and the whole coast for miles is clearly made out. Gasturi on its hill is detached and prominent. Santi Deca, the high mountain at no great distance, looks as if one might reach the top in half an hour. A deep and rich valley separates Gasturi from the mountain, and far away over the fertile plain of the middle of Corfu, broken by many picturesque hills, and covered with its tens of thousands of olive trees, and hundreds of acres of vineyard and corn land, rises the broad, massive range of San Salvador, with its two culminating points, and its continuous ridges, to Karagol in the east, and the Castle of St. Angelo in the west. Turning round, the view is equally extensive, and not less striking. The flat plain of Lefkimo is seen, and the high cliffs behind, terminating in Cape Bianca, loom like a distant island. Paxo is clearly marked, and beyond it the high lands of Santa Maura may be recognised in the extreme distance, while the mountains of Albania, ever present and always beautiful, form a graceful border to the picture towards the east.

I descended from Stavró to Benizze by a different

and easier path than that by which I had climbed. A sheer naked precipice of limestone rock, several hundred feet high, and perfectly vertical, forms a singular termination of the hill and cliff of Stavró. This precipice does not look towards the sea, but faces a ravine between the hill of Stavró and that of Gasturi. Below this cliff is a long natural talus, formed of innumerable fragments of rock that have fallen down from the precipitous face. This talus extends to the sea, and is covered everywhere with the richest vegetation.

One of the roads diverging from that to Benizze leads to the village of Santi Deca, from which the mountain of that name can be conveniently ascended. The village lies on the shoulder of the mountain, about a third of the way from the base, and has nearly eight hundred inhabitants. It is not very clean, and the streets are rough, unpaved, and irregular; but there are several houses and gardens indicating material wealth. The land about the village, also, is cultivated, and the sides of the mountain are made available whenever soil enough can be heaped together for the purpose.

Santi Deca (ἡ Ἅγιοι δεκα, or the ten saints) has derived its name from a local tradition. It is sometimes, but quite improperly, corrupted into Santa Decca, as if the ten male saints had been miraculously rolled into one virgin, as some compensation for the much more remarkable and celebrated case in the city of Cologne, where one maiden saint named *Undecimilla* has left behind her, for the veneration of the faithful,

the bones of eleven thousand.   However this may be,
the summit of the mountain before us certainly exhibits a monastery where ten holy men may have lived
without being too closely jostled, and we may, therefore, accept the name in whichever way inclination
suggests.

The mountain is of considerable elevation, but I
know of no attempt at measurement either by the
barometer or other means.   It is by no means difficult of access, a perfectly good path leading up from
the village to the monastery, which is within a hundred feet of any one of the three summit peaks of which
it boasts.   It is nearly detached, the pass of Garuna,
which separates it from the high ridge running southwards to San Mathias, being not very much above the
level of the village of Santi Deca.   On the east and
north sides the olive-trees extend high up the mountain side; on the west side there are chiefly vines
cultivated in terraces.   The whole mountain is of
limestone.

Of quite a different character from San Salvador,
which is the higher of two culminating points of a
long ridge and table-land, Santi Deca represents the
angle formed by the meeting of the east and west
coast ranges of the southern division of Corfu, or
rather, perhaps, of the south middle, since the
southern part more properly consists of the hills
terminating with Cape Bianco.   The eastern range
appears in Stavró, and is separated by a somewhat
wide ravine from Santi Deca, through which runs
one of the roads from Corfu to Lefkimo.   The

western range is the loftier, and from the mountain
of San Mathias, some miles to the south-west, the
ground sinks till it dies into the cliffs which run all
along the west coast of the island to Cape St. Angelo
beyond Paleocastrizza. San Mathias is probably little,
if at all, inferior in elevation to Santi Deca, but no
one seems to have estimated the height.

Regarded in this light, Santi Deca is interesting, as
opening out a view of the south of the island, which
cannot be seen from any point further north, and I
was therefore anxious to reach the summit. The
views towards Corfu and the sea are, perhaps, hardly
equal to those from Stavró, but those on the other
side are instructive.

The beautiful pass of Garuna is immediately below
the steep western face of Santi Deca. On this side of
the mountain, as I have already remarked, there is a
succession of terraces covered with vines, and at the
foot of the cliff is a somewhat wide expanse at an
elevation sufficiently above that of the village of Santi
Deca to make it a steep pull for a carriage. Here is
the pass between the mountains, and the cliffs beyond
which are somewhat higher. A picturesque road
through the olives leads over the pass into the valley
beyond, and so to the lake of Corissio, passing the foot
of Santa Mathias.

The vine and fig flourish in all this part of the
island; and they are even cultivated at the monastery,
close to the summit of Santi Deca, where there is a
small plot of level ground. At the time of my visit,

the men were busy tending the vines, and the women carrying brushwood.

From all the heights in every part of Corfu, the same general structure may be observed; and, as with this chapter I take leave of the island for the present, it will be desirable to take this opportunity of alluding to a point in its physical geography, on which much of its characteristic beauty depends, and to which also much of its present want of salubrity may be referred. If, in this way, I can offer any practical suggestion to those, whether in the island or elsewhere, who have it in their power to improve the sanitary state of this very important and most beautiful spot, it will be well worth while to diverge a little from the mere narrative of my travel, at the risk of being thought tedious by some of my readers.

Looking down from the highest peak of Santi Deca, the eye is attracted at once by a large sheet of water, at a distance of several miles to the south, nearly corresponding with, but not so large as the Val di Roppa, already described in the last chapter as one of the points of greatest interest in the view from the cliffs of Pelleka.

This large sheet is called the Lake of Corissio. I was not able to reach it,—my time in the island being limited, and the distance from the town considerable; but I saw it, and made enquiries concerning it, which satisfied me of its real nature. It presents conditions by no means identical with those exhibited by the Val di Roppa, and, indeed, more like those observed at

Govino; but it has its own peculiarities. It is a marine marsh of great extent, very little below the ordinary level of the sea, receiving the drainage of a considerable mountain district, but having natural outlets that have sometimes been obstructed. At such times, the lake has become a source of malaria, and has rendered the neighbourhood absolutely uninhabitable.

Besides the Val di Roppa, the harbour of Govino, the Lake of Calichiopulo, and the Lake of Corissio, I saw, at least, a dozen similar examples on a much smaller scale in Corfu. Some are perfectly round pools, such as are seen below Scripero, on the way to the pass of Pantaleoni; some irregular marshes, seen on the road to Pelleka; some swamps by the sea-side; and some large flats south of Santi Deca, before the Lake of Corissio is reached.

The Lake of Corissio had always for many years an outlet to the sea; and, in old maps, it is marked as a bay rather than a lake. This outlet has been long since choked up, and the lake has become enclosed; and as the level of the bottom of the basin is not very different from the mean sea level of the Mediterranean at that point, it is always subject to be choked. The Val di Roppa and most of the other swamps are, in some respects, similarly circumstanced, being near the sea level, but not draining naturally into the sea.

It must be remembered that, although there is little true tide traceable in the Adriatic, and, indeed, in the Mediterranean generally, beyond Malta, the waters of that great inland sea are subject to considerable and, apparently, to periodical alternations of level, sometimes receding so as to leave bare extensive breadths of mud and sand, and sometimes advancing much beyond their usual limits. In embayed portions of the sea and in the channels between large islands and the main land, where one end of the channel is much narrower than the other, or is choked up, this difference is, of course, liable to be multiplied.

The question of real tidal influences in these waters must be regarded as still subject to discussion, although a large amount of careful observation was, many years ago, brought to bear upon it by Admiral Smyth. It is certain that there is a diurnal change of level, and extremely probable that this is due to lunar action, but the amount of flux and reflux is small, and greatly interfered with by winds and currents. Thus, at Venice, it is considered that the time of high water takes place about an hour and a-half before the moon reaches the meridian, and again after an interval of twelve hours, while the times of rising and setting of the moon are the periods of low water. The change of level is stated to vary from one to four feet at the head of the Adriatic, but is probably less, and is so completely interfered with by occasional currents, produced by local winds, as often to be altogether masked and lost sight of.

But while at the head of the Adriatic the tide due to the moon's attraction is thus masked, it is even less clear in the Ionian sea, where the water is more open. In Corfu, as at Argostoli, in Cephalonia, it is only in embayed seas that the effect is determinable; and it

generally only ranges between two inches and a foot.
Still there can hardly be a doubt that there does exist
a periodical rise and fall of the water; and the result,
even of this small wave, ought to involve a corresponding change of the air, and secure good health. That
this is not the case is probably due to the interference
of prevalent winds with the real tide.

There are many causes acting to produce a change
of level in these waters, and each helps to complicate
the others. Thus, in some places and during some
seasons, the vaporisation of the water in the open
parts of the sea may help not a little, while sometimes the continuance for an unusual period of some
prevalent wind, and even the earthquakes, by producing large waves, are enabled to influence greatly
the level of the water at enormous distances. The
whole subject, though of much interest, is surrounded
by difficulties, which render it difficult to determine
accurately the meaning of local observations.

On the whole, however, we must regard the Mediterranean as being subject to one or more direct
small tides, besides having its waters disturbed by
occasional storm; but as the regular tide is very
small, and the flux and reflux of the tide in a large
ocean is accompanied by the disturbance, equally
regular, of the great atmospheric wave, so this occasional change of level may, perhaps, be accompanied
by small oscillations in the pressure of the air, and be
connected with winds. Certain winds prevalent for a
long time must inevitably drive the water into, or out
of, the various embayed portions of the Mediterranean;

and the reflex action of the wave thus produced may act again on the atmosphere.*

It is in the districts where the prevailing rock is limestone of a nature very easily cracked and certainly very cavernous, that these dangerous swamps, whether freshwater or marine, are known. That the limestone rocks of the whole of Corfu contain much water is evident from the fact that at the tops of all the mountains where monasteries are built, wells are sunk, and water reached with the greatest ease. When I was at the top of San Salvador, after a drought of eight weeks without a drop of rain and with little cloud, the water was within eight feet of the surface in the monk's well, at the very highest point of the island. The springs that issue from the sea, at the foot of the mountain near Ipso, are further proofs of the state of the case. Limestones, cavernous in themselves, and constantly giving passage to water that dissolves the rock while it passes through it, must inevitably tend to form funnel-shaped valleys; and the bottoms of such valleys becoming filled with

---

* I may, however, state a result of personal observation in the island of Santa Maura during the equinoctial gales of the present spring (1863), which were unusually severe and prolonged, owing to there having been no change of weather and little rain for three months. During the whole season of the gales (extending over ten days), during which calms, hurricanes, torrents of rain, bright sunshine, and fearful thunder-storms rapidly alternated, the indications of a sensitive aneroid barometer showed no rapid change of pressure ; and the total range did not exceed nine millimetres. The lowest reading was ·736, and the highest, after the worst weather commenced, ·745. The usual reading throughout was ·741. During this time, the level of the water in the sea changed about two feet.

detritus, brought down from the adjacent hills, assume a dead level constantly rising. From the nature of the case, it would be a comparatively easy task to carry off the water retained on these bottoms by deep cuts, kept clear from time to time; and there cannot be a doubt that, with the removal of the stagnant water, the malaria derived from them would not exist.

The periodical occurrence and heavy fall of rain in the island of Corfu, the nature of the rock of which the island is chiefly formed, and the rapid growth of vegetation immediately after the spring rains, followed by the intense heat of summer, combine to produce malaria. A thorough and systematic drainage of all the valleys and swamps, whether fresh water or marine, free access given to the sea in the saline marshes, and a rapid removal of the rain water draining into these receptacles, preventing the accumulation of organic matter in stagnant pools, could not fail to have a favourable effect with reference to the villages of the interior, and very greatly improve the sanitary state of the island.

On the other hand, the marine swamps, such as those of Lake Calichiopulo, Lake Corissio, and Govino, are becoming silted up, and are subject to the occasioual and irregular rise and fall of the water in the Channel of Corfu, besides receiving fresh water during the rainy season. So long as a large quantity of organic matter reaches and enters these tracts of shallow water, or grows on the broad line that intervenes between the highest and lowest levels the sea reaches, so long will they remain poisonous, and nothing but the constant and free access of the sea can keep them clear.

Probably nothing short of the absolute silting up, and the conversion into permanent land, of these lakes, will altogether remove the causes of insalubrity, but with care much of the mischief might be prevented. It is very doubtful whether a saline marsh on an ordinary sea shore where the water is not extremely shallow is of itself injurious, and it may be regarded as certain, that by the removal of the shallow stagnant pools of brackish water, all that is seriously injurious would be got rid of, and the coast of Corfu would become healthy.

The movement of the population of Corfu is so slow, and has been so unsatisfactory since the census in 1848, that some effort is clearly required to improve the healthiness of the island. It is true that the statements for the intermediate years given without detail are somewhat contradictory, but if any reliance can be placed on the returns, the native population of Corfu in 1861 had certainly not increased at the rate of one per cent. per annum for many years, and scarcely then exceeded 64,000, being at the rate of 281 per square mile. There is reason to suppose that in former times the population has been at least four times as great, and I have already expressed an opinion that before the silting took place to the extent it has now reached, the saline marshes were less unhealthy than they are at present.

It may be a question whether the cultivation of the olive to the great extent it has reached in Corfu has not also helped to put the air in a state to receive and propagate malarious gases. The principal tree vegetation in all parts of the low lands being of this kind, the trees not being trimmed, and the dead wood seldom removed, there is a constant slow decay almost everywhere. The luxuriant vegetation of spring, followed by a long period of summer heat, cannot but tend to increase the danger in localities where the ground is low and flat. The absence of forests in the mountains, is another cause affecting the state of the atmosphere, by increasing radiation and evaporation.

On the whole, it would seem that while there are several causes sufficiently accounting for and explaining the frequent and serious attacks of summer fever in the island of Corfu, many of these causes are capable of removal, and others might be so far modified as to give reasonable hope of effecting a great improvement in the sanitary state of the island at moderate cost, if the attention of the authorities could be seriously directed to the subject. It may seem difficult to understand how a matter so vitally important should fail to receive the consideration it deserves; but the explanation is at hand, for political gossip is to the Corfiot a much more important part of public business than any honest inquiry as to the best measures of attaining any great practical good.

There is one district in Corfu about which I have hitherto said little, and which is, perhaps, the most unhealthy of all; I mean the whole of what is called Lefkimo, comprising the southern extremity of the island, which terminates in the bold headland of Cape

Bianco, formerly Leucinna, where the Athenians are
said to have erected a trophy on the occasion of their
first naval victory on the breaking out of the Peloponnesian war.   The soil and rock here is much more
marly than elsewhere in Corfu; the produce is chiefly
oil—always a bad indication, and the villages, which
are numerous, are almost all in decay, and most of the
houses in ruins.   So little stone is there hereabouts,
that the stone for the houses has to be brought from
the opposite coast of Albania.   Long ago, the miserable appearance of the people, their dirt, and squalor,
and poverty, attracted attention.   Dr. Davy, speaking
of the people of this part of Corfu, remarks, " Agues
are common amongst them, so is scurvy, particularly
among the men, and dropsy, and visceral disease.   It
is remarkable, that they are also very subject to gout,
a complaint elsewhere exceedingly rare in the Ionian
islands.   I was told, that in the whole population of
the five principal villages, which are contiguous,
amounting to about 2,000, there were when I visited
it, in the spring of 1825, forty cases of the complaint,
many of them severe and chronic.   I saw one man a
complete martyr to the disease, who had been confined
to bed three or four years, a cripple from concretions
of lithate of soda in the joints of his hands and feet."
This terrible state is attributed to the position, the
marly soil, and the stagnant water in the neighbourhood.   Dr. Davy is inclined to attribute the result to
the food and habits of the people.   He says, that
during the time of making oil they will eat from one
to two pounds of oil a day, and at other times from

six ounces down to two ounces, according to the plenty or scarcity. There is a marl district in Cephalonia, near Lixuri, and another in Zante, neither of which is unhealthy in a remarkable degree.

That the island of Corfu is inevitably unhealthy, in the strictest and most practical sense of the word, is as clear from the statistics of the population as from a common sense view of the case in connexion with these large marshy tracts (see chapter iv.). The increment of the population for the last four years is at the rate of only one per cent. per annum, and there had previously been a diminution. The proper increment would be at least treble that rate in a healthy, thinly-peopled country; and the conclusion I think is, that until some other cause can be pointed out, the malaria must be looked to as the cause. I have not been able to obtain even a suggestion as to the possible existence of any other cause.

At the same time, it would give a very unfair and incorrect notion of the climate of Corfu if it were dismissed thus summarily. To the feelings of most of the English residents, who can select their position, and who avoid certain imprudences of exposure, the temperature and state of the air are generally pleasant. The winter is short; and though the rainfall seems to be very heavy when it does come, the number of rainy days is small. The quantity of cloud, except at certain brief seasons of change, is also extremely small. The air is clear, bright, and dry,—very stimulating to the membrane lining the throat and lungs; but this is not always unpleasant, and those who escape fever suffer little from other diseases.

As a proof of the sanitary condition of the lower classes, I may state, on the authority of the best authorities, native and English, that during summer and autumn, the whole of the suburb towards the Lake of Calichiopulo is one mass of low fever. This fever is *never* absent; and both grown up people and children show, in their general appearance, the badness of the air they breathe.

A strong contrast is apparent when we compare this with the medical statistics of the troops stationed here. Many of them suffer less than in any other Mediterranean station; and, generally, there is nothing to complain of. This is doubtless due to the position and good ventilation of the barracks and the nourishing food supplied. A good deal of fever of all kinds seems common among the sailors and marines on board the men of war in the harbour, when they remain long on the station.

It has often been stated, and is, indeed, practically admitted, that Corfu itself forms an admirable intermediate station between England and the tropics. For troops sent in good health from England, some care no doubt is needed to avoid malaria in summer and autumn. During those seasons, also, the heat is excessive,—probably quite as trying to the constitution as either India or the West Indies. Those who escape in Corfu would probably escape if removed at once to the tropics, and those who there receive the seeds of low fever and malaria may not die, but are so far injured in constitution that they can never after be of much value for severe work.

PAXO.

I conclude this chapter with a brief notice of the two islands of Paxo and Antipaxo, which the short stay in the country and the unfavourable state of the weather did not allow me to visit. Paxo is a little island about ten miles south of Corfu, measuring nearly five miles long and two miles across, and having, at the last census, a population of 4,635 souls. It is hilly, and covered almost entirely with olives, the rock being everywhere limestone, as in Corfu. There is only one small stream, called, as usual, the Potamó. The houses of the only town are neat, whitewashed, and embosomed in gardens and olive trees, offering, on entering the little harbour, a very agreeable sight. It is on the east side of the island opposite the Albanian coast. The harbour is merely a narrow passage between two detached rocky masses of limestone and the larger island. It cannot be entered in bad weather. On the outermost of the islands is a small chapel, and on the innermost a fort.

Paxo, although so small, ranks as one of the islands forming the Septinsular Republic. It has, therefore, its Resident, or representative of the Lord High Commissioner, a municipality with its Regent, judicial courts, and other machinery of government. A small detachment of troops has generally been stationed there. It is subject only to the Lord High Commissioner; and it sends its representative to the Assembly.

Antipaxo is a rocky islet south of Paxo. It contains about 100 inhabitants, chiefly shepherds and fishermen. Asphaltum exudes from between the strata of limestone in a liquid form. On exposure, it becomes hard and brittle.

A curious legend concerning Paxo is given by Plutarch, and is alluded to by Milton in his grand " Ode on the Nativity," in these words:—

> " The lonely mountains o'er,
> And the resounding shore,
> A voice of weeping heard and loud lament:—"

The following is an account of the legend, given by an old annotator in Spenser's "Pastoral in May:"—

" Here (in Paxo), about the time that our Lord suffered his most bitter passion, certain persons sailing from Italy to Cyprus at night, heard a voice calling aloud, Thamus! Thamus! who, giving ear to the cry, was bidden (for he was pilot of the ship), when he came near to Pelodes (the Bay of Butrinto), to tell that the great god Pan was dead; which he doubting to do, yet for that when he came to Pelodes, there was such a calm of wind that the ship stood still in the sea unmoved, he was forced to cry aloud that Pan was dead; wherewithal there were such piteous outcries and dreadful shrieking as hath not been the like."

Paxo is described as possessing a certain amount of mineral wealth, chiefly in sulphur and sulphur springs.

It has, also, some fair building material. Its inhabitants are among the best looking and most comfortable of the whole group, and are different, in this respect, from most of the small islands. Its olive trees are celebrated as among the finest trees and as yielding the largest crops and the best oil of any of the islands. Seen from the sea, it offers little to remark upon; and its small town, Gaja, and nearly land-locked harbour are more picturesque than useful. Besides the town, there are numerous small villages. I ought to mention that the town is said to have received its name from the early Christian disciple, Gaius, mentioned in the Acts of the Apostles.

Paxo is without springs of water sufficient to supply the inhabitants, and what there are seem to be inconveniently placed, while some of them are brackish. Large cisterns, or tanks, have been constructed out of the rock to store the water in dry seasons, and these seem to have proved very useful. I cannot but think that as the prevailing rock is the common limestone of the islands, artesian springs might be discovered by boring.

The air of this little island is regarded as very healthy, and the people attain a great age. The women are remarkable for their good looks when young; but, as elsewhere in this part of the world, the beauty of the lower classes is worn off before the girls are out of their teens. In dress, they were formerly picturesque; but costume is rapidly dying out. Both sexes are rather idle and very inoffensive, but ignorant and superstitious; spinning thread, but

hardly able to make cloth.   They are often seen
knitting in the open air.   They are tolerably well
off, and few, or none, are absolutely unprovided for.
It is said that many of the poorer families possess
olive trees without owning land.   A few years un-
disputed possession of the fruits of a tree substantiate
a claim to permanent ownership, or, at least, to ownership as long as the trees last, and thus anyone having
been lucky enough to appropriate a neighbour's property for a time without notice, becomes the legal
owner of the trees he has robbed.   This, however,
gives no claim to the land on which the trees grow.

There is a bishop of Paxos, and many very small
chapels are distributed about the island.   As elsewhere, they are chiefly used on certain special
festivals, being those of the saint to whom the chapel
is dedicated.

Paxo is remarkable for its caverns.   They open
from the west and south-west, and are situated in the
lofty perpendicular cliffs of that part of the island.
They can only be entered in boats, and in calm
weather.   The largest of them is about 100 feet high
at its mouth,—nearly a third of the height of the cliff;
and its width is also about 100 feet.   It enters more
than 100 yards; and when inside, the view outwards
is described as very peculiar—"not without grandeur
and a certain beauty, produced by a combination of
circumstances, such as the great arched lofty roof—
the vast perpendicular walls—the deep and transpa-
rent blue water beneath, heaving up and down—the
gigantic cliff skirting it on the outside, almost shutting

out the sea and sky—the beautiful and vivid tints of the rock—the extraordinary play of light on the roof —and that clear obscure which belongs to deep shade in a clear atmosphere under a bright sun."* This cavern is covered with the beautiful "maiden-hair" fern.

Other caverns, not far distant, are highly characteristic of limestone districts and very picturesque, being divided into compartments, with openings in the roof admitting the light of day. The cliff scenery connected with these caverns is very fine, and is said to be superior to anything of the kind in the whole range of the Ionian Islands.

Besides Paxo and Antipaxo, there are several other small islands situated to the north of Corfu, and belonging to that island. Of these, Fano is interesting, as possessing a large and roomy cavern, difficult of access, except from the sea, and during very fine weather. This cave was long the resort of robbers and pirates. It was called by the French the Cave of Calypso, but without the smallest reason. It opens on the western side of the island. Fano also contains one of the curious, circular, hollow valleys, entirely enclosed, of which mention has already been made, and which recur in most of the other islands. It affords good quail shooting in the spring.

* Davy's "Ionian Islands," vol. i, p. 67.

MAP OF CORFU AND PAXOS.

C. Drasti

dara

Scale of English Miles 69 1=1°

0 1 2 3 4 5   10 MILES

P. St. Katherine

Spagus

Kasopo

Pantaleone

S. Angelo

MAVIONA

Light

Scripero

SALVADOR

Sganes

Sparilla

Gupho

Karkazi

Ipsa

Val di Ropa

GOVINO

Durmula

Lazaretto

Pelleka

Vido

Potamos

Hepa

CORFU

Lake Calichiopulo

Castrades

Vrosu Rock

S. DECA

Gastari

C H A N N E L

Benizze

S. MATTHIAS

Salvara

O F

L. di Corissa

C O R F U

A L B A N I A

L. of Butrinto

LEFKIMO

Solines

C. Bianco

SANTA MAURA,

OR

LEUCADIA.

———◆———

Lo! next, where Acarnania's shores extend,
Leucate's pale and broken rocks ascend.
Ah, fatal scene! by Venus doom'd to prove
The last sad refuge of despairing love,
For ever sacred be the foaming tide
That breaks against thy hoarse resounding side.
What though thy long forsaken steep retain
No mould'ring vestige of its marble fane,
Yet shall thy cliffs derive eternal fame
From Sappho's plaintive verse, and hapless flame.

WRIGHT'S "Horæ Ioniæ," p. 30.

CHAPTER V.

THE island of Santa Maura is the third in magnitude
and the fourth in population of the islands of the Septinsular Republic; but it is rarely visited, and has no
town of importance. Its area is estimated roughly at
180 square miles, and its population at 24,000. It
is the LEUCADIA of the ancients, a name which has
been very disadvantageously exchanged for Santa
Maura; but as the latter is that by which it is now

generally known, and is the name mentioned in modern maps and geographical books, I suppose it must here be retained.*

Santa Maura is a mountainous island, its highest elevation exceeding 3,000 feet, and there being within it several hills exceeding 2,000 feet. It consists, for the most part, of two principal and several subordinate mountain chains, trending north and south. It is twenty miles long from north to south, and about ten miles wide; but, as will be seen by the map, the western side is the longest, and it contains, or, rather, is connected with, the loftiest ridges.

Properly speaking, the island belongs to the mainland of Greece, although, politically, the adjacent shores of Greece belong to it, so that the Santa Mauriots claim, and possess, the whole of the valuable fisheries in the shallow waters between the north of the island and the continent. We shall presently see on what law, and for what reason these curious rights exist and have been retained.

I have said that the island properly forms part of Greece. It can, indeed, hardly be said to be separated from it, although no doubt a small part of the

* It is a curious fact that while the old Greeks denominated the island *Leukos* (λευκος *white*) from the colour of the cliffs, the more recent inhabitants have named it *Santa Maura* from μαυρος or σμαυρος, black. The latter name, however, is supposed to be that of a lady from Constantinople who died in the fort, and has no reference to physical appearances. It ought only to be used in speaking of the fort; but custom has proved stronger than reason; and, as stated in the text, it has gradually superseded the old and modern Greek names for the island and town.

connecting isthmus, or causeway, is permanently covered by a few inches of water.* The northern boundary of this isthmus may be said to extend from Teki Castle, and the islands and rocky reef in front of that land, to the cliffs below the north-western headland of Santa Maura. Outside this line there is everywhere deep water. The southern boundary of the isthmus is between Fort Alexander in the island and the opposite shore, a distance of about 350 yards; outside, (to the south,) there is also rather deep water. The distance from north to south, marking the width of the isthmus is somewhere about two and a-half miles, and the area is for the most part covered by very shallow water, divided artificially by causeways, which shut off a portion to the north-west, described and spoken of as "the lagoon."

It appears that by treaty, and by a fair interpretation of the old maritime law of the Mediterranean, of which the basis is to be found in the "Institutes of Justinian," all the sea at the northern extremity of Santa Maura, as far as the highest point to which the water ever rises, and therefore all the land that has been at any time laid bare by the retirement of the sea within

---

* I am aware of more than one instance, on a small scale, of this doubtful separation, and in tidal seas there are small islands, sometimes joined, sometimes detached. In most cases the island designation prevails even where there is this alternation. I know of no island so large and important in a non-tidal sea that is circumstanced like Santa Maura, and I think it indicates a remarkable permanence of level in the district for at least 2,500 years, unless, indeed, there has been a slow elevation, and a paring away of the surface corresponding to the elevation.

those limits, belongs to the island of Santa Maura. A curious result follows, for, as the sea-bottom seems to be shallowing · by the deposit of mud on the Greek side, and it is very rarely indeed that the waters reach their full height, a portion of the mainland of Greece is included among the island possessions. Thence the right of constructing a harbour; and so, again, the right of protecting such harbour by a fort, if it should be formed naturally. The capacity of benefitting by that portion of coast, is, ´indeed, thus lost to the Greeks. A somewhat valuable fishery is included among the rights possessed by the islanders, and absolute possession is secured by this arrangement. As a proof that this is no barren right, it is on record that on one occasion, before the liberation of Greece, when the Turkish Government commenced, and nearly completed, a strong fort, too near our frontier to be agreeable, they were called on to dismantle it, and were forced to do so. The ruins of this fort still exist.

The classical history of Leucadia I will allude to presently. Its more recent history has been written by Dr. Petrizzopulo, a learned native of the island, long resident in Italy, and a member of the Academy of Padua. His book, a small pamphlet, was published, in 1824, at Venice. Commencing with an account of the island under the Romans, for the accuracy of which classical authorities are quoted, he proceeds to narrate the events that followed the accession of Constantine the Great, and the christianizing of the island by the appointment of Agatarcus as its first bishop. As is usual in the account of conversion of that period, the people were more anxious to be baptized than the bishop could be to baptize them, and the change from Paganism, whatever its value might be, was effected with an almost miraculous rapidity.   Then followed the irruption of the Vandals under Genseric, and until the fall of the eastern empire various bishops seem to have been appointed, and to have attended the councils from time to time, summoned up to the close of the tenth century.   At this time the Ottoman empire was rapidly gaining ground, and had obtained its greatest victories in the east, and a century afterwards the crusades commenced. Leucadia was then selected as a safe spot in which to deposit the body of St. Donatus for a time; but after that, there was an interval of great confusion, during which little notice was taken of so small and unimportant a locality as this island.   It became in later times the fighting ground of the Turks and Venetians, until the former were finally driven out. The new city of Santa Maura, or Amaxiki, was founded in 1445, and has since undergone many important changes.

With a large and sheltered bay, and several ports in the south of the island, it seems to have been almost an act of perverse stupidity, especially in a maritime people, to have selected as the site of the chief town a bare, unmeaning, unhealthy spot, a mile away from any place to which it is possible for a ship to approach, and with no conveniences, or any redeeming points. As in many other cases, however, accident has had more to do with this position than intention.   At a very early period—so early that it is described by Homer—there

K

stood on the healthy and pleasant hills, behind and above the isthmus, a city called *Nericos*, sufficient remains of whose Cyclopean walls still exist to mark its limits. I believe that at the time this city was founded, the station may have been much less subject than it now is to malaria, for the lagoon, which is rapidly silting up, was then certainly larger, and the greater part of it must have been deeper than it now is. At any rate there was free access to the sea from the south to the foot of the hills, and fewer olive trees covered the flat land between the hills and the water, and there is no reason why the water may not have remained untainted during the whole summer. It is easy to understand the advantage of a position like that of Nericos in early times, for it was easily accessible, and yet perfectly defensible against any means of attack then known. Homer described this large tract of land, which was and is so nearly connected with the mainland that one can easily walk across it, as a peninsula and not an island, but as I shall have occasion to consider this question at greater length presently, I will not here pursue it further.

Much later than Homer's time, but still some two thousand years ago, there was a city on the same spot, probably much larger, built by the Corinthians, and called LEUCAS, whose remains are also traceable, and of which the coins and pottery and bronzes are in various collections.

It is worthy of remark that Homer speaks of Leucadia as Ἀκτὴ Ἠπείροιο, 'the peninsula of Epirus' (a name formerly including Acarnania, the present designation of the opposite shore of Greece). We also learn that the Corinthians cut a canal through the isthmus, which, however, in time became silted up, so that, in the Peloponnesian war, Thucydides describes the galleys as conveyed across the isthmus, and the same was done by Philip, son of Demetrius, in B.C. 218, as is described by Polybius. Livy, also, in describing the siege of Leucas by the Romans shortly afterwards (B.C. 197), gives the following description of the locality: "Leucadia, *nunc insula*, et vadoso freto quod perfossum manu est, ab Acarnaniâ divisa, *tum peninsula erat*, occidentis regione artis faucibus cohærens Acarnaniæ. Quingentos ferme passus longæ fauces erant; latæ haud amplius centum et viginti. In his angustiis Leucas posita est, colli applicata verso in orientem et Acarnaniam. Ima urbis plana sunt, jacentia ad mare, quo Leucadia ab Acarnaniâ dividitur. Inde terrâ marique expugnabilis est. Nam et vada sunt stagno similiora, quam mari; et campus terrenus omnis operique facilis."—T. Liv. xxxiii., 17.

"Leucadia, now an island separated from Acarnania by a shallow strait, which is a work of art, was then a peninsula, united on its eastern side to Acarnania by a narrow isthmus (this isthmus was about 500 paces in length, and in breadth not above 120 paces). At the entrance of this narrow neck stands Leucas, stretching up part of a hill which faces the east and Acarnania; the lower part of the town is level, lying along the sea, which divides Leucadia from Acarnania. Thus it lies open to attacks both from the sea and from the land, for the channel is more like a marsh than a sea, and all the adjacent ground has a depth which renders the construction of works easy."—BAKER's Translation.

After a gallant defence, Leucas became a Roman city, and in due time the seat of a Christian bishopric. It remained so till seized by the Turks in 1467.

Of the low flat that I have called the isthmus, only a part is permanently above water. It consists of a spit of sand reaching from the north-western end of the present island to within a couple of hundred yards of the mainland of Greece.

The belt of sand is, for the most part, narrow; but it widens in two or three places, one of them affording space for the construction of a large fort. Here the Turks, and after them the Venetians, made their head-quarters, as it is approachable from the north by ships of considerable burden; and before the modern improvements in artillery, must have been exceedingly strong. It was held alternately by the Turks and Venetians; and the former constructed an aqueduct, nearly a mile long, across the shallow waters between the fort and the plains below Leucas, where are excellent and abundant springs. The Venetians living in the fort traded with the Greeks and others inhabiting the island, and kept their magazines and certain cars, used for conveying produce and other purposes, at the nearest point of land to the fort. By degrees, a settlement was made on this spot; and as the Greek word for a car is ἅμαξαι, the town that arose was called Αμαξίχιον, or, in Italian, *Amaxiki*. The modern representative of this town, much altered, enlarged, and rebuilt, is the present capital of the island, and is still the only town it can boast of.*

* For the sake of convenience, I have sometimes retained this older name, in speaking of the town, in order to distinguish it from the island generally, and from the fort. Practically, both by the British and the islanders, it is now abandoned; but to speak sometimes

To improve the communication between the fort and the town, and to enable boats to reach the town, which the occasional shallows would otherwise prevent, a narrow canal has been constructed, the causeways on the banks of which nearly enclose a large part of the water between the sandy belt and the land. Thus is formed the present lagoon; and unfortunately for the health of the place, it is shut in by reeds, so as to become a fishery,—the water being nearly stagnant. At the furthest extremity of the canal, seawards, close to the west side of the fort, a larger and deeper cut has been made, which forms the present harbour; and there was an attempt (under British protection) to continue this cut, as a ship canal, entirely through the isthmus. The work was stopped within a very short time of its anticipated completion, and is now useless, as there is a bar at the south end, and the bottom is gradually filling up. It is believed, and is not improbable, that if an opening had once been established there would always have been sufficient current to scour the channel; for whatever wind blows, the water will always be higher on one side of the isthmus than at the other.

What is called the lagoon of Santa Maura is, then, really a low flat beyond the extremity of a bay, or gulf, running up between the peninsula of Leucadia and the mainland of Greece. Receiving the drainage

---

of the town of Santa Maura, sometimes of the fortress of Santa Maura, and sometimes of the island of Santa Maura, and be unable to do other than call each simply " Santa Maura," would be so confusing and in. convenient that I venture to revert to the earlier designation.

of a considerable tract of land, much of it hilly, the heavy rains that occasionally fall carry into it a good deal of silt; and marine currents coming in, either from north or south, help to increase the deposit which is rapidly forming and hardening at the head of this gulf. Unless interfered with from without, the whole tends, ultimately, to form a wide tract of dry land. The narrow passage near Teki Castle does not tend to become deeper; and, indeed, the water is already so shallow there that it can easily be waded across. The passage at Fort Alexander is both wider and deeper, but still has no tendency to check, but rather increases the deposits within the present area of shallow water. The completion of the ship canal, if successful, might slightly check the filling up of the lagoon.

The usual approach to Santa Maura is from the north, comparatively few ships coming up the south channel to the head of the gulf, except a war ship now and then, and the vessels intending to load with salt at the Salinas, just within the southern passage at Fort Alexander. A steamer of the Austrian Lloyds Company leaves Corfu for the island on Saturday evening, arriving early on Sunday morning. It then proceeds to Previsa, a small Turkish town in the Gulf of Arta, about eight miles distant; comes back in the afternoon to Santa Maura, and returns to Corfu during the night. There is no other regular communication, and very little chance indeed of occasional visits. Yachts rarely touch at a place so inconveniently situated and so poorly provided; but the classical interest of Leucadia brings, from time to time, a few travellers, and sportsmen are occasionally tempted by the shooting on the mainland, immediately opposite, which is said to be very good.

Seen from the deck of a steamer, Santa Maura appears one unbroken mass of mountainous land, fringed with a few narrow strips of cultivated ground near the sea. As the ship approaches and anchors in the little harbour, one is surprised at the appearance of the long spit of sand and reef, and the wide space by which we are still separated from the town, which looks in the distance more like a collection of low hovels than a capital city. On entering the boat that is to convey one to shore, one feels confused at the multitude of lines and sticks that just rise above the water's edge; and on entering the narrow canal—a canal cut through water—there is a curious feeling of incongruity, not diminished when we find ourselves towed and pushed along by a couple of boatmen, who jump upon one of the causeways enclosing the canal, and with their boathooks propel us towards land. There are, however, no other means of reaching the shore, unless, indeed, we prefer a walk of nearly four miles over a narrow belt of shingle, and afterwards a further long walk through an olive grove. We resign ourselves to be towed and pushed along, and in time are landed on a kind of quay, in front of an incongruous collection of low wooden houses and sheds, which are the custom-house, the health-office, and the police-office of Santa Maura.

The town was described to me by one who knew it

well, and who had travelled much, as the third worst
real town to be found in civilised countries. He knew
of two only that were more wretched. I think my own
experience could add but one or two more to the melancholy list. There is in it no house of public entertainment in which a stranger can take up his temporary
abode. Such a thing as an hotel would be simply
ridiculous. I had an introduction to the Resident,
the title given in all the seven islands of the republic
to the official representative of the Lord High Commissioner; and though I arrived at a most unreasonable
hour in the morning, and had to rouse up the whole
house, I had no resource but to proceed there at once,
and there take up my abode. The open-handed hospitality, cheerfully and instantly rendered, is not easily
to be forgotten. It would clearly be impossible, if
stray travellers often visited the island; but there
seems no danger of its being converted into a heavy
tax.

Although, however, Amaxiki does not boast of an
hotel, it has its public buildings. There is, first—the
Palace, or Residence, where the representative of the
protecting sovereign takes up his abode. Then there
are the Law Courts next door; there is the Mansion
House, the residence of the head of the municipality;
the Casino, or Club; the churches, of which there are
many; the Market-place; the Health-office, including
the Post-office, and the Prison. The principal street
is called the Bazaar, and is, in so far, fitly named, that
it is full of open sheds from one end to the other.
Not a pane of glass in a shop front; not a decent

looking shop of any kind is to be found there. All is oriental and dirty. Certainly it does not abound in silks and gold or silver ware; there are no rich scarfs, or amber beads, or handsome arms. It is not luxurious, in fact, in any sense; but it is not the less oriental.

And the public buildings are not models of architectural beauty. There are few constructions of any kind in the whole place that are more than one storey high; there are hardly any that are built of anything much stronger than wood, ten feet above the foundations. The town was destroyed by an earthquake in 1825, and built up afterwards with a view to the return of a similar convulsion. Thus the foundations of most of the buildings are laid deep in thick walls of solid stone, and the superstructure is a plain, stout framing of oak, filled in with brick and stucco. In case of future earthquakes, it is hoped that the damage would be trifling, although, should fire occur, the result would be very serious. Slight earthquake shocks are very common.

The style in the better class of buildings is more Italian than anything else, and is by no means unpicturesque, the lines being much broken, and no two houses that are detached being alike. All but the principal streets are narrow, dirty, and badly paved. The better houses have large, airy rooms, with French windows, which are sensible enough, for the climate rarely requires much shelter from cold, and the heat is said not to be excessive. The smaller houses are dark and dirty, and the rooms are small and miserable. The churches are not large, and are built in the style

common in the East, except in rich and luxurious
cities. They are oblong, barn-like constructions, with
a small detached bell-tower holding two bells. Exter-
nally they are quite without ornament, and inside the
decoration consists of a number of figures painted
on the screen that, as usual, not only shuts off the
high altar, but reaches to the ceiling. The number of churches is large compared with the size
and population of the town; but Santa Maura is an
archbishopric, and there is a goodly array of town
priests, all of whom seem to belong to the class of
celibates.

Outside the town is the commencement of a handsome stone building, in the style of an ancient temple,
which was intended to be dedicated to the patron saint
of the town, whose name is Santa Maura. After the
foundations were laid and the walls raised to the
height of about four feet from the ground, and when
there had been brought to the spot a vast number of
squared and rough blocks from the ruins of Leucas,
the work was stopped, and seems likely to remain a
monument of folly, extravagance, and the barbarous
and needless destruction of one of the grandest remains of antiquity. One would have hoped that no
one having the smallest pretence to liberal education,
or who could appreciate the value of ancient monuments of art, would have destroyed, wilfully and
utterly, one of the very few remains that exist of ·
the complete gateways through Cyclopean walls.
Such a gate, however, existed at Leucas till destroyed
for the sake of this modern temple, and the stones

of it may still be recognised among the large blocks
by the roadside adjacent.

In front, and on each side of Amaxiki are the
shallow waters of the lagoon, gradually diminishing
in depth, and in many places already reduced to a
few inches. Less mischief arises from this lagoon
than might be expected, and sometimes a summer
and winter will pass away with much fever. So little
unhealthy, indeed, is the mere shallow sea water, that
the fort, which is entirely surrounded, is said to be
singularly salubrious. Probably the small amount of
population, and the distance of the fort from the
town, may have something to do with this exemption.
There are large salinas, or salt pans, in the neighbourhood, and these also are not considered to poison the
air. It would seem that during the whole of the
summer, at a time when most of the islands suffer
greatly from malarious fever, the never-failing land
and sea breezes keep the town and its neighbourhood
in good health. Little organic matter finds its way
into the water, and there is always a good supply
of fish.

The old fort, built on one of the principal expan-
sions of the generally narrow strip of land enclosing
the lagoon, is interesting, and in the middle ages must
have been capable of making a good fight. It could
not, however, stand against modern artillery. It covers
much ground, and includes several outworks. It bears
marks of its successive masters, who, in each modification in the building, employed the old materials, of
whatever kind they were. There is a Turkish mosque,

perhaps originally a heathen temple, ultimately Chris-
tianized by the Venetians.   As a Christian church it
has, in its turn, been occupied by Greek and Roman,
popish and orthodox congregations, and now, at last,
under the English rule, is converted into a store-
room.   There are walls of all kinds, bastions, and outworks, chiefly constructed by the Turks; but the
prisons and oubliettes were added by the Venetians,
the old tyrants, but now the slaves of the eastern
Mediterranean.   To these have been added modern
barracks and earthworks.   It is interesting rather
for its historical recollections than for its actual
remains.

Viewed from any of the neighbouring hills the
lagoon, the spit of white sand running out to Teki
Castle on the Greek land; the tract of cultivated land,
with a house, and church, and olive trees upon it,
which projects from the sand spit into the lake nearly
opposite the town; the large enceinte of the fort with
its bastions and outworks; the salinas to the south,
and a conical hill crowned with the ruins of a dismantled fort erected by the Turks opposite the salinas:—
these together form a pleasing and striking group.
Immediately behind the town, and extending almost
the whole distance to the foot of the hills, some miles
inland, is a flat plain somewhat above the level of the
sand-spit, covered almost entirely on the west side
with magnificent olive trees, and on the other side
partly cultivated for garden produce, fruit trees, and
corn.   Here also, however, are other olive groves.
This rich tract affords large and profitable crops,

and combines great beauty with material sources of wealth. The olive groves are very ancient, and contain trees of almost fabulous growth. In one place I observed three trunks, each of the largest size that a sound young single tree ever attains (seven or eight feet in girth), growing together within a single bark; the total girth could not have been less than thirty feet. The age of some of these old trunks can only be guessed at; but certainly must be exceedingly great. No order is observable in the planting of these trees, and young trees are mixed up indifferently with old, but all are. well cared for, and the ground beneath them, which is generally very good soil in this part of Santa Maura, is for the most part under tillage, or is at least available for grazing sheep and horned cattle.

The olive groves now extend nearly to the edges of the lagoon; but they must have advanced by degrees in this direction, as the area of water has been gradually becoming less considerable for a long while.

Remains of an old wall, partly Cyclopean, partly of that somewhat newer construction called polygonal,* are found at intervals, and some towers of similar construction have been destroyed within the present century. These clearly mark the ancient limits of land towards the lagoon, and show that the water is now more than a quarter of a mile further back than

* By this term is meant large blocks, of various shapes, closely and neatly fitted, and having artificially smoothed surfaces in contact. The true Cyclopean wall is one in which the blocks of stone are selected as nearly adapted, but are not chiselled so that the surfaces in contact correspond. Both terms are limited to walls constructed chiefly of gigantic blocks.

it was two thousand years ago.   Besides these walls and
towers, remains of an ancient temple of Neptune just
within the old walls still exist, and have been converted into the foundations of a modern chapel.   The
walls seem to have been continued so as to include
most of the present olive groves, and they are traceable outside, but at no great distance from the modern
city.

It might be supposed that in a place so out of the
world as Amaxiki, the events going on in England
would possess little interest.   This is not, however, at
all the case, and ample proof was established of its
loyalty and good feeling on the occasion of the marriage of the Prince of Wales to the Princess Alexandra.   Perhaps this might not be uninfluenced by
the great question of the day, which to every one
speaking the Greek language must certainly be, union
with Greece; but, whatever the cause may have been,
the effect was very marked, and it will give some
insight into the Greek character, and may afford some
amusement if I conclude the present chapter with an
account of the rejoicings that took place in the island
on that day of universal holiday wherever the English
flag was hoisted.

I arrived at Santa Maura about the beginning of
March, within a few days of the wedding of the Prince
and Princess. Days before this, the preparations for celebrating the grand event had been going on to the utter
stoppage of all business. This might no doubt have
been a much more serious matter if the business interfered with amounted to other than wandering about,

'hearing and saying some new thing.' The streets had
been crowded with Greeks of all classes, in every conceivable variety of picturesque shabbiness.   Even the
ladies had been seen in public, and as for children and
dogs, they had constituted themselves permanent guardians of the principal preparations, and steadily kept
guard at every point where work was going on. The pre-
liminaries consisted in bringing in on the backs of old
women thousands of loads (none of them too heavy)
of green branches from the adjacant hill sides.   From
these hills any quantity of myrtle, ilex, and other beautiful materials for decorative purposes may be obtained,
and there will still be enough left for celebrations much
larger even than this.   When brought, the loads were
thrown down in front of the public and private buildings that were to be adorned.   Looking on at these
preparations, I see other Greeks, chiefly men, squatted
down in the middle of the road, weaving the branches
into interminable strings, which, in course of time,
are suspended in wreaths round windows, doors,
and other places.   While this is going on, a car-
penter appears with a comfortable ladder, on which
he can sit at ease, and having provided sticks and
nails, he proceeds to do his share in getting ready for
the illumination.   Fortunately, the weather is dry, and
progress is not checked by any untoward event.
After many days of such labour, relieved by the occasional shouts of little boys and the gaping wonder of
every peasant of the neighbourhood, long lines of brilliant green vegetation may be seen decorating the

market-place. All this confusion and bustle does not
interfere with business, for as it is now the great fast
of Lent, the sales consist chiefly of oranges and beans,
and the transactions are so small that they can afford
any amount of interruption. The wreaths extend
over the whole façade of public buildings occupied by
the Resident, the Tribunals, the Public Offices, the
Schools, the Churches, the Casino, or Club, and others;
and at length things are beginning to get into something like order. Meanwhile, the weather looks
treacherous, and much alarm is experienced by those
who are supposed to be weather wise.

I have said already that the houses in Amaxiki are
not lofty. The island generally, and especially these
low plains at the foot of the hills, on one of which the
town is built, is subject to frequent and troublesome
earthquakes. In 1825, much of the town and part
of an aqueduct crossing the lagoon to the castle were
almost destroyed by a convulsion; and in the houses
that were rebuilt, care has been taken by deepening
and rendering very solid the foundations and diminishing the upper works, to avoid serious risk should such
a catastrophe recur. The result is that, with few exceptions, the houses are either entirely on the ground
floor or with only one storey above the ground. Thus,
though the façade of the public buildings alluded to is
certainly extensive, the elevation is not commanding.
The palaces, in a word, are more safe than ornamental.
But as the public eye of the Amaxikians has not been
educated to any other style, they are quite prepared to

admire this; and no complaint is made. On the contrary, all the newest constructions vie with the palace in simplicity.

Exhausted, perhaps, by the excitement of the preparations, and in anticipation of the work of the day, the morning of Tuesday, the 10th March, is ushered in by unusual calm. Even the little boys have deserted their posts in front of my window—perhaps attracted by more exciting scenes elsewhere—the municipality having decided at the last moment to do something more than they had previously intended. My windows, it must be said, are part of the Palace façade, decorated for the occasion. I am thus enwreathed with myrtle; and, indeed, I may venture to say that, independently of the myrtle, I am the object of great wonder and of much discussion to the worthy people of the town. Your true Greek of the islands is behind no one in curiosity; and his intelligence and acuteness are so developed that he sees motives and meanings without number in everything that happens around him. Thus, when an Englishman arrives, who does not deal in currants, or wine, or oil; who is neither soldier nor sailor, judge nor physician; and especially if, as in my case, he carries a box round his neck, by the aid of which he measures the heights of the hills, and who, moreover, when he walks out of the town, has a policeman as a guide to help him look at, and knock about, the rocks by the sea-side, and climb hills that lead nowhere, the native is too clever a great deal to be puzzled, and at once discovers deep political motives, utterly unknown and unguessed at by any one but himself. The

stranger is the precursor of Alfred. He is going to
make the islands of the Septinsular Republic and the
mother country rich and great by a stroke of the pen.
There is nothing he is not capable of. It is true he
professes not to speak modern Greek, but then he is
only the more mysterious because so utterly incomprehensible; and wise men shake their heads when they
find that he can read the Greek Testament and write
the character and yet pretends that he neither speaks
nor understands what is said. But I am forgetting
the events of the day. The performances, besides the
grand exhibition of garlands and wreaths, and the illumination, were to include a considerable distribution
of money to the poor, that they also might bless the
happy occasion. More than a hundred families had
been thus supplied on the day preceding; and none
can help feeling how much this added to the satisfaction, both of those who gave and those who received.*
Within the residence, there was much to be done. A
grand ball and supper, to which two hundred of the
principal Leucadians had been invited, was to take
place in the evening. A *levée* was to begin the day,
a grand performance at the church to come next, and
in the evening the illuminations and transparencies
were to precede the ball. Such was the general pro-
gramme, to say nothing of royal salutes from the
castle, bands of music in the town, and the marching
to and fro of soldiers and police. Everybody, in a
word, was to be rendered happy; and the excitement

---

* It ought to be mentioned that the expense of most of this was
borne by the municipality.

was to know no end. The ladies had already trans-
lated into the best modern Greek, for immediate use,
the well-known lines—

"We won't go home till morning,
Till daylight doth appear;"

and the gentlemen were fully prepared to assist them
in keeping their word. Balls are not events of every
day at Amaxiki; and it was shrewdly supposed that
the supper might have its charms also. It was well
known that most of the invited had been practising
the dances for a long time; and for the last three
evenings there had been regular rehearsals in the
little theatre. One of the great difficulties in the
way was, indeed, the want of gloves; and I was informed, ou good authority, that this might have the sad
effect of diminishing the number of the ladies present
at the ball, for gloves were understood to be *de rigueur*,
and all gloves of all colours had long been bought up
from all the shops in the place. It was too late to get
more from Corfu.

Precisely at eleven, the business of the day commences, the whole police force of the island, fifty in
number, marching up to the house of the Resident with
their band playing, and forming a guard of honour.
Then the principal officers of the municipality appeared, and waited the arrival of the archbishop,
whose approach was soon heralded by the striking up
of the band to a lively air. At this moment, the Resident descended, accompanied by the regent and the
judge, and on their appearance, the guard saluted.

Close to the door was the archbishop, in his robes of state, heading a procession of priests, and holding in his hand a very ancient and curious crosier. His robes were long, and the train was held by the chief deacon. The archbishop was followed by his grand vicar and chancellor; and the three made a noble group, being all remarkably fine handsome old men. They were followed by the priesthood of the town, some of them fine and interesting-looking men, but others of a lower caste.

The Resident and the archbishop having bowed, they joined company, and marched on side by side, followed by the mayor, to a room in the Tribunal, or Courts of Justice, a building adjoining the Residence. Arrived there, the Resident stood in the middle of a small room with two doors, the archbishop on his left hand and the regent, or préfet, on his right. I, as a stranger, was placed next the archbishop. When the court was arranged, the priests came in at one door, each bowing to the archbishop, and shaking hands with the Resident. They went out by the other door, remaining, however, at hand. After them, came the judicial officers, and then other town functionaries, and, at length, private gentlemen. The scene was rather disorderly; and the bows were, some of them, awkward enough. The stock of black coats and white gloves seemed also to have been distributed by some freak of fortune,—the small coat with short sleeves, terminating in gloves with ample room for the hands, while the man with a coat and trousers hanging about him like a bag had split both gloves in the vain attempt to force his hands

into them.   Still the affair went off very decently.
Last of all came the primates, or head men of the
villages, who form a kind of police establishment, and
are generally the most respectable persons in each
neighbourhood.   These were particularly interesting.
They wore a national costume, and looked much better
than the town gentry. .They were, many of them, fine
old men; and I noticed some long, venerable, curly
locks among them.   Most of them behaved very well,
—entering slowly, stopping when they approached,
putting the hand on the heart, and then bowing in a
grand oriental style.   This was the best part of the *levée*.
As soon as the reception was over, a move was made
towards the church.   The archbishop headed the procession, and the clergy followed in something like order.
· The Resident and his party, after a short delay, also
proceeded through the bazaar under a triumphal arch
of evergreens, to a large square at the end of the town,
where was the church selected for the coming solemnity.
The streets and windows were lined with people, all of
whom uncovered as we passed.   About half way down
the street, we met the officers of the garrison from the
fort, who had been prevented by the strong wind from
coming across in time for the *levée*.   They turned back;
and we reached the square, and there found the police
with their band, and also the soldiers from the garrison,
drawn up.   As the archbishop entered the church, the
band commenced playing, and continued until the resident and his party had also entered.   The principal
visitors were placed in the stalls on each side of the
bishop's stall, and the priests were crowded together

in the part behind the screen, coming out only now
and then.   There were a vast number of candles in
the church, which were being sometimes lighted and
sometimes blown out during the whole service, a
beadle having a long stick, provided with a taper at
the end and a little fan close to the taper, so that he
could amuse himself in this way and produce endless
occupation very conveniently.   The service consisted
of prayers sung in a nasal, disagreeable tone, in
something like a very bad Gregorian chant, and the
responses were made by the whole body of priests.
The body of the church was quite full of men and
boys, some of whom were rather unruly, and a constant squabble went on as to places and other matters
without much reference to the service, and not always
sotto voce.   There was a large latticed gallery, in which
were as many ladies as could be crammed.   They did
not appear on the ground floor.

After the prayers, the Gospel was read by the archbishop, the book being held by the grand vicar and the
chancellor.   This book was said to be an old Alexandrian
manuscript, and was handsomely bound in embossed
silver.   It was brought after the reading to be kissed
by some of the principal persons, the Resident, the
regent, and myself being selected for the honour.
Then followed a special Litany, that had been drawn
up by the archbishop and his secretary for the occasion.
It is interesting as a specimen of the style of the Greek
Church on such occasions, and also for the good feeling
it exhibits throughout.   The original Greek is not remarkable as a composition, but the substance may be

thus rendered in a free translation. The officiating chief deacon chanted the versicles, standing outside the screen before the door that leads to the altar, and the priests present joined in the response, which consisted of the well known *Kyrie eleison! Kyrie eleison!*

THE LITANY.

Officiating chief deacon. O Lord have mercy upon us; and in the multitude of thy mercies, we beseech thee to hear us and help us.

Response. Lord have mercy upon us.

D. Bless, O Lord, we beseech thee, Thy Holy Orthodox Church.

R. Lord have mercy upon us.

D. Bless, O Lord, thy servant Gregorius, our archbishop, and all Christian people throughout the world.

R. Lord have mercy us.

D. Bless, O Lord, we beseech thee, thy servant Victoria, our protecting sovereign. Preserve her in health and strength for many years, and keep, also, under thy charge, her faithful army.

R. Lord have mercy upon us.

D. Bless, we beseech thee, thy servants, Albert Edward, Prince of Wales, and Alexandra, Princess of Denmark, who have, this day, been united in the holy bonds of matrimony.

R. Lord have mercy upon us.

D. Vouchsafe, O Lord Most High, to preserve these thy servants in strength and power. Grant them, we beseech thee, long life, and endue them with all the blessings of thy goodness.

R. Lord have mercy upon us.

D. Keep them, O Lord, in health of body, in peace of mind, and in uprightness of heart.

R. Lord have mercy upon us.

D. Grant unto them, O Lord, a numerous offspring, and that they may enjoy length of days, even for ever and ever.

R. Lord have mercy upon us.

D. Grant unto them that their children's children may remain on the earth, and that they be multiplied as the stars of heaven.

R. Lord have mercy upon us.

D. We beseech thee, O Lord, to hear these our humble petitions, and to have mercy upon us, miserable sinners.

R. Lord have mercy upon us.

The Archbishop.

Hear us, we pray thee, O God, our Saviour. Thou who art the hope of all the ends of the earth and of them that remain afar off in the broad sea. Be merciful unto us. Forgive us all our sins and be gracious unto us. Amen.

At that verse in the Litany in which the names of the bride and bridegroom were introduced, a signal was given, and the band, stationed outside the church, broke forth into an outburst of music fitted for the occasion. After the Litany had been sung, the Lord's Prayer was repeated, and the Archbishop concluded the ceremony by pronouncing a short blessing. When he had taken off his vestments, he came and sat down for a short time on his throne in the stall next to me, and conversed. I noticed that he alone had a veil on his hat, but he did not use it. The other priests, as well as the Archbishop, were all celibates, and this seems to be generally the case in the towns, though not so often in the country. The whole floor of the church had been strewed with laurel leaves and other evergreens, and the general effect impressed one as exhibiting oriental, or rather barbaric, splendour, although without the smallest attempt at that order and decency which, among northern people, seem so essential to the performance of a religious ceremony.

After the service the people dispersed, and we returned home, making on the way a visit of ceremony to the lady of the Regent, who was to act as lady patroness of the ball in the evening, the Resident not being a married man. We found her evidently prepared for the visit. She was a simple-mannered, well-informed person, young and good-looking, and well fitted for the occasion. The commandant of the fort was selected to assist this lady as master of the ceremonies, and, with her, superintend the dancing part of the entertainment. The day had now pretty well advanced, and there was a lull in the entertainments, everybody looking forward to the evening as the next great event.

Rather unluckily, as it then appeared, the weather, which had been threatening for some days, seemed inclined to break up and terminate in rain. A rough wind blew, and an uniform coat of grey completely concealed the sky; a few drops of rain also fell, and looked very ominous with reference to the evening's illuminations. A town council was held, the result of which was that the illuminations were officially postponed till the next day.*

After our return to the Residence a sound of distant music was heard. I was at the time talking to one of the officers of the garrison, and I stopped to ask if they had any Highlanders, as I thought I recognised bagpipes. The error was soon explained, for the sound proceeded from a drum and three fifes played on by villagers from the mountains, whose national music and some of their other peculiarities have a singular resemblance to those of the Scotch. Even when the men were standing, dressed in their pic-turesque costume, before the door, and I saw the instruments in their hands, I could hardly feel satis-fied that they were not bagpipes after all. The pipe must be nearly the same as an acoustic instrument, and thus the effect is similar; but the more acute Celt has distanced the simple Leucadian by raising the wind at the expense of something else than his own lungs. This peculiar music of drum and bagpipe, if so it is to be called, sounds somewhat oriental, and we find it in the mountains of Albania, as well as in the wilds of Leucadia. I ought to add, that the drum was played Chinese fashion, the art seeming to consist

* From what I was afterwards told, I am inclined to think that the ladies lent their influence to produce this delay, for they were obliged to be in the agony (or delight) of preparing themselves for the ball at the time when the illuminations would have been chiefly effective.

only in striking a succession of unmeaning bangs;
but I was told that in the old national dances it is this
martial sound that brings forth all the most violent
efforts, and stimulates to the utmost the excitement of
the performers.

By dusk, the elaborate preparations made at the
residence for the expected visitors, were complete.
The wreaths were suspended, the rooms decorated
with flags; stars, composed of bayonets and ramrods,
were placed in prominent positions; bouquets, consisting of flowers and mandarin oranges, were arranged,
and supper was laid.   Long lines of tables were prepared in the dining hall, and were so closely covered
with eatables, that there was barely room for plates.
It was expected that nearly two hundred guests might
arrive; and, as a good many hangers-on had also to be
provided for, and appetites on such an occasion are
proofs of loyalty, the supply was by no means so extravagant as it seemed.   What would an English lady
say to providing a wild boar and half-a-dozen young
pigs (the latter roasted whole), half-a-dozen turkeys,
and as many hares; sundry quarters of lamb, a score
of meat, pigeon and game pies, and a few other such
trifles, as the foundation of a ball supper.   Countless
dishes of smaller articles and sweets were at hand to
fill up every spare corner; and a good reserve was retained in the kitchen in case of need.   Such was the
scale of hospitality provided for Her Majesty's protected subjects in the Ionian island of Santa Maura;
and the event showed the wisdom of the provider.

Long before nine (the hour named in the invita-

tions) the guests began to muster. The majority of
the ladies were dressed in the fashion of the day, the
dresses having been obtained for the most part from
Corfu. These dresses were almost all in excellent
taste, but of course offered nothing for remark. Some
of the ladies of the old school appeared in national
costume, and were more interesting. These were all
married ladies, the wives of merchants and landed
proprietors. The costume they wore was very old,
and rather Byzantine than Greek. It is, however, an
island costume, and is considered to have been introduced originally from Constantinople several centuries
ago. The dresses were of silk, but the colour seemed
unimportant. All were bound with an edging of
rich gold embroidery, more than half an inch wide.
The dresses were not worn with much crinoline, but
they stood out well from the figure. From the back
of the neck, long lappets seemed to fall, also bound
with gold embroidery of the same kind and width.
The sleeves were of curious shape, fitting tight from
the elbow to the wrist. At the elbow, a double gold
band, or fillet, was seen, but the bands were of different patterns, although in the same general style in
all the dresses. Above the elbow, the sleeve was
puffed into the shape of a small balloon, with many
plaits. A very broad and rich gold band encircled the
waist; a chemisette of peculiar shape reached from the
waist to the neck, and the head dress was a long strip
of fine cambric and lace, curiously arranged, and
hanging behind below the waist. On the left side of
the head was a gold ornament, or cap, shaped like a

shell, and put on so as to form a part of the dressing of the hair. On the whole, the costumes were more interesting than beautiful, though they did not lack a quiet dignity, and an indication of very comfortable resources. I have since seen some of the wedding dresses, which are singularly beautiful and costly. They are now rarely worn.

Very few of the gentlemen from the town appeared in costume. One, a cousin of General Grivas, a name well known in the history of the recovery of Greek freedom, made his appearance in an extremely handsome dress, something intermediate between the usual Greek and Albanian costumes, as known in England, but more like the latter in the extremely full short petticoat and gaiters. His jacket was of a pale coffee colour (café au lait), covered with beautiful embroidery. The various chiefs of the country villages were in their ordinary costume, though of a better quality than is worn every day. They looked exceedingly well in their dark blue jacket and short full trousers, with a coloured sash round the waist, their white stockings showing from the knee to the ancle, and their large, curiously shaped shoes, oddly contrasting with the thin pumps of the other gentlemen. Over the jacket, the villagers generally wear a kind of pelisse or long sleeved coat. This is thrown off sometimes in society, but rarely, except when dancing is going on.

Dancing commenced in due time, and was kept up with the spirit that might be expected, in the case of ladies whose appetites for this amusement had been sharpened by long fasting. The real young Leuca-

dians are believed to have known balls hitherto only as
historical events, and those who had been educated at
Corfu, though more instructed by experience, were by
no means less active or less inclined to enjoy themselves.

I was much struck by the large number of pleasing
faces among the young ladies present, but not less so
by the fact that hardly any one of them possessed the
slightest degree of what is called classical beauty, or
Greek style of countenance. Their style was, in fact,
much more that of Eastern Italy and Venice, than of
Greece. Some of the prettiest were remarkable for
bright dark eyes and dark hair, though lighter and
bluer eyes and fine complexion were numerous. The
gentlemen of the town were also strikingly different in
physiognomy from the Greeks of the villages, the latter
much better representing the recognised types of their
country people. The primates, who were present,
were not accompanied by wives or daughters; and it
was considered rather a stretch of authority on the
part of the Resident to bring together, on any terms,
in a room honoured by the presence of the descendants
of old Venetian aristocracy, these real indigens of the
island, who had so long been depressed. They did
not join in the regular dances, and sat all together in
one room, scarcely moving the whole evening; but,
just before the ball broke up, a request was made that
they should take their share, and, a proper instrument
being obtained, they favoured the company with a
specimen of the remarkable and most ancient *Romaika,*
a curious measured movement, probably identical with
the Pyrrhic dance, and certainly handed down from

very remote antiquity. The dance was thus conducted:—A number of persons, all of whom were men, stood in an uneven line, and each took hold of a handkerchief held by his next neighbour in one hand, and held a handkerchief in the other. The two outside had, of course, one hand free. All then moved together in a monotonous step, first slowly and soon more quickly. They retained throughout a wavy serpentine line, changing every instant, and from time to time the dancer at one end would detach himself, and perform gesticulations much more violent. They afterwards danced again, each holding the sash of his neighbour, but all the effect seemed to depend on the wavy line in which moved.

Balls, like everything else, come at length to an end; and, by half-past four o'clock, a long line of ladies, escorted by their cavaliers, might have been seen by the bright moonlight wending their way to their homes. Wisely wrapped up, so that nothing was left exposed but the tip of the nose, it might have been a procession of nuns, or an eastern pilgrimage. Gradually, all sounds died away, and the morrow of the wedding was left to commence its history of happiness or disappointment. If the wishes and hopes of half the civilised world can give happiness, the former is insured.

But I have said nothing of the supper. It disappeared as if by magic, and hardly left a trace behind. Turkies and wild boar, jellies and cakes, all came alike to the consumers. The great majority created for themselves a special dispensation from the fierce Lenten fast on so auspicious an occasion, and allowed them-

selves thorough enjoyment of the good things provided
for them. It must be admitted that most of them
ate their fill, in spite of the unlucky fact that Tuesday
night had passed into Wednesday morning before the
meal was announced, and that they thus greatly increased the enormity they were committing. To the
honour of human nature be it said however, that
there were many of the country people whose con-
sciences were stronger than their appetites; and thus,
while the residents in town devoured all before them,
I observed some, and knew of other excellent, but
superstitious men, who would touch nothing but bread,
nuts, olives and oranges. One, in particular, an old
man, after supping in this way, and sitting up all
night, followed me on foot the next day to a mountain
top, half-a-day's journey from the town, and, after this
act of politeness (for his attendance was nothing more
than a compliment to me, as the friend and guest of
the Resident), he still would take no other breakfast
than a cup of coffee. He looked worn and exhausted,
as he well might; and one could not help respecting
his scruples of conscience thus acted on at extreme
personal inconvenience, and with an example of such
different conduct before his eyes. This man was
wealthy, and lived on his own estate.

The final event of the celebration of the festival took
place the next night; and, certainly, the illumination
of the town did the greatest credit to the loyalty and
good taste of all the inhabitants. To all intents and
purposes, it was universal. Hardly any one was so
poor, that he could not show by a little lamp of some

kind, placed in a prominent position, that he partook of the general feeling.

All the principal public buildings were lighted at the expense of the municipality; and the houses of the Resident and Regent, as well as those of the principal gentlemen of the place, were resplendent. The effect was not broken by street lamps, of which there are hardly any.

The Resident's house, situated between what may be called the Law Courts and the schools of the town, forms, with these, a long uninterrupted line, occupying the whole of a terrace looking towards the lagoon, and with only a few houses opposite the schools. This terrace is seen at a distance, and is detached from the town. Every window lighted with candles, a continuous chain of lamps on the balconies of the upper rooms, each doorway marked by a large arch of light, and some coloured lights ingeniously placed in a row of vases on the balcony of the Residence, formed a combination, which, for simplicity and effect, deserve the highest praise. Even transparencies were not wanting; one being placed in each of the windows of the dining-room on the ground floor. Wonderful transparencies they were; and they were as much admired as they deserved. They quite carried the palm over all other attempts, and ensured the Resident the credit of having excelled everybody. One was a not unfamiliar representation of St. George and the Dragon, a legend as well known in the Ionian Islands as in England. The drawing was very fairly done. The other was a sketch of Sappho, floating majestically away

M

from a celebrated cliff, bearing her name, from whence she is said to have leaped into the sea, and where there still remain fragments of an ancient temple of Apollo. Dressed in one long lemon-coloured garment, of which the idea seems to have been taken from those invented to cover the youngest babies, this classical young lady has already left earth behind her, and has nearly reached the main top of a British vessel of war floating in the blue water below. The royal standard of England is of course flying at the mast head, and one solitary British tar, with glazed hat, blue jacket and white trousers, is energetically dancing a hornpipe, in anticipation of her arrival. British protection to the sons of Apollo, thus worthily represented, was a fertile source of the loudest expressions of delight from all who passed; perhaps not the less so, as it was known to be the work of a native genius.

The Market Place was the next in importance of the illuminations of the evening. Continuous lines of lamps here, also, produced a fine effect, especially when straight, and not too close. This was the style generally selected, and was wonderfully effective, the broken outline of the architecture of the place, and the fact that few of the houses are exact counterparts of their neighbours, preventing the smallest approach to monotony. I had, indeed, no idea that the forms of the houses were so picturesque, until I saw them thus indicated.

Although candles were used in many windows, the great effects in all these cases were produced by lamps, of which three kinds were employed. One—the best known, readiest, and most usual, consisted of common tumblers half filled with water, on which oil was poured. Small wicks, passing through cork, were floated on the oil; and the oil used being the olive oil of the country, it burnt with a pure, bright, clear flame that was extremely pretty.

When all the tumblers in the town had been bought up, an ingenious potter manufactured and sold a multitude of little lamps of the prettiest antique form imaginable. I doubt whether anything better designed was done anywhere. But neither was this enough; and, at last, a tinman entered the field, and, by stamping out little saucers of tin plate with a small lip, which he sold at the rate of about three farthings a piece, this patriot laid the foundation of his own fortune, and met the demand that had arisen. Hundreds of these were turned out in a few hours; and they answered all the purpose, so long as the weather was fine. Most fortunately, the evening turned out clear, calm, and warm; and the whole population was in the streets from dusk till ten o'clock. From time to time, a band of music was heard, and everybody was delighted.

I have omitted to describe the illumination of the "Bazaar," as the Regent Street of Santa Maura is called. It is the principal place of business of the town, which it crosses from one end to the other; and I believe there was not in its whole length one shop or shed, however poor, that was not lighted up. There was no attempt at designs, which would, most likely, have failed, though for want of experience rather than from absence of taste; but there was plenty of variety, and abundance of light. Regent Street, no doubt, is wider and longer, and looked more brilliant in its gas, and more elaborate in its costly decorations, but I doubt whether, in proportion to its resources and means, our little Bazaar and its inhabitants—representing the poor widow with her mite—did not exert themselves as much and make as much sacrifice in honour of the Queen and her son on this occasion as any one of the hundreds of islands that prosper and are happy under her much-loved sway.

In this true history of an interesting exhibition of loyalty, good feeling, and affection, on an occasion fraught with interest to every one connected with England, however remotely, there lies a moral that has special reference to the group of dependencies, of which the island of Santa Maura is one. Although it is true that the inhabitants of the Ionian Islands, for various reasons and at various times, have intimated a strong desire that they should form part of a free Greek people, it is not true that the majority of the people dislike, distrust, or object to the government of England. England and the English are well liked, and are respected for their solid qualities. They are not always popular, for an Englishman abroad has the art of seeming supercilious, and his reserve is taken for pride; but when occasion arises, and when, as is the case in Santa Maura, the highest English authority is a prudent, considerate, firm, and intelligent gentleman, understanding the people and understood by them, it is hardly possible to exaggerate the amount of influence he possesses or the good feeling reflected upon every-thing connected with his country. Whenever the right person is selected to hold authority, England need fear nothing. Her only danger lies in the placing of weak, idle, incompetent officers in posts where individual character and influence have weight. Numerous illustrations of this truth might be drawn from the history of the Septinsular Republic within the last quarter of a century; but I believe that, in spite of many mistakes on our part, there will be found amongst the inhabitants a general feeling of admiration and respect, if not of affection, for the western race, who have dwelt among them and who have ruled them without domineering over them.

CHAPTER VI.

IMMEDIATELY outside the town of Santa Maura we
enter a tract occupied chiefly by olive groves and
enclosed gardens.   These outskirts are almost without
inhabitants, for the town itself is not only small, but
it is not straggling, and no houses extend beyond the
last of those that form the main street.   We pass,

in fact, immediately into the olive groves on the right and the gardens on the left. The former I have already mentioned, and shall allude to again immediately; the latter are evidently very productive, and go down close to the edge of the water. One branch of a small stream (one of the largest in the north of the island) passes through these gardens, and from time to time enables the owners to irrigate them; and there are a few strong springs turning mills that come out at the foot of the hills, and assist the supply of water. But generally during summer the stream is altogether absent, and spring water alone is available for all purposes. Part of the water of these springs is conveyed to the town, as in Corfu, by a system of conduits; but as the distance is much less than in the sister island, the engineering works have involved no difficulty. The water is calcareous.

The cultivation of the gardens and grounds, as observable around the town of Santa Maura, is decidedly superior to that seen in the island of Corfu. The work is done in better style, the limits of property are marked, and the crops obtained are said to be, and no doubt are, proportionably larger and more profitable. Fruit of all kinds are especially abundant, and excellent. The date ripens, though not well. In May there are already fruits ready for the table, and the supply continues abundant and varied till late in autumn, when the orange only remains to carry on the supply till the next season. Figs, grapes, currant-grapes, pomegranates, apricots, pears, apples, plums, quinces, and many others, all ripen to perfection.

There is no want of interest in the neighbourhood of Amaxiki in whatever direction we turn, and to whatever subject of ancient or modern history, antiquities, picturesque scenery, or natural history, the attention and taste of the traveller may be directed. I will describe a few of the walks, to give the reader an idea of the island and the country.

The ruined walls of the ancient town of Leucas are among the first objects of attraction; and on the way to see them one is struck by the neat and well cared for appearance of the country. The old Greek town was built on one of the amphitheatre of hills embracing not only the lagoon but the large tract of richly cultivated plain around. All this at some former period has been recovered from the sea, and at least half the space is now covered with olive trees, which yield every second year an important crop. Estimating roughly, there cannot be less than half a million of fine trees in this part of the island, and the crop is exceedingly valuable, though, unfortunately, very speculative. I have already observed, and must now repeat, that in this island property of all kinds is more cared for, and all kinds of agricultural work is much more advanced than in Corfu. The olive trees are kept in good order, the dead wood being removed every spring; the roots of the trees are annually laid bare and manured; the properties are all carefully marked, generally by trenches, but sometimes by walls, and the ground under the trees is often rendered available for other crops instead of being left to run to waste, or covered by all kinds of 'weeds. Sheep are often seen feeding in these localities.

The field work in Santa Maura is also neater and cleaner than in Corfu, and the people are said to be more intelligent as well as better off. The crops at the time of my visit looked healthy, and were well advanced, in spite of an unusual drought from which the land was suffering.

The first thing one sees of ancient Leucas is a Cyclopean wall, of great beauty, near the foot of the hill on which the ancient city of Nerikos was built. This wall may be traced at intervals all round the old town, and it seems to be the lowest of several that rise in successive steps, or terraces, according to the form of the ground. The part first met with is for at least thirty yards in a very good state. The stones are for the most part closely fitted, so closely, that it would be difficult to find room for the blade of a knife between them; but some of the blocks certainly contain fifty cubic feet, and must weigh more than two and a-half tons. They consist of the white limestone of which the hill is composed, but this stone contains numerous flints and lumps of chert, and is troublesome to cut by the tools now used owing to its irregular hardness.

Past this fragment of wall, which is, indeed, in better preservation than any other, one emerges on a rocky, bare-looking hill, and a few modern cottages with a bee garden. The people I found very friendly, and I took the opportunity of entering one of their cottages. But first, I must say a word on a bee

garden which met my eye on climbing the old wall of
colossal stones that is the first evidence of the ancient
city.

Bees are celebrated in Greece, and have been so
from time immemorial. The great extent of limestone, of which almost the whole country is made up,
the rocky and fragmentary state of the rock, which is
eminently favourable to the growth of those flowering
herbs that bees most delight in, and that communicate
the most pungent flavour to the honey, and the fact
that, once established, bees give little or no trouble, are
all reasons why these useful insects should be encouraged. The honeys of Hybla and Hymettus are at
this day almost as celebrated as they were in the time
of the classical Greek poets; the honeys of Cerigo, of
Zante, and many other places continental and insular,
are all fine, and each has its admirers. The honey of
Leucadia is perhaps almost as good as any, and the
descendants of the bees that fed Ulysses deserve some
consideration. I was interested, then, in the little bee
garden on the site of the old city of Leucas. It was a
rocky, barren-looking spot, and did not at first sight
seem very promising, for the whole ground, for a
great distance around, looks naked, and without vegetation. But it is not really so. Every little crevice
or interval between two stones, whether large or
small, and not a few holes made by vegetation in the
solid rock itself, contain some little flowering plant
especially patronised by the honey-bee. I was not
much surprised, therefore, to see the bees, but the
hives rather puzzled me at first. They consist of

small oblong boxes placed on end on a low stone, each box being covered by two or three tiles, evidently to keep off the heat of the sun in summer. Two round holes, each about half-an-inch in diameter, sufficed for the bees to enter and emerge, and it did not seem to matter much where these holes were pierced. The boxes were run together in the roughest manner, and seemed to have two or three cross sticks within them. They were placed not two feet apart, and each box was about twenty inches high, and nine inches square in section. The bees were exceedingly busy, and perfectly good-tempered.

I noticed among the bee plants that there was an enormous quantity of a large kind of rosemary, of which the spikes of flower were so large and numerous as to conceal the leaves; there is also an abundant supply of sage on all the rocks.

In the way of actual remains, there is not much now to be found at Leucas, with the exception of ruined walls; these, indeed, are met with in abundance, and are interesting, as presenting all the various styles of construction, from the early Greek to the time when Rome was exercising its influence. As in Corfu, there seem to have been two old cities on the same site, one very early, the other about the second century before Christ. Most of the material that remained available of the former was worked up in constructing the latter, and thus, practically, it is the fragments of the latter city that we meet with everywhere. Coins and pottery of both periods are obtained, though rarely; and now and then fragments of stone with inscriptions. Works of art in sculptured marble do not seem to have reached this somewhat remote corner. Of the few things that have been found, some are curious enough. Within the walls, at various places, are several excavations, and one or two good remains of a line of foundations with large squared stones. The excavations include a singularly small adit, or tunnel, run into the solid limestone for a long distance, and communicating (apparently with intention) with the outer air at several points. This tunnel is admirably constructed with a vaulted roof, but it is so exceedingly small, that it seems impossible that a man of ordinary size could have used tools to work in it. It is not more than about eighteen inches wide and about three feet high, dimensions that seem almost impossible. There are other larger and less perfect adits offering fewer difficulties of construction, and a few well-cut chambers in the rock, not communicating with each other, no doubt used either as vaults, cellars, or prisons, according to circumstances.

In addition to these there are numerous chambers for storing grain, also cut out of the rock, and of the shape of large jars formerly used by the Romans and still used in Spain, which were buried in the ground for a similar purpose. Those at Leucas are just large enough at top to admit of being entered by a man; but inside they are from ten to fifteen feet diameter, and from six to ten feet deep: they seem to have been lined with cement, the surface within being beautifully smooth.

An afternoon is pleasantly spent in wandering

among these few but curious reminiscences of a past age. The distance from the town is within a walk, and lies through rich gardens and olive groves.

Some doubt has been expressed as to whether the more modern city of Leucas, established or adopted by the Romans, was not on the lower ground between the hill and the sea, the real isthmus of the ancients being between the little building called Fort Alexander and the village of Paleocaglia opposite on the main land. No doubt at this point the channel is very narrow, though the distance across is still between three and four hundred yards, but no natural cause is likely to have removed an isthmus if once existing there. All the tendencies are rather to choke up than to widen such a passage, and if at the present day the channel were closed, the waters in the lagoon would certainly evaporate very rapidly, and probably induce a current from the north by Teki Castle, deepening that channel. It is, however, difficult to understand how an isthmus can have disappeared anywhere in the neighbourhood of either spot, without some depression connected with earthquake movements, and had any such event taken place, we should look for evidence of it in the place where the water is now most shallow and deepens slowly in all directions rather than where it is deep and deepens rapidly in one direction only, as is the case near Fort Alexander. One can hardly conceive a depression to cause a neck of land to be converted suddenly into a deep channel, except where a strong current or a heavy tidal wave is at hand to remove to a distance all the detritus, and increase a channel once made. The tendencies here are in the opposite direction, owing to the rapid accumulation of transported matter. This clearly shows that an isthmus if it were once formed near the latter place, must tend to be rapidly enlarged, and could hardly become obliterated. If it is remembered that every south wind that blows drifts into such a channel from the south, a quantity of silt which cannot but be deposited before it is carried through to Teki Castle, and that every north wind must drive other silt in the opposite direction, both meeting in the lagoon, it is clear that, unless it were carried through a deep channel and deposited at the other end in deep water, no canal or natural cut could long remain open without being kept clear by artificial means, and that no isthmus once existing at this southerly point could be naturally removed. After all, it is perfectly conceivable that the exceedingly shallow, fordable channel to the north might have existed as it is now even at the time when it is described as an isthmus. It is still so easy to traverse, that even a child might, with care, be enabled to walk across the ford; and there are numbers of persons, men, women, and children, who, from time to time, during the first Greek revolution of modern times, thus succeeded in securing the shelter of the British flag when disposed to do so. The depth at the other end of the channel, or rather outside the lagoon to the south, is quite enough to render it certain that there are here no remains of a broken communication.

Besides Leucas, there are other places in the island

where remains of some of the ancient Greek cities have been found; and, from time to time, collections of antiquities have been made. It is to be regretted that all these have been distributed, and that now no one on the spot possesses more than very meagre and comparatively valueless examples. The various articles of which I heard, include funereal and other vases; small articles of pottery, chiefly such as were used in funeral ceremonies; lamps, and small statuettes. These are the most common; but medals are not rare, and possess some interest; slabs with inscriptions, belonging to the second city, and a few other objects, more curious than valuable, are also to be seen in the possession of one or two gentlemen in the town, but they call for special description. A few bronzes have been turned up at times; but considering that a city existed for two thousand years on the hill, where now hardly one stone is left upon another, it is certain that larger and more important antiquities might have been expected. Perhaps one reason of their rarity is the state of the rock and the absence of any depth of soil in which objects of moderate size might lie concealed. The completeness of the desolation is almost startling; for over almost the whole area, nothing can be detected above ground but fragments of the walls.

The style of art exhibited in the antiquities is not of the highest order, as, indeed, might be expected. Most of the remains are funereal; but even the sanctuaries of the dead have not often been met with, and a few vases, partly filled with calcined bones, indicate the reason why there are no sepulchres. A

minute silver coin is common enough.   It is the coin
usually put in the mouth of the dead.

Medals have at one time been more commonly
found than they are now at Leucas and other places in
Santa Maura, and many of them seem interesting.   A
work on the subject was published in Padua in 1815;
and, since then, additional medals have been found.
Some few of these are very ancient, the letters on the
legend being of a form different from that afterwards
used.   In some, the writing is from right to left, instead of in the usual way; but they all belong to the
second city of Leucas, founded by the Corinthians in
the sixth century before Christ.   Many of them exhibit, on one face, the prow of a galley; many more
a Pegasus, or winged horse; and many the club of
Hercules.   Heads of Apollo, Minerva, and Diana,
seem also common.   Many of them have the name
ΛΗΥΚΑΔΙΩΝ, or part of it, in characters of the
ordinary form.   Indications of the story of Sappho
appear, also, on some of the medals; but they are
rather doubtfully expressed.

The houses of the villagers near the town of Santa
Maura are small, but remarkably neat, and perfectly
clean.   I visited one, consisting of a single room and
a very small dark shed adjacent, used, apparently, for
the oven, and for holding tools and other odds and
ends.   The room had an unglazed window, and
seemed to be about fifteen feet square.   The floor
was earthen, but scrupulously clean.   There were
two large double beds, very comfortable looking, and
provided with really handsome counterpanes; two

good and large chests; a table covered with tin and brass cooking utensils; a small fire-place in the corner; a number of jars and bottles, and some other odds and ends. This house was occupied by two families; but whether they were two generations of the same family, or other relations, I did not make out. The roof was moderately high pitched, and the rafters were strewn with a large kind of reed, forming a kind of floor, on which stores of various kinds could be kept. I had no sooner entered the house, and sat down, than coffee was offered; and as I would not give them the trouble to make that, it was necessary that I should taste a glass of *raki*, the spirituous drink of the country and of Greece. I cannot say I felt inclined to do more than sip it, in acknowledgment of the compliment.

Although, at the time of my visit, the olives had long been ripe, and ought to have been made into oil some months before, I found one oil-mill, close to the town, at which work was still going on. The process there adopted was singularly inartificial, but is little varied, even in the best establishments. The fruit is not collected till quite ripe, and is then often kept for some time. Within a shed, a large and wide cylindrical stone was revolving upon its edge, on a flat stone table. The olives being thrown on this table are swept with little rods under the vertical stone, which is turned by a horse, mule, or ass. They thus become crushed, and a portion of the oil runs off; and the operation is continued till they are thought fit for squeezing. The crushed mass is transferred to small round baskets, made of soft grass or matting, and rather

smaller at the opening than within. A number of
these are placed upon each other in a frame, and a
powerful pressure is produced by a strong and large
wooden screw, worked by leverage. The oil is thus
squeezed out, and runs down through a spout into a
trough. Nothing can be imagined more unpleasant
than the appearance of this product; but it is put into
jars to settle, and afterwards drawn off fine into skins
or barrels. The crushed and squeezed cake that remains after pressing, and which ought, if properly
pressed, to be as hard as wood, is of loose texture,
and full of oil. It is used as fuel. No doubt, in
some of the larger establishments, the mechanical
apparatus is on a better scale, but the principle is
the same, and the result is not satisfactory either as
regards quantity or quality. Still, notwithstanding
these drawbacks, Santa Maura, which also grows currants and sells wine, exports its thirty thousand barrels
of oil, and provides, also, a supply of no small magnitude for its native inhabitants.

Very primitive little corn mills are dotted about,—
some worked by wind, some by water. The former
are on the spit of sand separating the lagoon from the
open sea—the latter are wherever a suitable fall of
water can be secured. The little water mills consist
only of a pair of stones of very moderate size, with a
little feeding hopper, and a box for the flour as it
emerges. Nothing can be conceived more classical
and inartificial; each person bringing his measure of
Indian corn, waiting his turn to grind, looking on
during the grinding, and carrying away his flour on

his back. There is always a little group of idlers to be seen gossiping in these mills. Horizontal and undershot wheels seem most common; and, indeed, I am not aware that any others exist.

A stroll on the sea-shore by the town of Amaxiki will not be without interest to the naturalist and geologist. Sea-weeds are not abundant; but there are some interesting species. Large sponges are occasionally thrown up, and sea-eggs—their spines of the richest blue colour—are common. They and other shell-fish —such as the *pinna* and a species of *spondylus*—are liked as food by the islanders, though there is an unpleasant and prevalent idea that they disagree with strangers.

A very curious and completely honey-combed kind of limestone is seen on the sea shore; and a rich variety of flints, jaspers, cherts, agates, and other forms of silica may be found there. These have been washed out of the compact cherty limestone that forms the chief mass of the rock, and a much larger proportion of the siliceous stones has been preserved than of the calcareous in this reconstructed rock, owing to the greater hardness of the former. The occasional presence of large angular blocks, as well as the numerous rounded boulders of unaltered and compact limestone, clearly indicate the origin of the conglomerate.

There is an interesting walk from Amaxiki towards the south through the olive groves and past the foot of the hill on which stands the old city, past a fountain of the period of the later city of Leucas, and then

between the foot of the hills and the sea to a curious
hill having a face of conglomerate rock dipping towards the sea at a high angle. Throughout this tract
the low land is on a gentle slope, the highest point of
which is about thirteen feet above the present sea level;
but at the last hill the conglomerate is thrown up to
a height of nearly two thousand feet. This evidently
belongs to a different and earlier elevation. The last
movement was no doubt slow, and may be going on
now. It certainly has taken some thousands of years
to rise the last thirteen feet, since there is reason to
suppose that it had commenced long before the first
Greek city was founded. The other belongs to a
period when all was under water.

That this latter change is quite unconnected with
the earthquake disturbances that have troubled all the
Ionian islands for many years, but especially those
belonging to the southerly groups, is more than probable. It is, as I shall presently explain, an inevitable result of the exposure of the mountain sides and
tops to the effect of rain and atmosphere, lasting
for a long while, and always proceeding on a large
scale.

An important and interesting question arises here
as to the effect of the earthquake shocks in producing
permanent elevation or depression on the coast of
Leucadia. That all the chief results obtained are due
to silting up and not to earthquake action, I have no
doubt whatever; and I have seen no sufficient evidence of elevation. Indeed, I think that if there had
been elevation, it could hardly have failed to affect the

whole plain between the hills and the sea, so that Amaxiki itself would have been lifted, and the walls of the fort of Santa Maura must also have been affected. Neither of them shows marks of having once been lower than they now are, nor is any change of level perceptible in the ruins of the aqueduct constructed by the Turks and destroyed in 1825. Nor, on the other hand, is there proof of depression; no doubt evidence of this change is more difficult to obtain than that of elevation; but, apart from the unmistakeable fact that the lagoon is rapidly filling up, neither the piers of the aqueduct, the spit of sand, nor the cliffs at the western extremity of the lagoon, show indications of such phenomena.

On the whole, I think it the most probable explanation of the phenomena to assume that the earthquakes have been simple vibrations producing no permanent result; and that the changes recorded are due to a natural accumulation of detritus, partly owing to the position of the island in reference to the mainland. Geological changes of very great extent have taken place within the later tertiary period, and these may have produced the original separation of the island from Greece, for they have thrown up the east coast at an angle of twenty or thirty degrees, or even more, thick beds formed in the sea being now two thousand feet above it. Since that elevation, the tendency has been to fill up with detritus and silt the large gap then made. But it is equally certain that the great coast elevation was an operation that took a long while to bring about, and that it has been long since completed. There is nothing to prove that great change of a paroxysmal character has taken place within the latest of the great geological periods.

A ride into the country reveals one great want of Leucadia, for the roads are very bad. It is true that several good roads have been commenced; but it is thankless work, for the whole communication being kept up by horses and mules, the old steep mountain paths are used, and will continue to be used, until carriages can be taken to the different villages. As the island is very mountainous, it may be doubted whether the result would justify the cost. Certainly, the experiment is not likely to be tried should the island pass from under British rule.

Very soon after quitting Amaxiki in any direction towards the interior, it becomes necessary to leave the strip of low cultivated land near the sea, and rise upon rough and steep hills, full of broken rock, and thoroughly wild and picturesque. But it is not here as in Corfu. These mountain sides are carefully and well cultivated, vines cover every available spot, corn crops are seen here and there, and to avoid loss of soil and economise space, the whole hill sides, even to a great altitude, are most carefully terraced. Thus, though there are fewer olives, and this picturesque tree is rarely seen away from the low plains, there is no want of vegetation and cultivation.

A very steep and rocky path conducts up the side of one of the hills behind the town across the first or coast range, revealing, at intervals, the beautiful lagoon, the narrow strip separating it from the sea

and running out far towards the bay of Arta, the
causeway separating it from the channel on the east,
and the salt works. The masts of the ships are
visible, should any be in the harbour or the roads.
Dotted over the blue water are many white specks—
the lateen sails of fishing-boats, and far away the
mountains of Albania, above the lake of Joannina, begin to mark the horizon with a white line. On reaching the top of the ridge we look towards the country beyond, and, at first sight, the antiquary might
fancy himself in some vast amphitheatre of giants, so
perfectly circular is the sweep, and so regular the
apparent seats in two or three valleys at his feet.
Two such valleys are seen nearly adjacent, one a little
beyond the other. The nearest is the most perfect,
and might well deceive any one whose faith in the
magnitude of human works was sufficiently great.
A much larger one is close at hand. The bottom is
perfectly circular in its outline, and is absolutely flat.
It is, indeed, the bed of a lake; and at the time of
my visit the water had only just left the bottom. I
had no means of measuring the dimensions, but I
think the diameter could not be less than half a mile
at the bottom, and the depth to the bottom I estimated at a hundred and fifty feet. The apparent seats
were natural terraces, carried round at intervals at
various heights, produced by the action of the water
that had rested at those levels. The resemblance to
an artificial construction is admirable. Without de-
taining the reader here with learned disquisitions, it
may be well to say, that there are good reasons in the

geology and physical geography of the district where these curious valleys should exist, and that they represent very closely the kettle-shaped valleys already alluded to as common in Corfu. They are, in fact, portions of the limestone of which so much is seen in this part of the world, and they indicate places where hollow cavities have been produced in the interior by infiltration and the passage of water, and where probably the roof of some cavern has fallen in.

Leaving these curious valleys behind, and passing numerous vine-dressers and other peasants cultivating their fields, I had to make my way from point to point, the horses climbing up and down the rough stony paths like wild cats, until at length I wound round the foot of a hill and came in view of the picturesque monastery of Scarus, or Carus, at the foot of the low mountain group of that name, which it was the object of my journey to visit. The monastery is situated about fourteen hundred feet above the sea, near a wide and wild opening towards the north. It occupies part of the west slope of one of several hills almost deserving to be called mountains. The path to it is steep, stony, and long, and winds a good deal both up and down before reaching the monastery. Beyond the monastery there is a good hour's walk through some of the finest forest trees of white oak that exist in the island, up and down steep and difficult paths, always affording grand and fine views, both near and distant. The forest was till lately in a very valuable state, and much money might have been made of it by judicious thinning, and removing only the trees then at their prime. There was much timber of very unusual size for this kind of wood, and perfectly sound, and probably a succession of valuable timber might then have been secured. Left too long to the carelessness and ignorance of the village population, many of the best trees have been spoilt by burning and charring, and thus the value of the forest is much reduced.

But the forest is still well worth visiting. When the green leaves are freshly out in spring, and in the early days of summer, its shade must be delicious. At all times it is a glorious object, interesting in itself for its own great beauty; interesting still more as pointing out the probable condition of the mountain sides in all the islands in the ancient time.

As in so many cases in the Greek mountains, there are here several detached summits, or pyramids of rock, some higher than others, but all affording good points of view. The most lofty summit is about 2,300 feet above the sea, roughly estimated by the aneroid barometer. It affords a charming view of the numerous fine islands between Santa Maura and the mainland. Meganisi looks low, and is flatter than the others. Calamos is very lofty and frowning. Sparti, Scordi, and Scorpio are picturesquely spread out, and are close at hand. Ithaca is barely seen, but the lofty mountain chain of Cephalonia—the Black Mountain —lifts its head far above every other elevation in the neighbourhood.

The sweet little bay of Vliko is the prettiest object of all within this wide range. You look down over a sea of rocks, and see, completely enclosed in hills of moderate elevation, a small, square, well-proportioned basin with a very narrow outlet, its shores covered with wood to the water's edge, and calmly buried at one's feet. Not a sign of human occupation is visible, for, though occasionally used as a port, it is neither very accessible, nor does it lead to accessible places; but it is wild, natural, and classical, and impresses one very strongly by the contrast it affords to the surrounding scenery.

The path from the monastery to the summits of Scarus is obscure, and my guide was less inclined to push on than I was. When more than half way I was in doubt about the direction I should take, and, while waiting for information, heard myself called. I then learnt that some time after I had left Amaxiki the primate of the village nearest Scarus being informed of my movements had followed me on foot by a much nearer but very rough mule track, and by dint of running had succeeded in catching me up. The poor man was nearly exhausted, but still insisted on showing me everything. He had been up all night, had eaten nothing but a little bread and some olives, but his extreme respect and regard for the Resident had induced him to exert himself in this way to be of use to the Effendi's friend. When he had pointed out all the beauties of the mountain, and was returning, I induced him with difficulty to take advantage of my mule, and ride down to the monastery. I have already alluded to this trait of character in the respectable primate of Scarus.

Most of the mountains in the Ionian islands have a religious house either at the summit or at the nearest convenient point. Some are large and regularly inhabited; some are only occupied during a part of the year when a festival of the patron saint is likely to attract a large multitude; some few are residences adapted only for one or two monks or nuns; and others are mere hermitages. Few of them have till lately been kept up in the old style, and, as in Roman Catholic countries there are scandalous tales afloat about the goings on when a convent and a monastery were adjacent. Nothing of this kind has tainted the fair fame of the monastery of Saint George of Scarus. The building is large, and there is fair accommodation for strangers. There are at present only two monks, venerable, kind, intelligent old men, knowing little and caring little for the world outside them. Their habitation is convenient, safe, and healthy. They possess all reasonable comforts, and they are willing as well as able to accommodate strangers in case of need.

The monastery being on the mountains is required to be made defensible against brigands as well as wolves. It is walled, and has double gates. There is a small court-yard on entering. On one side is the chapel, large in proportion to the population, and round two sides are the dwellings. These are perfectly plain, and very barely furnished. Opposite the chapel is the refectory, or feeding-room, and this serves as a place of extra accommodation in case of need. Near it are sleeping-rooms for strangers, and the

cells, or rooms, of the monks. These are small, and
often mere bare walls with a roof, a hole in the wall to
let in air and light, and a door by which to enter.
The floor is earth; but this is no great hardship in a
warm climate; and as the Greeks all dress warmly, they
can bear the temporary cold that sometimes occurs.

I have mentioned that there are only two monks
regularly inhabiting the monastery of Scarus, and
they are pleasant, honest-looking, and hospitable. On
first entering I was greeted warmly, with much
shaking of hands, and proceeded to the chapel, where
the different pictures were pointed out. I was then
shown into the refectory, and seated on a kind of sofa,
the two priests sitting opposite, while an attendant
was preparing coffee. A decanter containing a little
raki was first brought. I tasted a little, mixed with
water, and found it very refreshing. Soon the coffee
succeeded, and with it half-a-dozen slices of bread that
had been air or sun dried so completely as to be perfectly hard and crisp, and nearly mouldy. This dried
bread is a kind of biscuit   The coffee was excellent.
After partaking of it, I asked to see a certain manuscript of the Gospels, of which I had heard, and both
that and another in the possession of the brothers was
brought out. Both were admirably written, and in
excellent preservation; but they were not old. The
curiosities of this kind that may once have existed in
the Greek monasteries have long disappeared in the
Ionian islands, and, indeed, except at Mount Athos,
and in a few other places, there is little now to be learnt
in such depositaries, so far as Europe is concerned.

The monks are simple, pleasant people, and one sees them with pleasure. They believe in the forms of their religion, and really practise their fasts, no doubt to the great mortification of the flesh; but the old celibates of this kind are few in number, and seem gradually dying out. It is impossible to go far in any direction without seeing some building devoted to religious purposes; but, in most cases, these buildings are only occupied once a year, on the occasion of the festival of the saint to whom they are dedicated.

Before leaving the monastery of Scarus, I was asked to give my name, which I wrote in the Greek character. As I had previously read a verse or two of the Gospel in one of the manuscripts, I found that it was considered very remarkable that I could read and write the Greek language, though I could neither speak nor understand Romaic. So completely is this the converse of the usual state of things in the country, where all, of course, speak, and very few read and write, that it was quite a phenomenon.

After quitting my friends, the monks, I went back from Scarus towards the town, by a shorter and more precipitous road than that by which I had come, and, on the way, stopped to look at a very striking and picturesque block of the conglomerate of the hills, which had fallen down, and stuck out from the mountain side in a singular manner. The exposed part of this vast block, as it projects from the ground, measured full fifty feet square, and nearly twenty feet thick. Underneath it was a large space, which had been walled in to make a shed for cattle, part of the

stone forming the roof.   Near the top, in a recess in
the stone, was a little chapel, constructed in honour of
three saints, whose portraits had once been painted on
three little boards hanging up in front of an altar.
Nothing remained of the paintings but parts of the
gilt rings of glory that had once encircled the heads of
the figures.   All the rest had been long since kissed
away; but my companions, like many other persons,
still most reverently saluted the dirty boards.   The
most curious thing was the presence of a well in
the heart of the boulder, the water of which fills a
cistern, said to be the coffin of one of the saints, and
performing marvellous miracles.   This must be a
small, natural, artesian spring, derived from some
crevice, perhaps connected with the falling of the
rock from above.   Besides this gigantic boulder,
looking like the cap stone of a vast cromlech, there
are many large stones, on the side of the hill, that
have fallen down after being undermined by atmospheric action.

A curious appearance has been noticed in some of
these blocks, both in their natural place on the rock
and when fallen.   Many of them are scooped out vertically, as if drilled by some enormous tool; or part of
the stone being broken away, they look like gigantic
seats sculptured artificially.   This is, however, to
be accounted for in a natural and easy way; and
hundreds of cases of the same kind, in different stages
of progress, may be observed on the rocks all round.
They are the result of vegetation commencing on the
surface of a block of the conglomerate, and eating its

way down into the substance of the rock by the dissolving power of water.

Near the town of Amaxiki, there are lovely shady walks among the olive groves, which occupy almost the whole of the available land between the lagoon and the hills. Winding about among these old trees, we come at last to a steep face of naked limestone rock—the ancient sea cliff, against which the waves of the Mediterranean have dashed before the lagoon existed, at a time when the island was smaller and lower than it now is. Caverns abound in this cliff; and one of them is said to open into a village a mile or two distant. At present, these caverns are the dens of the owls and jackals, which abound in the neighbourhood. They are not stalactitic, and do not seem to contain much beyond the recent remains of their inhabitants. But the scenery on the hill tops and amongst the little villages adjacent is singularly pretty, for it affords numerous contrasts of vegetation and varieties of form that are sure to please. I obtained a sketch of part of one of these villages,* a very pleasing and creditable specimen of Greek art, by a Corfiot artist, resident in Santa Maura. The houses of the village are sprinkled about here and there with extreme irregularity, no two being together, or in line. Most of them are of moderate size, and, though with-

---

* Φρήνη, phrene, or frini (the brain), is so called because the dwellers therein are considered unusually stupid, and are said to have no brains. This mode of giving nicknames—equivalent to the lucus a non lucendo of the Romans—is especially Greek, and is characteristic of their style of joking.

out much of the comfort of an English cottage, are
sufficient for the purpose required. They afford
shelter against weather, and thieves, and wild animals. They are storing places for grain, wine, and
oil, and sleeping places for the women, and sometimes
for the cattle; but of these latter, there are few of any
kind, except goats. This and other similar old villages
are wisely built on the steep slope of the hill, where
there is abundant natural drainage. Of water, there
is not often serious want; and there cannot be a doubt
that the health of all such places must be greater than
of the villages on the plains. Besides the village of
Frini, there are others larger and richer between it
and Leucas. One rarely sees the human inhabitants;
but the dogs are sure to present themselves. They
are, as everywhere in eastern countries, fierce, noisy,
and troublesome; cowardly and wolfish in their habits,
and annoying beyond measure. There is, however, nothing to be done but threaten them with stones. It
is curious to see how instantly they turn tail and run off
if one merely stoops; but they come back before long,
unless actually pelted and warned off by their masters.

The heavy rains had already detained me longer
than I intended in Santa Maura, when, during a
temporary lull, I crossed the plains, in order to visit
one of these villages. The stream from the mountain, though never very large, was yet fierce and
irregular enough to have carried away and distributed over the plain a large and wide area of stones.
A few hours after the heaviest rain, there was no part
of the stream that one could not jump across, and

certainly none in which the depth was more than nine
or ten inches; and yet there were acres of land covered entirely with large stones, all removed from
the mountains and distributed within a period which
could not possibly have extended over three days.
These stones and the mud, or silt, which inevitably
accompanies them, are either retained on the surface
of the plain, thus permanently elevating it, or are carried out into the lagoon, and there help to bring that
into the condition of dry land. The filling up of the
lagoon is thus easily and clearly accounted for, without bringing in the aid of earthquakes, of whose results there is as little evidence in this direction as in
the others to which I have already alluded.

A picturesque and favourite monastery is situated
on one of the hills behind the glorious olive groves of
Amaxiki. A steep zigzag road, in good condition,
leads up to it; and, from this road, there is a blind
path, of about a quarter of a mile, but almost impassable, into an excellent road, wide enough for carts,
and continued for several miles into the interior and
to a village on the west coast. The case is singularly
illustrative of the slipshod and unpractical habits of
the people. As far as the mules are concerned, for
whose benefit, chiefly, the road is needed, I am convinced that they very much prefer a road in which
every step offers a difficulty and presents danger; and
judging from the way in which the old paths up the
steep hill side are preferred to the new zigzag, I am
equally certain that the foot-passengers and mule
leaders partake of this preference. It may thus seem

that roads are thrown away in the island; but it is not
so, and those that have been constructed have unques-
tionably, after a time, civilised and humanised the
people.   Indeed, were it only that they afford a free
course to the police and open the country in spite of
the country-people, there would be a great advantage
gained.   The Greeks would not be brigands, nor, perhaps, would the inhabitants of South Italy be brigands
if, in those countries, there were free and fair means
of communication between villages, and from the towns
into the recesses of the country, such as now exist,
thanks to British protection, even in the smallest and
least peopled of the Ionian Islands.

But I have not yet done with the shady olive groves
and their numerous points of interest.   They are the
every-day resort of the present inhabitants of the island, and have probably always served, during nearly
four thousand years, a somewhat similar purpose.
Even when a great Cyclopean wall* extended from
the cliff that juts into the sea, along the inner margin
of the ancient lagoon to the old city of Leucas, the
old groves, whether then of olive or of ilex, were the
sacred resort of the divinities of classical antiquity;
and the foundations of their temples dedicated to the
old gods still exist, though the superstructure bears

---

* Remains of this wall and of some of its towers, all of Cyclopean
work, may be distinctly traced far within the present margin of the
lake. Remains of the ancient temples exist in the foundations and
walls of the existing chapels, and are seen from time to time. These
fragments and the gigantic stones, many of which are broken, are sometimes arranged along the present road. Each ancient construction has
served as a quarry for that of subsequent date.

the name of an early Christian or mediæval saint. Still,
on the occasion of the festivals of these saints, perhaps
on the day once devoted to a heathen sacrifice to
Neptune or to Apollo, to Venus or to Diana, the
people, with their habits and customs marvellously
little changed, come down from the country and
march in long procession; still, perhaps, do they
repeat, not knowing why, and not caring about its
former meaning, the slightly-modified hymn, or the
never-forgotten chorus; still do they tread the same
labyrinthic dance, slowly and painfully imitating the
movements of their far distant ancestors, while they
mix with these unmistakable marks of antiquity some
of the latest results of civilisation, which, in so far
as they are natural, clash and jar but little with the
ancient myth, and leave the mass of the people very
much in the same state, both physically and intel-
lectually.

At other times, these sacred groves are the resort
of more lively groups. Each day in summer, the
towns-people of Amaxiki stroll out after their early
dinner, and meet in a spot where a well of delicious
water reminds one, by its name, of its Turkish masters.
This well is surrounded by half-a-dozen sheds of the
rudest kind, where coffee is made in oriental fashion;
and a little cup of this ever-welcome stimulant may be
had for a penny while seated on a rude bench under
the foliage of some gigantic tree. Not like the coffee
served in an English hotel, or a Parisian or Vienna
café, is the delicious thimble-ful here offered. The
pure bean from Mocha, well and recently roasted;

crushed between two stones; heated, but never boiled,
in a most unpromising tin pot, by the aid of a few
burnt embers of olive roots; then cleared for an
instant by a couple of drops of cold water, and
finally poured out to be eaten rather than drank,—
such is the coffee to be got at the Turkish well in the
olive grove.   Nor is such a draught to be despised.
It is astonishing how soon and how completely one
gets accustomed to a change of habit in articles of
food, when the material itself is excellent; and I
confess that, when on the last day of my stay in
Amaxiki, I made a pilgrimage to the well, tasted its
sweet waters, and refreshed myself with the accustomed cup, I could appreciate it thoroughly, and shall
never complain if I can obtain a draught equally
well flavoured, and equally answering the purpose
as a stimulant.

A curious instance of the effect of vegetation in
lifting stones is seen in one ˜of the fragments of the
Cyclopean wall, just alluded to.   An olive tree has
planted itself, or has been planted, close to the wall,
and its roots and two of the principal branches have
pushed their way through some little crevice, or
through the grouting between the stones, preferring
this to a more open course.   In growing, they have
succeeded in displacing the gigantic stones of which
the wall was built; and one stone, about three feet
long, thirty inches wide, and as much deep, is altogether removed from its original position in the wall,
and, in the course of years, has become built into the
tree, and raised at least a foot higher than it was

originally placed.   Two other larger stones are much disturbed.   The Dryades have thus succeeded in over-turning the work of the Cyclops; and nature has shown that the subtle influences of life, long con-tinued, and unappreciable within the period of a few scores of years, may yet, in time, bring about results which affect~ and destroy the combined efforts of a multitude of human beings, who have endeavoured in vain to produce an abiding monument of their skill and labour.

According to the political division that now obtains, MEGANISI is the only one of several large islands that adjoin Santa Maura, and lie between it and the main-land, that belongs to this government.   The rest belong to Ithaca, to make up to that island a respect-able population.

Meganisi is a long narrow island of the shape of a bent bow, the back of which is turned towards the south-east extremity of Santa Maura, from which it is only separated by a channel about a mile wide.   It is remarkable for quarries of excellent stone, and for the very fine quality of the corn grown there.   It has been celebrated for the latter from time immemorial; and its building stone is exported to various islands and the mainland, besides being almost exclusively used for the newer buildings in the town of Santa Maura.   Like all the islands, it is hilly; but much of the coast is readily accessible in fine weather.

CHAPTER VII.

THE more distant excursions that can be made from
the chief town of Santa Maura require some arrangement. The country is wild, mountainous, and little
peopled; the villages few, and there is no accommodation whatever, except at the houses of those proprietors of the better class who cultivate their own lands,
or, which is more usual, who cultivate the lands of
their family, while other members of the family are
occupied in the towns, or are even abroad and engaged
in totally different departments of business. Where

such families are found, the houses are generally of some size, adapted to receive a larger number of persons than generally live in them. Visits to villages where there are proprietors of this kind are often pleasant enough, for the manager and part owner of the principal property is necessarily the great man of the district. He is always extremely hospitable, and would on no account allow a traveller to put up in any other quarters, and still less would he accept the smallest remuneration.

A curious and highly interesting feature in the social state of the island is exhibited in this habit of leaving the management of the family estate to some one member of the family, not always, or generally, the eldest, but rather the one who most willingly and naturally takes to it. It is connected with a state of society so much more oriental than western, that a short account of it is necessary, and cannot fail to be interesting.

According to Ionian law, all the members of a family share equally in the family property after the death of the father; but it does not follow as a matter of course that the property is divided. It is much more usual that the brothers and sisters, if young, continue to live together till they either marry or undertake some employment or business at a distance. If a sister marries, she is dowered with a sum equivalent to her share. If a brother, however, earns a separate income, from whatever source, whether he be married or remain single, and whether he live in the same or a different house, or even remove to another town or island, he pays in all his income to a joint fund, the foundation of which is the income obtained from the paternal estate. Those who do nothing else manage the estate. One brother, perhaps, remains in the village as a cultivator, another lives in the town acting as factor, or merchant to the estate, receiving and selling the produce, and managing the proceeds, whatever the case may be; and, in addition, selling, exporting, and otherwise conducting a general business in the same department. A third may, perhaps, receive and sell the goods in a foreign country. A fourth may be a member of legislature, and a fifth a judge. Some marry and have families, others remain single; but the incomes of all are united, each draws out a reasonable share, according to his needs, and a very close account is kept of all transactions. If one brother dies, his children come into the partnership; and, as time goes on, these again will grow up and marry, the daughters receiving a proportional, and often large, dower out of the joint fund, entirely without reference to the special property of their own parents. This may go on indefinitely; but as family quarrels will arise, there are always means of terminating the arrangement, and closing the accounts, either entirely as regards all, or partially, as with reference to a *mauvais sujet*, or troublesome member of the partnership. So extensive are the accounts in many cases, that one or two years are required to bring out a result, but no ill feeling or doubt seems to arise as to the system, or as to the accuracy of the accounts; there being a kind of family audit from time to time.

This curious patriarchal system, though obtaining more perfectly and frequently in Santa Maura than in the other islands, exists in Cephalonia, and is said to be not quite unknown in Zante, where the state of society approximates far more to that common in the western countries of Europe. Santa Maura being the most isolated of all the islands, and that which retains all ancient customs most tenaciously, is naturally that in which this sort of communism can exist with smallest risk of interference.

I have remarked that one result of this system is to keep up a kind of aristocracy in the villages, and almost to produce that peculiarly English institution, a resident gentry. Without the education, wealth and luxuries, or rather with much of the wealth and a very infinitesimal proportion of the comforts, and little of the education of the landed gentry in England, the patriarchs of the villages possess great influence, which they sometimes exert favourably, helping and improving the poorer members of the population of their districts. Sometimes they behave badly, lending these poor wretches small sums of money on their land or growing crops, at exorbitant interest, or buying up the crops at unfair prices, or by petty tyranny of other kinds, grinding the poor, and rendering themselves hated. I believe it may be said, to the credit of Santa Maura, that there is, on the whole, rather more of the former and less of the latter in that island than in the others. It is not, however, in human nature that the country should be free from such pests as extortioners and usurers, and where there is power there will always be abuse of it. The bad tendency of the system is clearly to give power to some one person of a district at the expense of the rest, and the favourable result is to keep property together rather than to break it up into small holdings.

I left the town of Santa Maura in the hope of fine weather, a hope doomed to be disappointed, although I delayed my start till after the close of some of the heaviest rains and fiercest storms that affect temperate climates. Accompanied by my kind host and excellent friend the Resident, I endeavoured to make my way at once across to the high central range, and thence to the west coast. The country is picturesque, but peculiar. A long and steep rise brings us to the first ridge at a moderate elevation; this ridge continues as far as Scarus, and is there cut off by the sea. In the interval between this ridge and the next, which is at least 800 feet higher, there are two or three lakes and hollows of the kind I have already spoken of as occurring at lower levels in Corfu. Here, however, they all form part of a wide valley in a table-land 500 feet above the sea. There was water in them at the time I saw them. It was already yellow, and very shallow, and it would no doubt very soon sink down, and perhaps pass off in springs at the foot of the mountains towards the sea. A picturesque village was planted on the slope of the hill above one of them, and just at the foot above the water I observed the foundations of a large ancient temple, said to have been a temple of Apollo. Most of the stones have been

worked up into use in the adjacent village, but coins
have been found in the neighbourhood.

Crossing the head of this high valley, which is in
parts very romantic, and terminates towards the sea
in a narrow, precipitous gorge, we have immediately
before us the principal and central range, along the
side of which an admirable road has been constructed
under the superintendence of the present Resident.
This road makes a steady ascent for three miles without a turn, rising one foot in eighteen, and thus
enables the inhabitants to perform in an hour, without
difficulty, the ascent to the village of Engluvi, which
had formerly taken three hours.

The construction of this and many of the country
roads in this island deserves special allusion. Although still very imperfectly provided with means of
communication, and from its mountainous character
difficult of access, and especially troublesome to provide with roads—having, moreover, a population who,
if they do not fancy a road, will not use it,—there are
difficulties in the way of improving Santa Maura. Very
often, however, the country people, who are the most
deeply interested, will give free labour for such purposes as they desire to see accomplished, and such
labour is of an excellent kind. If to that a small sum
is added by the local authorities, or the central government, a road can be made at very small cost.
But for this the people must have confidence in the
road engineer, and if, as is too often the case, he is
utterly incompetent, having been appointed by friends
in the municipality who merely desired to find him a

place, the scheme will fail. Stories of incompetent
engineers are unfortunately very common. One was
pointed out to me who undertook the construction of
a road close to the town of Santa Maura communicating with some villages on the high table-land.
When he came to the mountain side, this original
genius carried his road in a straight line up the face
of the mountain at such a gradient that on the first
trial of its qualities by a loaded cart drawn by one
horse, the cart rolled back before it got half-way up,
dragging the horse with it, till the whole tumbled
into a ditch, to the destruction of the engineer's reputation as well as of the vehicle and the poor quad-
ruped. In another case, an engineer, of equal experience and intelligence, undertook a bridge. Proceeding by the light of his nature, he secured a supply of
thick slabs of heavy stone, and laid them on the centering like a pavement. He was surprised when the
centering was removed to find that the pavement did
not support itself in the air as he imagined other
pavements of bridges usually did. A fourth engineer was farther advanced in his studies, and placed
his material, properly shaped, on the centering, but
provided piers so ludicrously inadequate to support
the weight, that the whole construction fell on the
first commencement of the removal of the centering.
In these cases warning had been given, and even the
masons employed knew the absurdity they were committing; but the work went on, and it did not appear
that the *employé* received his dismissal, or was the
worse thought of for his failure.

The road in question was not, however, either laid out or constructed by an engineer of this class. Though now somewhat in want of repair, it is an admirable work, and cost scarcely any money. It is completed to the village of Engluvi, whence it is continued by an inferior hand to the top of the pass, another 500 feet above.

Engluvi is a small, dirty village, like most of the straggling grey villages on the mountain sides, but it is charmingly placed. It has one of the most elaborate and complicated bell-towers that I have seen in the islands, built somewhat in a Palladian style, and not much unlike the lower part of the well-known 'Gate of Honour,' clothed with ivy, at Caius College, Cambridge. We paid a visit to the head man of the village, and, as usual, were expected to take coffee; as usual, too, the coffee was quickly made and excellent, far better than one would get at any hotel in London or North Germany. With the coffee was served a plate of broken walnuts and a curious confection made of the must of wine, enclosing whole kernels of the walnut. This sweetmeat is made in skins of the same kind as those commonly used for small sausages. A slice of it looked something like a slice of common German sausage. The flavour was rather pleasant though faint.

The house was a fair specimen of its kind. As usual, the inhabited part is on an upper floor, being built over low stores and stabling. The staircase is outside, and constructed of rough limestone slabs, of which there is any quantity in the neighbour-

hood.   There was a sort of half-enclosed ante-room,
used as a kitchen, containing a most curious and
ancient mechanical contrivance in the shape of a loom.
It should have been sent to the Great Exhibition as
a contrast to the elaborate contrivances of the present
day.

The principal chamber opened out of this ante-
room, and contained three beds, several chests, a few
chairs, and a table, several sacks of flour, and a
number of vessels of crockery.   The fowls and children had free access everywhere.   A third small room
opened beyond this.   It contained the oven and various utensils.   There was no other accommodation.

The owner of this house was well off.   He had
land, trees, and very likely some money lent on mort-
gage at high interest.   The men of the family were
decently clothed; and both men and women, and
indeed the children also, all wore a peculiar gaber-
dine, which I have not often seen in its perfection out
of Santa Maura.   It is something between a coat and
a pelisse, having slits for the arms but no sleeves,
not meeting in front, but covering the back from the
neck to the ancles.   It is made of a peculiar coarse,
black, homespun cloth or serge, bound with red
braid.   When new it looks well; but it does not seem
of much use, owing to its scantiness.

Generally, the women of the lower classes of this
island are clothed in the most miserable rags that
it is possible to conceive.   A long chemise, of the
coarsest and dingiest canvas, that can hardly have
been washed since it was first made, is tied round

the waist with a strip of similar canvas, and fastened round the neck with a string. This is the foundation and the only describable part of the dress. The younger girls, and even grown-up girls, sometimes have little else, but the women are generally wrapped and covered with sundry odds and ends that seem to have neither form nor meaning. Over all is a short, torn blue skirt reaching to the knees, which is indescribably hideous. The feet are generally covered with slippers, and the legs sometimes swathed in rags. No description can exaggerate the wretchedness of this attempt at clothing; and it is rare, indeed, to observe the smallest effort made by the women to do the best with the miserable material they possess. In all this the oriental character is manifest. The men are both better looking and better clothed than the women, and evidently try to make the best of the materials at their command to set themselves off.

The daily costume of the Leucadian women of the better class is, however, different, and very peculiar. A tight-fitting shirt and jacket, with much rich embroidery on the jacket, and a deeply-frilled skirt, are the principal articles seen. There is no crinoline, and nothing of Dutch extravagance in the under garments. The effect is more quaint than good. The lower classes in the towns wear generally a skirt of some coarse, blue material, fitting closely, and a kind of chemise, tightly drawn in front, is seen above it. A handkerchief, of some gaudy colour, is not unusual; and a cloth is generally distributed in some way over

the head, covering it more or less according to circumstances, and according to the taste of the owner. As
in Corfu, the women, except when young, are extremely ugly; but the men are handsome, and often
seem to improve and gain an appearance of dignity and
intelligence as they become old, which is not observable
at an earlier period of life.

The full dress of the Leucadian ladies is again quite
different, and has been already alluded to. Originally,
it was exceedingly elaborate and beautiful. No one,
however, now wears it in society. It is a costume
derived originally from Constantinople, and is Byzantine in its character. The under garment was embroidered over the bosom down to the waist, and also on
the sleeves, either in silver or gold, or in coloured
silks, in exquisite patterns. Round the waist was a
girdle, made up of massive links of chased and sculptured silver, filled in with fine filagree work, and in front
was a still more massive and handsome triangular plate.
A jacket, deeply embroidered, did not conceal these,
and a curious narrow coat, with short sleeves, fitted
the back tightly, but scarcely appeared in front. The
skirts were full, and also very rich. Some of the girdles
that I have seen contain more than sixteen ounces of
silver, and the workmanship is exquisite. Few of
them now remain, and they are never worn.

From Engluvi there is a rise of several hundred feet
to a plateau, from which again rises the loftiest part of
the island chain. There are two mountain tops that
have divided the honour of being regarded as the culminating points; Stavrota, rising immediately from

this plateau, is one of them,—and St. Elias, a short distance to the south, is the other. Unfortunately, by the time I was near enough to think of reaching the top of Stavrota, now considered the loftiest peak, the weather, which had been threatening for some time, become unmistakably bad. The whole mountain top was enveloped in cloud, and there was no hope of improvement.

I was therefore obliged to proceed to my destination through the pouring rain, which now set in. An exceedingly rough path over large loose stones, across the plateau and up the little shoulder of a hill opposite, introduced us to a break-neck descent; to accomplish which it was necessary to dismount, and let the horses pick their way while we jumped from one stone to another,—now in water, now in mud, and always in difficulty,—till we reached a village, where we waited for a time, hoping the weather might change. Below us was a deep valley, entirely enveloped in cloud; and it was only at intervals that the opposite hills loomed through the mist. Finding that there was no improvement, we at last started once more on horseback, and determined to make a final effort to reach our destination. The road was still of the same nature, and we had to cross much troublesome country; but we succeeded in getting on; and towards sunset, as we approached a narrow opening between the mountains and beheld the sea and the west coast of the island, the rain had almost ceased. This did not take place till we were all thoroughly soaked and made uncomfortable.

P

From one of the higher parts of the descent we obtained a view towards the north, and saw the sun shining on the hills of Paxo, the mountains of Corfu rising beyond it in great beauty. The coast of Paxo was marked by a border of brilliant white, probably occasioned by the reflection of the sun's rays from the breakers on the coast, and its outline stood out against the intensely blue sky just cleared of the clouds, so that the little island was presented under the most favourable conditions. Its well-covered hills gave that peculiar tone of colour that large patches of olives never fail to do. It looked calm and peaceful, lying in the broad sunshine, while all above our heads was storm and rain. The interval of sea, more than fifty miles, seemed trifling, and the forms were as sharp as if we had been less than half the distance in an ordinary atmosphere. Even the mountains of Corfu beyond were perfectly well outlined, and very beautiful, while the Albanian coast and mountains filled up the distance in that direction.

The beauty was no doubt enhanced by the gloomy masses of storm cloud that still hung heavily on the top of Stavrota, only a few miles from us, and from the rapid advance of storm and rain clouds from the south. It was long, however, before these had advanced far enough to shut off our view in the opposite direction; and we lost sight of Paxo by a turn of the road, rejoicing in its fine weather, while all around us the storm was closing in once more, and becoming again involved in mist and cloud.

Our object was to reach the village of Attané, one

of a number of similar and small places in the western district of the island. Owing to its position in a north and south valley, and sheltered by the high mountains from the east, this district is generally warmer, and of more equable climate, than those on the eastern coast; and being higher, and naturally drained, it is both healthy and fertile.

The first acquaintance I made of the actual details of the interior life of the rich natives of Santa Maura, was on this occasion. We put up for the night at the house of the chief person in Attané. It is near the coast, and only about four hours' ride from Sappho's Leap, and two hours from the ruins of Basilike. We arrived under somewhat unfavourable circumstances— the son of the family, a member of the Assembly of Santa Maura, having by an accident been prevented from proceeding a-head to announce us, and allow of due preparations being made. Unexpected, however, as we were, we were received with the warmest welcome, and with every possible hospitality. The house is charmingly situated near the opening of a lateral gorge in the coast chain, at a height of nearly a thousand feet above the sea. It is surrounded by gardens and cultivated land. As we dashed along, after a tiresome and wet journey, and came into the village at a hand gallop, we saw the owner of the house, his brother, and the rest of the male members of the family, coming out to meet us. I believe they may have seen us as we rounded the hill at a little distance. Besides the human members of the family, we were met by a noble group of turkeys, who expressed their feelings in the usual manner,—little aware, probably, that they were to assist personally in the hospitalities about to be offered us.

The house is large, low, and straggling. The principal part inhabited by the family is built on the slope of a hill, and is entered from the front by a double flight of rough stone steps leading to a kind of verandah, pleasant enough in summer. A fine old mulberry tree stands in front of the steps. From the verandah are two entrances, both through short passages, into a large hall used as the eating room, and furnished with a kind of divan or sofa against the wall. A large table or press in one corner, a few chairs and benches, and some chests, form the whole furniture.

From this hall, to the right and left, we enter the sleeping rooms. On the left hand are two small rooms, one about twelve feet by ten, the other a little larger. The smaller room is only entered by passing through the larger. The larger has in it the family picture of the patron saint, with a lamp ever burning before it. The smaller has no picture, but it enjoys the luxury of glass in the windows; whereas the larger has merely a shutter, excluding or admitting light and air together. The walls, however, are very thick, and thus the quantity of light that enters is not very large. Not so with the air, which rushes in with terrible pertinacity, and will not be excluded.

The smaller bedroom with the glazed window was appropriated to my use, as the greater stranger. It is, indeed, the state room. I believe it to be exactly the size of the condemned cell at Newgate. By taking short steps, I can manage to extend my walk to eight paces, commencing at one corner, passing carefully round all the articles of furniture, and reaching the opposite corner. It is ventilated on one of those principles originally applied by Dr. Reid in the House of Commons, and there found inconvenient. I mean the introduction of air through the floor. Our legislators found, that air rushing up through holes in the floor, was apt to bring up dust as well as warmth. My contrivance was not subject to this objection, though hardly satisfactory in other respects. It consisted of holes in the floor, probably gnawed through by friendly and scientific rats, communicating with a pig stye, poultry house and stable, below. More senses than one were appealed to, and not always pleasantly.

The walls being thick and the openings narrow, all the rooms of the houses are necessarily gloomy. The interior walls and the doors are kept whitewashed, but the ceilings, consisting of stout planks laid across huge beams, are black with age, and have never been whitened or coloured.

The rooms, though small, were clean; and, indeed, I found my bed not only comfortable but luxurious. It was covered with an immense quilted coverlet, enclosed in a green watered-silk case. This coverlet was so large as to require to be doubled to put on the bed; and even then, it reached the floor on two sides. No doubt it was a valued family production, and only used on important occasions.

The furniture in the room, besides the bed, included only two boxes, a small chest of drawers of English

appearance, and a chair; nor was there space for anything besides. The other room was similarly provided,
and was about equal in the amount of conveniences it
held; but the window not being glazed, it was less
comfortable. There was no latch, or lock, to the door
of communication between the rooms. There was a
little table in the larger room, but it was covered
with oranges, biscuits, and garlic.

Besides these bedrooms and the others opposite,
both of which opened out to the hall, there was only
a small parlour about the same size as the smaller
bedrooms. Two long sofas against the wall, a small
table, and the invariable chest, left little room but to
sit down. This room, however, was carpeted with a
thick woven material that is common in the island,
and is used indifferently for carpet, table-cover, and
horse furniture. Some specimens of it were sent to
London to the Great exhibition of 1862, and were
much admired. The window of the parlour was
glazed, but it was very small, and the walls being
thick, little light could enter,—the less, as the window
looked out on the verandah, sheltered by a large pent-
house, convenient enough in bad weather.

The hall was large, and contained a few articles of
furniture, as well as the great table, settee, and chairs.
It was only lighted, and that very imperfectly, when
the doors were left open. In cold, rainy, and windy
weather, it would certainly be desirable to limit the
sitting at table to the smallest possible time. The
weather in this part of the country is often unmistakably cold, and sometimes continues so for weeks

together; but it is rarely thought worth while to do anything to remedy this inconvenience. A small brazier, or pan of charcoal embers, is sometimes brought into the sitting-room.

The chest is an invariable article of furniture in all rooms in every house. It is an oblong oak, or cypress-wood box, about three feet long and eighteen or twenty inches wide and high. The front is generally carved, —sometimes neatly, sometimes roughly, according to circumstances. It is provided with one, two, or three locks, and is the regular receptacle of all valuables of every kind.

The kitchen is outside the house, separated by a little paved passage, and as the doors of kitchen and hall are not opposite, and the passage is much interrupted by loose stones, tubs, and other obstructions, the navigation on a dark night would be dangerous. It is a large shed, but with no other apertures than the door and a hole in the roof to let out smoke and let in light. The hearth is a large space raised about four inches from the floor, and serves not only to hold the sticks that make the fire, but as the place where all kinds of scullery-work are carried on by boys, or girls, squatted down before it. I found a small female drab, clad in a filthy canvas sack, sitting there when I entered, having a dozen knives by her side and a scouring-brick close by. I watched her with some interest, she fully returning the compliment. At length, she takes a knife, rubs it vigorously on the brick for a minute, as if she had taken a vow to finish her job off hand. Not at all. She looks up and stares at the boy oppo-

site, who is engaged spitting in a little mass of black
dirt, holding a boot in one hand and a brush in
another. Then the girl rubs the edge of the brick
on a particular spot of the knife, and looks at it
earnestly, while the boy does the same with a spot
on his boot. During this time, the cook is getting
on with his preparations; and I am sitting toasting
myself and making observations. The kitchen utensils are limited to the smallest possible number, and
do not include a pair of tongs, or more than one spoon
and fork for cooking purposes.

But the house, thus simple and primitive, has been
the scene of stirring events. Not many years ago, a
gang of brigands attacked it, and succeeded in forcing
an entry. At the very moment when they were tearing
off rings from the hands of two daughters of the family,
whom they had dragged into the hall from their bedroom, two of the villains were shot dead on the spot
by the father, who had managed to reach the little
parlour, where were loaded arms ready for use.
Meanwhile, a son had made his way into the bedroom I occupied on the night of my visit (vacated, as
I had reason to suppose, in my favour by the identical
young ladies who were robbed), and was getting out
of the little window. It was barely large enough to
allow him to squeeze through; and while he was
escaping a bullet was sent after him which must almost
have grazed his leg, and which left a deep mark in
the plaster of the wall in the recess of the window.
This hole still remains perfectly manifest. The lad
succeeded in rousing the village and obtaining as-

sistance. The robbers were repulsed, and most of them have since been taken; but no doubt, had they succeeded, the booty would have been worth the risk.*

My little room had on a previous occasion been occupied by the Lord High Commissioner on one of his visits to this part of his charge, and the proprietor of the house did not fail to bring forward a magnificent many-bladed Sheffield knife that had been sent as an acknowledgment of the hospitality then rendered. The vicinity of the village to Sappho's Leap renders it more frequently resorted to than would otherwise be the case, and its beautiful situation well deserves notice. The approach is particularly grand and wild, and I was nowhere more struck with the fact that the vine delights in sterile ground than when I remarked here whole vineyards of enormous extent occupying a natural talus of angular fragments of limestone on the slope of the hill. This enormous heap of loose stones, disturbed after every shower and constantly moving by the action of gravity, is actually selected to plant vines upon, and, from the size of the stem, there is every probability that they flourish. These are grape vines, as the currant vine does not succeed in bare and stony districts, and requires a greater depth of soil.

* The owner of this house, in which he resides most part of the year and always in winter, possesses another house looking far more respectable, and even much more clean and comfortable, near the plain of Basilike. This house is a handsome Italian villa of two stories, with numerous windows shut in with jalousies. In accordance with the custom of the country the village residence in the mountains is preferred to this much more convenient house in the plains.

I slept well in my comfortable bed, but was disturbed before dawn by a violent thunderstorm and a rather sharp touch of earthquake. All that I felt of the earthquake was a long, loud, rattling noise like the rolling of a heavy waggon over stones, and a vibration of the frame of the bedstead. Such earthquakes are here very common, and it is said that in the central valley of the island the shocks are more felt than they are on the coast. I have seldom heard fiercer or more determined rain. It fell in torrents, and for so long a time, that I began to think the whole country would be inundated. Later in the day, when the weather had cleared and the sun was shining, I went out to look at an interesting bed of carbonaceous shale in the cliffs near the house. I then found that all signs of the torrent had disappeared, except indeed that a few rills were converted into small cascades, and made more show than they would usually have done. Throughout this country the effects of the heaviest rain last but a very short time, and an enormously large proportion of the water that falls must be absorbed into the cracked, spongy, chalky soil, which yields water in springs at every little puddle or cut that is made in it.

This great abundance of water in the rocks is beyond a doubt the cause of the large production in most of the crops that are well cared for, compared with the apparently stony, dry, and unprofitable soil. Rain falls only at intervals and in torrents, and in many countries would run off at once to the sea, so that after a week or fortnight the soil would be dry.

Here, on the contrary, evaporation from the great
sheets of water in the earth constantly keeps the soil
from becoming parched, and the greater the heat the
more complete and rapid is the evaporation from the
rarely-failing supplies beneath. The absorbing power
is increased after periods of dry weather longer extended than usual, and thus the proportion of rain
that passes out of sight is larger than elsewhere.

That the torrents of rain occasionally falling produce their full effect in one way is clear from certain
large valleys of soft, loose, sandy soil occurring between
the central chain of the island and the western hills.
I noticed several instances that must have been extremely recent, in which we passed round the head of
ravines in places where a child might easily and safely
jump across, although these same ravines a few yards
off had widened and grown rapidly impassable by the
eroding action of the rain. The moment that a channel
has been established, and the water enters it, it rapidly
widens and deepens; and within sight of the spot
where a crack first commenced, I have seen crevices a
hundred yards wide at the top and a hundred feet
deep. Every season certainly changes these both in
position and number as well as magnitude. New
ones replace old ones; old ones are filled up by the
falling in of their sides, and thus the face of the
country is constantly altering on a large scale.

From Attané, on the morning after the fearful
night of rain, thunderstorm, and earthquake, I proceeded to examine a series of deposits of bituminous
shale said to exist in the cliff adjacent. The approach

to the cliff, and the descent to that part of it that must be reached before arriving at the object of my search, were difficult; but very interesting, and highly picturesque.   Vast accumulations of small fragments of soft limestone were passed, wearing almost into a sand, and so easily acted on by the weather, that every shower must affect them.   These lie at the natural angle of fallen rubbish, and present an even slope for a great distance.   This slope ends in most parts by a vertical cliff, and in this the shale is seen. It is a promising and important deposit, provided enough raw material can be raised, and it is of a quality sufficiently rich to distil for the purpose of obtaining illuminating and lubricating oils, and paraffin. It is black, burns freely with a smell by no means disagreeable, and leaves a solid ash.   No doubt it might be obtained from the coast where the beds come out at the sea level, but perched between heaven and earth in the almost inaccessible spots where specimens can now alone be obtained, it is not easy to recognise more than the fact of its existence as a regular deposit.   About this there can be no doubt.   In order to reach the spot I had the assistance of a dozen Greeks with their usual implement, which is a very pointed spade, something between a pickaxe and spade; it is a tool answering the joint purpose of tilling and preparing the ground and laying open a rock.   It does not look very efficacious, but with it they rapidly made steps in the loose rubbish to assist in the descent and ascent, and then picked and shovelled away enough to lay bare the shale and clear the surface. They were extremely active, and it was really a beautiful thing to see them leap down like goats upon a narrow ledge of rock from some height with bare feet, and in case of need make a second leap before reaching a place where they could stand. The steep precipice immediately below would have given them small chance for their lives had they missed their footing, but they were perfectly fearless.

The geology of Santa Maura is as follows. The chief underlying rock seems to be a white limestone with flints, sometimes detached, sometimes bedded, which is occasionally (as on the west coast) exceedingly soft, but elsewhere (in the central ridge?) very hard and compact. It forms the lower part of the hills behind the town, and is there thinly bedded with regular bands of flint, dipping away to the south-south-west at an angle of about thirty degrees; these beds are covered unconformably by compact limestone, no doubt tertiary. Towards the interior there are shales that occupy the lowest position, but their age is doubtful; they are black, soft, and rotten, and alternate with hard bands of good stone.

The central range, culminating in Stavrota, is of hard, compact rock, and from the fossils shown me, said to be taken from it, it must be a tertiary limestone. On the other side are vast hills of soft rock, some reddish, but mostly white, very easily acted on by weather. Underneath, or perhaps forming the essential part of these, is a white chalky limestone (scaglia) with flints, in which are bands of harder limestone amongst the mass of bituminous shale. The

shale is very irregularly distributed, and the bands
are much contorted. It is said that there are two
distinct deposits of this kind, and this is not unlikely;
but the whole rock is much disturbed, and the deposit
thins out and suddenly expands, the thickness of the
shale having apparently some reference to the thickness of the limestone. The bed is well shown in natural
sections in two localities, more than a mile distant
from each other, on the coast. Both dip the same
way, about twenty degrees west, so that they are
either repetitions by fault or distinct deposits. The
limestone contains very broken and fragmentary remains of shells (bivalves, but not distinguishable);
the shale contains markings of an ammonite. No
doubt good fossils might be got by careful search;
and though, except from the sea, the deposits are
very inaccessible, there is no reason why large quantities of the mineral should not be obtained and removed at small cost.

From Attané a long ride of four hours over broken
ground conducts to Sappho's Leap, the southernmost
extremity of the western part of the island of Santa
Maura, and the rock from which it is supposed
Sappho committed suicide. A temple of Apollo
marked and rendered more sacred this celebrated
locality, and it has never ceased to be the object of
a pilgrimage to all those who desire to have any
credit for, or who feel any interest in classical investigation. Coins and medals have been found in this
locality, which has a real interest independently of its
legendary reputation, and is a very noble specimen of

cliff. Seen from a distance its whiteness is a striking
feature. It is not lofty as compared with the adjacent
cliffs to the north, but is a grand termination to the
promontory which it completes. The following account of it is at once accurate and picturesque. "The
rock, which declines gradually into the sea on the
south, presents a white and perpendicular cliff towards
the north of considerable elevation. There are the
ruins of a temple on the summit of one of the emi-
nences here seen, consisting, however, at present of
nothing more than the foundation and a few squared
stones of large dimensions. Not far from it is a platform cut in the rock, still on the verge of the precipice, and on a more lofty point. From its figure it is
not improbable that a circular edifice might have once
occupied the spot. The inhabitants imagine that the
altar of Apollo once stood where a few stones are now
piled together in honour of a Christian saint, and a
small vase of the size and shape of a pear was found on
the spot. The soil is covered with broken pottery."

Up the side of the mountain behind Attané is another road which leads near the foot of Stavrota
and then descends into the valley of Basilike. The
ascent is very steep but not long, and, the summit
once gained, the view, first of Stavrota and afterwards of the valley of Basilike, are extremely fine. As
a mountain, there are none within the compass of the
Ionian islands, and few elsewhere, that surpass Stavrota in form and general effect. Seen from the south,
it rises from the extremity of a valley or plain six
miles long and two miles wide, scarcely above the sea

level, and continued by a long and most beautiful bay, shut in by mountains. It is entirely detached for the greater part of its height, but connected on the east by a narrow neck with a lofty neighbouring mountain. Between these two mountains is a deep, wild and picturesque glen. The side of Stavrota, towards the south, is deeply furrowed by numerous water-courses, which give it (the mountain) a hoary and venerable appearance hardly justified when one examines it more minutely with a geological eye.

We passed through a small village on our descent. It was perched, as country villages often are, on the side of a hill, and we there had occasion to make some inquiries as to the arrival of a boat that had been ordered round to Basilike. At once we were surrounded by the whole population, of all ages, of men and boys. I counted more than a score, any one of whom would, I fully believe, have shown us any hospitality, and interrupted his own business to attend to ours, not only without expectation of reward, but firmly refusing it if offered. We learnt that our boat had probably arrived; and, as I was anxious to push on, we arranged, with some difficulty, to escape the inevitable half hour's delay and the cup of coffee that sweetens it.

There is something very peculiar in the perfectly dead level—a swamp, after the heavy rains we had lately had—that stretches out for miles at one's feet, and terminates in a noble bay that could contain with ease any amount of shipping. It occurs to one at the moment why the Venetians did not originally select it as their port, and the place for their city; and why, also, when Amaxiki was destroyed in 1825, that unhealthy and most inconvenient position was not abandoned in favour of one adapted by nature for a town and harbour. The unhealthiness that might be expected from the flat might easily be avoided by systematically carrying off the water. At present it is not only used for irrigation, but allowed to remain on the land.

A vast quantity of detritus is brought down on all sides, and must rapidly raise this large plain; but there seems a natural limit to the extension seawards, as the water is deep close in to the shore.

Melancholy is the contrast of the half-dozen ricketty houses that disgrace the name they bear (βασιλικὴ, royal), and the whole expanse of rich lands and wealth-bearing waters that stretch away to the right and left. But the Santa Mauriots, unlike the Ithacans and Cephalonians, are not mariners. They have no foreign commerce, and few boats of any kind; and the population is all in the villages on the mountain sides, or in the higher valleys far removed from the sea. To them the sea is a source of danger, not profit; they dread the pirate more than they love traffic. They, however, of all the islanders on these coasts, have most claim to be aborigines, and having been driven to the mountains for many generations as the only place of safety, they have not retained, and, perhaps, are not likely to acquire, the maritime tastes of their ancestors.

The climate of Leucadia is on the whole delightful.

Q

Snow sometimes falls during winter, and, occasionally, even so late as May, the mountains will be covered. On these occasions the winds are very sharp. Such seasons are, however, quite exceptional, for the crop of oats should be cut in May, and all the fruits are then well advanced.

In the town the summer heat is excessive. Whatever winds may be blowing outside and in the open waters of the Mediterranean, they are converted into one of two prevalent kinds, owing to the form of the island, and they are recognised accordingly. Thus the north wind, or a wind a point or two to east or west of north, is a regular wind during summer. The east winds are converted into north north-east, and come over Pindus and the rest of the lofty mountain chain of northern Greece. These are, therefore, always cool, while the west winds, converted into north north-west, come across from the Italian side, and are never oppressive. The latter of these winds blows steadily each day, beginning at 10 A.M. and not ceasing till near sunset. Then the other sets in, and the nights are always cool and pleasant. It is only the scirocco and Austral—winds coming from the south-east and south—that are dreaded. They bring storm and excessive heat, and not unfrequently electric storms usher them in. The appearance of the air immediately before one of these storms is peculiar, and the state of the atmosphere eminently uncomfortable. The wind blows a hurricane, the dust fills the air, the sky is so darkened that one can scarcely see to write, while a general state of distress pervades every living thing. It is considered that if in these conditions of the air a storm of rain does not very rapidly follow, there is imminent danger of an earthquake; but that after electric storms followed by rain earthquakes are not to be expected.

There is no winter of any severity, and the cold that is felt is only occasional. The air, also, does not often feel damp, so that a chill is rare. The unhealthy seasons are summer and part of autumn, and during August and September there is a good deal of malaria in some places. The malaria, however, is said never to reach the fort of Santa Maura, where the soldiers always enjoy excellent health.

In Santa Maura it is the custom for people to walk out after dusk with their wives to enjoy the evening breeze. In such cases the lady walks before her husband, and they do not address each other. Should a gentleman meet his friend thus accompanied, he would not think of addressing the lady, or alluding to her existence; he would not even take off his hat, though acquainted with and visiting the family. The lady is entirely incognito, and must remain so. This is a curious specimen of orientalism preserved intact to the present day, common enough in Greece a few years ago, but now confined to the less visited islands.

Superstition is rife in Santa Maura, especially among the country people. Not long ago a most respectable and wealthy proprietor, the chief of his village and district, allowed it to be known that he had been induced to give upwards of two hundred dollars to a woman who had a reputation as a witch, and who was known to have visited churchyards in the costume of Eve without her innocence. The poor man, being himself in authority, was forced by the higher authorities to give evidence on the subject, which he would willingly have avoided, and the woman was punished with imprisonment. The objcet in this case was to cure some complaint; but there was reason to suppose that the woman was a mischievous and dangerous character.

Another instance of superstition is seen in the mode in which they take an oath. They willingly swear falsely on the Gospels and in the church; but when called on to do so with their hands placed on the relics of some saint, they will, if possible, refuse to swear; but, if they cannot escape, the truth will come out. An instance occurred, not long ago, of an official maliciously and falsely accused. He desired an inquiry, but knew that no ordinary oath would be . attended to, as his enemies were very strong and determined. It was therefore ordered that each person should be sworn on the relics of St. Spiridion, after which there was no difficulty. Still it is believed that all these feelings are rapidly dying out.

MAP OF SANTA MAURA.

AND ADJACENT ISLANDS.

O Sesola Ro

Atiane

Basilike Bay   Ruins

"Basiliki"

MT. STAVRO

Engluri

Sta Mavra

LEUCA

Fort
Sta Maura

S. ELIAS

MT.
CARUS

MNIA

RKUDI

MEGANISI

C A R N I A

TOKO

ASTEO

0   1   2   3   4   5
Scale of English Miles 69 1 = 1°

MAP OF ZANTE.

C. Skinari

St Nicolo

Salines

ZANTE

Basilike Pt

Sulphur and
Naphtha Cave

Castle

KROKOS

Gulf of Cueri

VRACHIONI

Lagopodo

Luthad

Vroma

Pitch
Wells

Zieri Pt

3   4

10 MILES

ITHACA.

"Who brought thee, stranger, to the sea-girt land
  Of Ithaca? and from what foreign strand?"
"At dead of night, while fast asleep I lay,
  Phæacian seamen bore me on my way
  From Scheria's isle, in ship that oft before
  Hath men transported to this rugged shore."
ODYSS. xvi. 222—227.—(W. Mure.)

Horses I would not take to Ithaca:
In Ithaca, in sooth, neither broad runs
Are there, nor aught like meadow: goats it feeds,
And lovelier 'tis by far than feeding horses.
For of those isles that lie so steep in the sea
Not one is fit for horsemanship or driving,
Nor with good meadows one: and Ithaca
Is such beyond them all.
ODYSS. iv. 601—608.—(Norgate.)

CHAPTER VIII.

IF Corfu is the most beautiful, Cephalonia the largest, Santa Maura the wildest, and Zante the prettiest of the Ionian islands, Ithaca is, beyond all comparison, the most romantic. A pure and bright halo of poetry surrounds it—a poetry the most dreamy and the

sweetest, the most homely and the pleasantest—a
poetry that touches every feeling and harmonises
with every association—a poetry that is in us and
not in the place—a poetry that carries us back to
the earliest childhood of civilisation, and speaks of
men as strong, wise, and simple, and of women
as helps meet for a race of heroes—a poetry which
presumes each tree to have its Dryad, each spring
its Nymph, and each grove its sylvan god.

And there is no place in which this sweet spirit
of poetry is better preserved. Ithaca is now peopled
by a new race, and there is in all convenient parts of
it a certain amount of modern cultivation; but the
population is not large, and the people are collected
into a few groups. It is not difficult to find parts
of the little island where one can wander all day
without seeing a human face or hearing a human
voice, and certainly without seeing the impress of
a human foot. Small as it is, it abounds in charming
and retired spots, where one may fancy the old spirits
still haunt and where nature has not changed. It
is easy to appreciate the fondness of Homer for this
spot, which he certainly knew well, and which he
wisely selected as the home of the wise Ulysses.

But one of the great glories of Ithaca has departed.
No longer does the swineherd build his hut in the
dark forest and tend his charge on the wooded cliffs.
The ilex and the numerous other varieties of oak once
so useful in affording food for the pigs and supplying
wood for building boats, have long been destroyed,
and the rocks once green with their foliage are now

grey and naked, or at best supply for a short period a slight vegetation of herbs, on which goats, the supplanters of the swine, obtain their scanty meals. The goats will not allow the young wood to rise, and thus here, as elsewhere in small districts, they keep down the proper and natural covering of the soil, and at once diminish its productiveness and deteriorate the climate, by leaving no shelter to prevent the rain that falls from immediate evaporation. It must indeed be admitted that the goats are no novelty in the island, for Homer speaks of them in a passage of the Odyssey already quoted, but the number was then probably much smaller than it now is, and the forests being once established could protect themselves, whereas the young plantations have no chance.

That Ithaca was really the island intended to be described by Homer, and that he knew it himself perfectly in every nook, there will hardly be much doubt in the mind of the traveller who compares on the spot the poem with the reality. Admirably adapted as a place of resort for a small society; provided with a few ports into which the ships could enter and be securely housed; having a coast for the most part inaccessible and very defensible, and placed opposite and in sight of the mainland of Greece; it was also within a couple of hours easy sail of the city of Samos, on the island of Cephalonia, certainly one of the earliest and grandest of those most ancient Greek cities enclosed by Cyclopean walls. Besides these advantages, it also enjoyed all that could be needed in the early times of civilisation to tempt

occupation and provide a nucleus and a home for
his family and dependants, whence the restless and
curious Greek might wander in search of the novel-
ties of his day. Ithaca would thus naturally suggest itself to Homer as the home of Ulysses, even
if he had to invent the character, and find a spot
adapted to his conception of the hero. But it is
probable that tradition had from time immemorial
connected the wise and crafty king with the island,
and the few medals—the bare half-dozen that alone
properly belong to its history—all point in the same
direction, and prove that it has always borne the
same name since Homer's time, and has always been
regarded as having been the habitation of Ulysses.
The various direct proofs are supported by collateral
and independent evidence, showing how completely
Homer must have had this spot in his mind's eye
when he dramatised the facts, and adapted the tradition to his own purposes.

No one need suppose, however, that the so-called
'castle of Ulysses' in Ithaca was the actual habitation
of the husband of Penelope in any other sense than
that there existed in Homer's time, in a tolerably
complete state, that wonderful construction whose
foundations and enclosing wall are now, after some
thousand years have elapsed, still fresh and unmistakable. The grottoes and the fountains, also, that
bear familiar names, do not convert Homer's poem
into a bare, naked, and prosaic description. They
exist, probably, much in the state in which they
always were, and the country, the ruins, the grottoes,

and the fountains, sufficiently correspond with the general outline given by the father of poetry.

I left Basilike about four o'clock on a very calm morning, hoping to find a favourable breeze outside the Bay, which is sheltered from the east, north and west, and only open to the south. I could not but feel this quiet and almost solemn departure as a fit leave taking of Santa Maura, where I had met such extreme kindness and attention, and where I had seen such a contrast between the stormy weather and the peaceful homes. Indeed, the parting with my entertainer was rather that of old friends than recent acquaintances. He had not only housed and fed me, but had devoted his time to accompany me on my way; had introduced me to all those who could assist in my inquiries; and now, in the middle of the night, insisted on being disturbed, and would see with his own eyes that every thing was in the right way, so that I could have no unnecessary delay or difficulty.

Once seated on board, and the boat unloosed from her moorings, I had leisure to think and look about me, wrapped in my warm cloak, the stars shining overhead and the waves faintly rippling on the beach at no great distance. There was not a breath of wind; and after the rough weather we had had, the contrast was very striking. With four active pairs of oars, but a heavy boat, we moved along slowly and steadily, and towards daybreak were well away from Santa Maura. The sun rose above a bank of cloud, not angrily but heavily, tinting with pale pink the light clouds in the west, and gradually brightening, first, the distant but lofty mountain of Cephalonia, and then the nearer, but much lower summits of Ithaca. Ithaca, and the two headlands of Cephalonia, were directly before us; Arkudi, and the other islands belonging to Ithaca, to the left, and the last point of Santa Maura—Sappho's Leap—was not far off to the right. Each, in turn, became bathed in full sunlight; and the air, being heavy and damp, and the rays of the sun already extremely powerful, the heat was soon absolutely oppressive. I was glad to throw off every wrap and take all means to obtain a breath of air. As the morning wore on and we slowly advanced, Ithaca became more and more prominent, and absorbed my whole attention. Cephalonia was then hidden behind it. The position of these two islands is peculiar. Ithaca is not only much smaller than Cephalonia, but is as it were embraced by its near neighbour,—Cephalonia curving round and enclosing it on three sides. As, however, the mountains of little Ithaca, though not nearly so lofty as those of its larger neighbour, which indeed are the loftiest of all in the Ionian group, are still high enough to exclude anything behind them when they serve as a foreground, there is nothing observable from the sea but the cliffs and slopes of the hills immediately adjacent.

Ithaca measures about seventeen miles from north to south, and its greatest breadth is about four miles. It is in fact a curved ridge of limestone, highest near the middle, with several small spurs to the east. It is said to be healthier than the other Ionian islands, and its inhabitants live to a great age. It has few

streams of any kind, and none of the smallest importance, as they at once enter the sea, owing to the form
of the mountain ridge. The population is about ten
thousand, and is distributed over the island.

The first break in the line of coast, coming in from
the north, is that which opens into Frikis Bay. The
half-dozen habitations at the end, which form the village of the same name, are seen on turning into the
bay. Frikis is a small port, and several fishing boats,
besides some vessels of large size, were moored in the
roads or occupied sheltered nooks. Like most of the
other indentations of the land in Ithaca, it recedes to
some distance, and is connected with a natural valley
and little stream. I noticed, that the quantity of
water entering the sea from this stream, which is the
largest in Ithaca, is disproportionately small, even when
we consider the extent of land drained. This was the
case, although there had been much heavy rain for
many days previous to my visit. The houses of Frikis were remarkably well built, and neat; and there
was an air of comfort and ease about the place, very
different from the appearance of Basilike or the villages
of Santa Maura. The inhabitants of Ithaca are much
addicted to maritime occupations, and thus seem to
earn for themselves a better livelihood than their more
stay-at-home neighbours to the north. Ithaca has,
from earliest times, supplied boats and men; and its
people prefer boating to the cultivation of the land.

From Frikis, a good mule path goes up into the
country to a few small villages and through a considerable tract of cultivated land. At first it proceeds along

the banks of the little stream, which, from the occasional black sediment left by its water, is called Melænudros. This might be due to the presence of oxide of manganese; but as it receives the water of some mineral springs containing sulphuretted hydrogen, in sufficient abundance to be available for medical purposes, this may also have some influence on the result.

The path from Frikis, up the country, soon rises, and from it may be seen a number of small valleys, converging towards the little port, and all cultivated. To the right is a wide opening, terminating in the Bay of Affalis to the north; and a considerable promontory, of no great elevation, extends in this direction. The village of Oxoi stands on the hill opposite, and like Frikis, consists of very decent, clean-looking houses.

My object in landing at Frikis was to examine one of the curious remains of ancient times, existing near that place. It is called the School of Homer; though what connection it can have had with a school, or why the old poet should have gone there for instruction, it would be difficult to say. The way to it lies up the little valley for some distance, and the ruins are on a plateau immediately below the last rise of the hill. They overlook the Bay of Affalis, which lies immediately below; and in the immediate neighbourhood of it are two strong springs rising within a distance of twenty feet, but not connected. Both smell of sulphuretted hydrogen, but one of them more strongly than the other. The springs both rise at the foot of a low inland cliff, covered with rich trailing vegetation,

over which fresh water drips into a small pool close to
one of the springs.   The water, thus falling, mixing
with the waters of the springs, runs down the valley
over a broken rocky bed, and joins the somewhat larger
stream below.   A little further on we come suddenly
to the ruins.

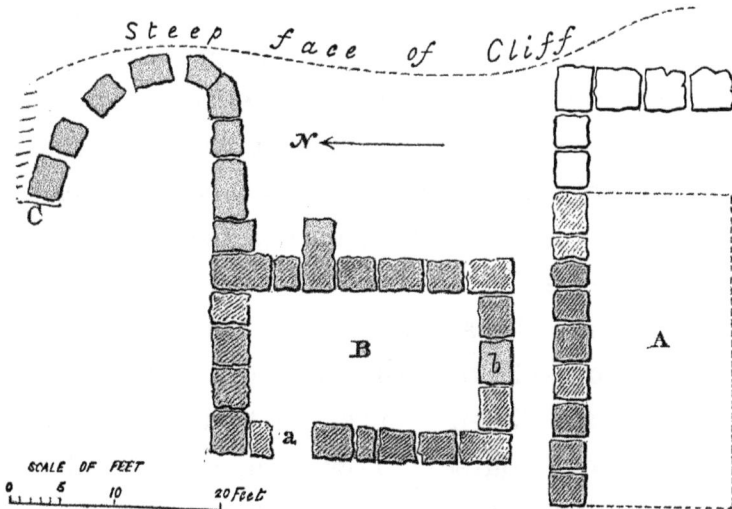

GROUND PLAN OF THE SCHOOL OF HOMER.

A.   A modern shed, built on the old Cyclopean foundations.
B.   The principal building, now in ruins.   (a) door, (b) window.
C.   Position of the stair down to the lower terrace.

These fragments of antiquity occupy a kind of plateau,
terminating abruptly with a steep face of rock.   Just
at the extremity, and communicating with a lower
plateau by a number of steps cut in the solid rock, are
the foundations of a somewhat extensive group of
buildings, all of which are constructed of large, squared
blocks, closely fitted, but not fastened with mortar.
Some of these are rectangular and some polygonal.

For the most part they are very carefully squared, and fit closely, without mortar or cement.

Some idea of the outline of the principal remains will be obtained by referring to the annexed ground plan and the sketches of the walls (see pp. 241, 243). These diagrams are not strictly accurate, the measurements having been taken roughly; but the chief features are preserved. The parts left without shade are those where only single stones lie on the ground. Of the enclosure B, in the plan, the walls are tolerably regular, and are all from five to seven feet from the ground. Fragments of the fallen stones lie about. Near the entrance (a), and at the point marked (b), where a window appears to have existed, these are somewhat higher. From the appearance on the north side, it seems not unlikely that the ground has been raised, perhaps by the fallen stones; so that the blocks, of which only one course is now seen, may possibly repose on another, which was really the foundation; and the walls may have one course of these large blocks more than can be seen. In that case, assuming that the whole height was at least that of the present highest stone, this gigantic architecture must have been fifteen feet above the ground. Above the large blocks, if the wall was required to be higher, smaller stones fastened with metal were probably used. There are not many of the largest stones on the ground, in this place.

The structure of the walls is simple, but belongs, probably, to a comparatively late period of Cyclopean work,—rather, indeed, to Hellenic than true Cyclopean. The largest stones are not more than five feet long, and probably none weighs so much as three tons. Several, however, certainly exceed two tons, and some of the largest stones are those that must have been lifted. Most of them are squared, and the angle stones are particularly well cut. Some of the middle stones of the wall are, however, irregular. The following diagram of the north wall will show the method of construction. A sketch of the south wall is given in p. 243. There are no uncut stones in the building.

ELEVATION OF NORTH WALL.

SCHOOL OF HOMER.

At the furthest point to the north, marked C in the plan, there is a descent by a number of steep steps cut in the rock to a terrace about twenty feet below. On this terrace, there are ruined fragments of smaller walls and a large rock which, so lately as the time at which Sir W. Gell visited the island (in 1806), seems to have been the part called Homer's School. All the remains described by that eminent antiquary cannot now be traced, but there are still some of the niches which attracted his attention. I observed a small cavern to

R

which he has made no allusion, and in this there is
said to be a well, but it is now choked up and difficult
of access.

The condition of these ruins seems to differ somewhat from that which they presented half-a-century
ago. The land around is under cultivation; and the
crops cultivated, being corn and fruit, involve a certain amount of digging and dressing. Few of the
trees described by Gell now remain; nor did I observe the base of the column he alludes to.

That the construction is the remains either of a
temple or fortified dwelling, or, perhaps, was a defended look-out, commanding the Bay of Affalis,
attached to a small temple, seems the most probable
explanation of its history and meaning. At any rate,
it is one of the very small number of well-marked
Cyclopean structures, of which there remains a
definite part of a building in tolerable preservation.
It possesses considerable interest. In the case of the
towns of Samos and Cranea in Cephalonia, and Leucas
in Santa Maura, little or nothing but the outer walls
of the town remain; and in Aitos, in Ithaca, although
there are clear indications of a dwelling, there is no
such complete fragment as here. I have, for this
reason, dwelt upon the details at some length; and
I have done so the more, because Gell, in his admirable and detailed account of the island, does not seem
to me to have done it full justice.

The following woodcut and that in page 241 will
help to give an idea of the two principal walls.
They face the north and south respectively; and the

latter is within three feet of a wall, also Cyclopean, now made use of as part of a shed, occupied by a farmer. A narrow passage is thus left between the two old walls, and, oddly enough, it must have been into this darkened and shaded passage that the window opened. The aperture for the window is, however, only conjectural. The wall of the shed is perfectly preserved and very regularly built. The south wall

ELEVATION OF SOUTH WALL.

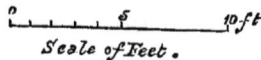

Scale of Feet.

SCHOOL OF HOMER.

of the principal building, except the two angle stones, is constructed of courses, each consisting of three smooth, well-proportioned, and carefully-squared blocks, five feet long by thirty inches high, and of about the same thickness. Four very large stones appear to have been originally placed as the foundation of the wall, and these four must have had a total length of eighteen feet. Only two of them, however, remain,—the others having apparently been injured. The stones of the upper course in this south wall are not large. The north wall is built of less regular stones but the upper course—the fourth course, measured from the earth, contains one stone of extraordinary size. This is,

indeed, the largest of all; and its exposed face is
about five feet square. It must be remembered that
these are the walls of a single apartment and not of a
city, and therefore the dimensions are proportionably
extreme, though many of the individual stones of
Cranea and Samos are far larger.

The sulphur springs already alluded to are situated
a few hundred yards to the south of the ruins. The
little village of Oxoi is about half a mile to the north.
The former are exceedingly interesting because there
is still a tradition that Homer came to bathe in the
mineral springs, by which his sight was restored.
That the waters are calculated to have a powerful
effect there can be little doubt; and it is within the
range of possibility that they may influence chronic
ophthalmia, supposing that common oriental calamity
to have been the disease the blind poet suffered from.
The spring, like the river that flows from it, is called
Melænudros, and for the same reason, namely, the
black sediment it leaves.

Oxoi, or Exoi, for the name is spelt both ways, is a
small but clean and pretty village, with several good
houses, situated on the hill side above the Bay of
Affalis. Leaving the so-called school of Homer and
entering the village, the first sound I heard was the
monotonous hum of boys learning their lessons, and
the first sight was the modern school-house. It
afforded a curious contrast to the ruin. It is a
well-sized, well-built room, in which was a much
larger young population than I should have thought
could have been obtained from the village; and all

were engaged in shouting aloud at the full pitch of
their voices. I have noticed the same curious mode
of conducting schools among the Arabs, and it seems
thoroughly oriental. I am not able to give an opinion
as to the degree of success it obtains, but it certainly
does not at all accord with our western mode of learning. I went into the school, and the noise was hushed
for an instant, for the presence of an Englishman was
quite an event in the neighbourhood. Very soon,
however, the work went on again in the same style.

It is right to mention that there exists in this part
of the island, not far from the school of Homer, a
fountain and rock, regarded by some as the fountain
of Arethusa and the rock Corax. The following is
the description of this locality by Mr. Mure, who
visited it in 1838:—

Immediately below the school, in the fertile land
among the olive trees, are traces of tombs discovered
by the peasantry in the course of their labours. From
thence we proceeded upwards of a mile northward to
another rock known at the present day by the name
of Corax. Beneath the rock springs a fountain possessing pretensions to be that of Arethusa. The
whole group of objects offers a counterpart in minia-
ture of their name-fellows in Amarathia—a bluff cliff
with a flat summit—below, a spring, from whence a
rivulet flows through a little valley into the sea.
There is this difference, however, that the sides of the
valley, instead of forming a precipitous glen, are here
a gentle slope, and the ground towards the sea, in
place of a rugged, bushy heath, is fertile and well

planted. The fountain is also far more copious, and has lately been adorned with a showy architectural front in a very barbarous style of art, with copious troughs for washing clothes and watering cattle. It is said that there formerly stood on the ground above a village called Corakini, the inhabitants of which have removed to Oxoi. However this may be, the general sense of all those who have expressed an opinion of late years has been rather in favour of the southern than the northern position of these localities."

We shall see in the next chapter how far the former answers to the description that remains, and what are the independent proofs of its being the Corax intended by Homer.

Below Oxoi, on the west side of the island, is a little port called Polis; from its name, the site of an ancient village. Near it are the ruins of a tower, and there is also a well. Two chapels are close by, whose construction is ancient; they are probably Roman, and are built of brick. Not far off, and on the rise of the hill, is the village of Stavros; above which are other antiquities. Stavros is a small group of neat houses, less important than Oxoi; it is on the road leading from Oxoi to Bathi.

Although I did not know any one in Oxoi, I found that I was expected to call at the house of the primate, or principal inhabitant, and I did so accordingly. As I went along and passed the open houses of the villagers, I was invited by more than one to enter and take refreshment. The house of the primate was a very comfortable villa residence, well

built, convenient, clean, and well furnished. It might
have been transplanted to the outskirts of a country
town in England without exciting much remark. It
had a long frontage, and only one storey above the
ground floor. The rooms were well-proportioned and
convenient. My host spoke a little Italian, and introduced me to his wife, whose Christian name by the
way was Basilike, or Royal. She was a simple-mannered, pleasant, and thoroughly friendly person. As
soon as she could prepare it, a glass of lemonade was
presented me, and it was with difficulty that I escaped sweetmeats, coffee, and biscuits. She expressed
her great regret that she could not talk to me, and
I won golden opinions, both from husband and wife,
by noticing their little girl—a sweet child, just three
years old, and one of the prettiest specimens of Greek
girlhood I had seen since I came to the islands. I
could hardly escape from these kind friends, and my
host accompanied me back the whole distance to
Frikis. On reaching there I was again offered coffee;
but this time by the officer of the health department,
who had been deputed to act as my guide; I did not
refuse it, supposing that I could offer some return;
but when I went on board the boat and endeavoured
to induce him to accept a trifling gratuity for his service, I met with a pointed and absolute refusal; he
only desired to have the honour of shaking hands with
me, and I need not say how cheerfully I recognised
the gentlemanly feeling thus expressed. This was by
no means the only occasion on which I met delicacy
and hospitality of that kind.

Leaving Frikis, I found the wind, of which there had been plenty on the hill, insufficient in quantity, and unsatisfactory in direction. We were therefore obliged once more to take to our oars, and, passing the headland of St. Elias, we soon entered the gulf of Molo. A bay opens at right angles to the southern shore of the gulf about three miles from St. Elias, and entering this sheltered nook, which is further defended from weather by a rocky island near its mouth, we are immediately in sight of Bathi, or Vathi, the capital of modern Ithaca.

Few towns are more pleasantly situated. It spreads out in a long, nearly semi-circular line close to the water's edge at the head of the little land-locked bay, which when entered has the appearance of a lake. The town consists of a number of white houses, all clean and neat, and either newly-painted or freshly whitewashed. Between the houses and the water is a fine quay, and, the water being deep, a few brigs, and schooners, and smaller craft in large numbers, come close up and discharge, or load, their cargoes alongside, close to the houses and offices of the merchants. Ithaca is a place of some traffic, and supplies sailors to many islands as well as to the mainland of Greece, besides doing some business of its own.

In the middle of the bay or pool of Bathi (pronounced Vathi) is a small rocky island now shorn smooth, and covered entirely by a circular building. This building contains the Health office, the Lazaretto, and the prison. It looks dull and melancholy enough, and from a distance seems a sort of excrescence stuck against the white houses, although really separated from them by at least a hundred yards of water. A similar island about the same size, but in its natural state and crowned with a cone of angular fragments of weathered limestone, is passed to the right on entering the harbour. It lies between the harbours of Bathi and Dexia. I was told, and fully believe, that the lazaretto island was once as rocky and lofty as this, and a small fragment of rock in the middle of the court-yard of the prison has been left as a sort of proof of this former condition. Certainly, whatever may be gained by the exchange, there is no improvement in the picturesque. Except round the little island there is deep water not only throughout the pool, but in almost all parts of the gulf of Molo. In this respect the harbour differs much from many of those in the Ionian islands, where the gradual silting up is the cause of much malaria. It is said that Bathi is particularly healthy and free from fever, and this is likely enough, since there are no streams to carry into the harbour decomposing vegetable or animal matter, and no shallows whose evaporation lays bare large tracts of swamp. The harbour, though generally safe and perfectly sheltered, is naturally subject to flaws of wind coming down from the mountains around, and these in summer are dangerous to the smaller shipping. The anchorage, however, is very good. Immediately after rain heavy torrents pour down into the bay and gulf from the mountains around, especially from Neritos, whose steep sides are deeply and permanently furrowed with the erosion of these water-courses; but except that at intervals a natural talus of angular stones is to be seen flanking the mountain, one might suppose the result to be undistinguishable. Beyond a doubt it is large and important; but, of whatever extent, it is quickly buried under deep water.

Besides the principal harbour, round a large part of which the town of Bathi is built, there is another smaller harbour a little beyond, only separated by a headland and narrow isthmus. It is the port of Dexia, with deep water and a shingle beach, and fair landing for small boats. A good rough road proceeds from the town across the little isthmus, and comes down on this beach, continuing round the shore to the end of the main gulf and branching off to Aito, whence there is a ferry to Samos, in Cephalonia. This is one of the principal roads in the island, and is kept in good condition. The road towards Arethusa's fountain, and that branching from the Aitos road to Stauros and Oxoi, and to Frikis, is almost the only other road constructed.

At the head of the Gulf of Molo the water is a little more shallow than elsewhere; and no doubt, the debris and detritus brought down after storm are here chiefly distributed. The deposit has not yet extended far, but is sufficient to show the nature of the operation going on. A certain breadth of flat ground is already formed; and in proportion to the extent of the deposit from the enclosing mountains will it increase. The water is, however, too deep to allow of

rapid advance; and the deposits coming in from the
head of the gulf are smaller than those from the mountain on the north side.   No villages have risen along
this shore, but there are a few detached houses at the
extreme head of the gulf.   On the higher ground, and
in places out of sight from the sea, are a few villages,
thinly inhabited; and perhaps the absence of people is
due to an old sense of the insecurity of living too
near a place to which there was easy access by water.

There is nothing remarkable about the town of
Bathi, beyond the almost uniform neatness and clean-
ness of the exterior.   The principal part is in the
Strada marina,—the marine parade,—a long terrace,
all the houses of which face the sea.   The houses are
neither regularly built, nor are they at all in the line
of an even curve.   Placed by accident or the convenience of the moment in some spot by the water side,
and with no regard to symmetry, they do not even
face in the same direction; but still the general effect
is good.   There are no public buildings of importance,
the churches being poor and small, and the municipal
allowance scarcely sufficient to do more than keep them
together.   A curious fragment of modern architecture,
now in ruins, faces the sea, near the barracks.   It was
constructed by the Turks, and seems to have been
meant for an official residence.   It was never finished,
and now there is a dispute as to ownership between
the government and the owners of the adjacent land.
It looks as desolate as land and buildings in chancery
are apt to do in England.

In the middle of the town, close to the sea, and with

a landing place of its own, is a neat house surrounded
by a verandah, and easily recognised by a statue placed
on a small pedestal in front.   This is the house of the
Resident.   It is a comfortable, roomy place.   All the
inhabited apartments are on the floor above the ground,
those below being stables, offices, and stores.   Besides
the residence, there are several other good private
houses, and many more that are occupied entirely for
business.   The mercantile interests in Bathi are evidently of some magnitude.

Bathi is, of course, the principal port in the island,
and the number of ships and boats that belong to it is
really very large.   Many of the ships are of considerable burthen.   The population of the town is between
four and five thousand, and of this a large part is entirely occupied in matters connected with shipping.
This is so much the case, that at certain seasons hardly
a man or boy is to be seen.

As in Santa Maura, the presence of strangers is so
rare in Ithaca, that no provision whatever is made for
their accommodation.   An English visitor is thus
obliged to claim the hospitality of the Resident, who
here, as in almost all the islands, exercises the rites
and virtues of this great public duty in a manner
worthy of the country he represents.   In Ithaca, as
in Santa Maura, and as afterwards in Cephalonia, no
limits seem to be set to the attempt to make the
stranger at home, and provide every means of assist-
ing him to carry out his inquiries.   The present Resident at Ithaca is one of the Counts Roma of Zante,—
an old, important, and wealthy family of the Venetian

oligarchy. There is no Englishman in the government, and but half-a-dozen foreigners in the whole island.

Bathi is entirely a modern town, and is so called from the hollow in which it is built. Not many centuries ago, the whole island of Ithaca was absolutely depopulated by the Turks, in a great endeavour they made to put a stop to piracy. But piracy is a natural occupation of the Greeks in time of trouble and difficulty. It is suggested by the numerous facilities afforded by the Greek islands generally, which abound with safe, sheltered ports, into which boats-can easily run, and whence their owners are not easily dislodged. Besides this, it is difficult to persuade a Greek that regular trade is more respectable and profitable than irregular and illegal traffic. The last colonising of Ithaca is, therefore, of comparatively modern date, and is due to the Venetians. Doubtless, there is a great mixture of race, but it seems a more favourable mixture than is to be found elsewhere. Most of the surrounding islands and the main land, both of Greece and Albania, besides some Venetian islands, helped to supply colonists; but the Greek element prevailed. In language and habits the island thus belongs to Greece; but there is something quite distinct in the features of the people. They are better looking, better dressed, neater, and altogether in better condition than their neighbours. Add to this, that they are far more active and laborious, and better governed than the inhabitants of the mainland have yet been, and there is no difficulty in understanding why they succeed better and are more respectable than their continental neighbours.

The population of the town of Bathi is not larger than that of the town of Santa Maura, but it is distributed over a mile and a-half of beach; and looks, therefore, much more imposing. The back streets, though less seen, do not contain worse built or poorer houses than the strada marina; and there is in every direction an air of life and comfort that is very striking. In all these respects, no town in the Ionian islands can compare with it.

The cultivation of Ithaca is not at all inferior to that of any of the islands; but, like all of them, the population is insufficient. Everywhere the valleys are well cultivated, and they are said to yield large supplies. The country is partly enclosed; and in places where it is important, irrigation is not neglected. Even the loose stones on the hill sides are made available for vines, and are arranged in steps, or terraces, to a great height. But the supply of corn grown is not equal to the demand; and were it not for the migratory nature and habits of most of the islanders, those who stay at home would come off but badly. As it is, what with the fish, which is plentiful and good, and the corn and meat imported, there is no want of food.

The fisheries are large and important, and extend for some distance towards Greece. They include during the summer, besides eatable fish, a considerable fishery for fine sponges, of which many, fully equal to fine Turkey sponges, come into the market. I was fortunate enough, during my short stay, to obtain a specimen of the finest kind, a foot in diameter and ten inches high. Such sponges are rarely found; but the ordinary sizes are very common. The price asked me for my sponge was eight shillings; and it was considered high, the reason being that the season was over, and there were none in the market. Besides sponges, much valuable red coral is also obtained in the neighbouring seas; but it is dived for by Neapolitans, who come here for the purpose from time to time, and carry away the result of their labours to Corfu.

Like all the islands, Ithaca is not only thinly peopled, but the population increases very slowly. It may not always have been so, though it is hardly likely that the island can ever have been very much crowded, except for some special reason and for a short time. At any rate, the repeated and entire removal of the whole population, which has taken place several times within the last two thousand years, and the sparse population of Greece and other adjacent countries, would naturally prevent a rapid advance in modern times. Nor is there much prospect of change or improvement in this respect in the future. Under English protection, there has been some increase, but it is useless to speculate on the probable effect of union with Greece. This may even check the slight increase lately noticeable. The men of Ithaca are certainly active and busy; its women are also active, and are comely and clean. The families are not small. In these important respects, the island of

Ulysses is ahead, not only of the land of Greece, but of most of the Ionian Islands. The cultivation of land for grain crops or fruit is, however, of necessity limited to a small part of the island, and is even there confined to crops more valuable for exportation than food. All the essentials of life, except oil, have to be imported; and should the Greek government find it necessary to tax imports, the people would probably rather smuggle and resist than pay. On the other hand, a heavier export duty would certainly check trade.

A certain amount of boat-building is done at Bathi. The craft there built, though not very handsome or with approved lines, are probably well-enough adapted for the rough work to which they are devoted. They are fishing boats,—rather broad in the beam, and not remarkable either for strength or speed. They are chiefly coasting vessels. Probably, under less unfavourable circumstances than are afforded by the presence of British cruisers, and if it were not for the outcry raised at the slightest appearance of such a thing, these boats might be found not ill adapted for a little piracy. Not that the Ithacans are worse than their neighbours; but with such creeks and small harbours—such caverns and recesses for storage—such weather and such a population on the coast as is found in the Eastern Mediterranean,—it really must be difficult for Greek nature to resist the forcible appropriation of property on the high seas. It belongs to their history, and is deeply engrained in their nature; and one can hardly look on the ragged picturesqueness of themselves and their craft without almost excusing them for following their instincts.

I could not discover that Ithaca had much opinion on the matter of annexation. That the Ithacans will agree to cast in their lot with Greece when called on to give a vote on the subject, is almost certain; but that they may regret it afterwards and be thrown back in their advance to wealth is also very probable. I imagine, too, that some of the merchants who are interested in the material prosperity of the island already see that they at least will not gain by the change of government.

CHAPTER IX.

THE chief excursions from Bathi are four,—all more
or less connected with the classical interest with which
the island is so completely surrounded.   It is as difficult to forget Ulysses and Homer in Ithaca as it would
be to forget Shakspeare in Stratford-on-Avon.   They
meet us at every turn.   True or false, the stories of

the island all hang upon them. It would be difficult to resist the conclusion that much of the description by Homer in the Odyssey really is, and was meant to be, an account of what the poet had seen in Ithaca, even were the question to be calmly and dispassionately discussed by the stay-at-home critic in his easy chair; but when the decision has to be arrived at by the traveller visiting the spot, to doubt the identity is simply impossible. The Ithaca of our day is, and must ever remain, the Ithaca of Homer.

> "Sunny Ithaca
> Where rises clear with woods of quivering leaves
> Mount Neritos; and many isles lie round
> Full close together,—Samos and Dulichium
> And forest-crowned Zacynthus. Towards the West
> With peaks o'ertopping all, lies in the sea
> My low-delled Ithaca, while to the East
> And mid-day sun lie the others all aloof.
> 'Tis rugged, but a kindly nursing-mother;
> And nothing sweeter, to my sight at least,
> Can I behold."
>
> ODYSS. ix. 22, *et seq.*

Taking a boat and rowing out from the little bay, or port, of Bathi to the larger Gulf of Molo, into which it opens, Mount Neritos is seen directly before us, rising boldly and almost vertically from the water's edge. Towards the top is seen the Monastery of Cathara, and in the sides are the deep furrows made by the rushing waters of many a year's storm and rain. To the left is the extremity of the gulf closed in by the mountain of Aitos, crowned by its *castrum*, the site of the ancient palace of Ulysses.

On the same side of the gulf and immediately to
the left in coming out from Bathi is seen the picturesque and quiet little recess of Dexia,—a pretty,
sheltered cove, like the Bay of Bathi, but much
smaller.. Hence Ulysses took his departure. Here
he was brought when loaded with the treasures of
Alcinöus. The cavern into which he was received
was on the further side of the cove. It is, indeed,
now almost obliterated, having been greatly altered
in making the excellent road which skirts the shore
and is continued through the north-west of the island
to Oxoi and Frikis, branching to Aito and Cathara.
That this is the real cavern alluded to by Homer, and
his grotto of the nymphs, is at least highly probable.
It is thus described by Gell in his "Geography and
Antiquities of Ithaca," published in 1807.

" The projecting rock on the north of the entrance
exhibits the vestiges of a cave of considerable magnitude, in the formation of which art has been called in
to assist the ordinary operations of nature. From this
cave, the interior of the port of Dexia presents a beach
consisting of sand and pebbles, and sloping so gradually into the sea, that boats may be drawn upon the
land without difficulty, a circumstance the more remarkable as a sandy shore is rarely to be found in
Ithaca. At the head of the port are a few cultivated
terraces and vineyards, spotted with olive and almond
trees. The cave has now lost its covering, the stone
lying conveniently for the use of the masons employed
in building the town, and I should have quitted the
island without seeing it, as no one imagined we could

wish to see its remains, if one of the persons who had
been active in its demolition had not fortunately heard
of our anxiety to discover a cavern near Bathi.

" The old people recollect the roof perfect, and
many about the age of twenty-five remember it only
half-destroyed.

" The rubbish occasioned by the removal of the
covering has overspread and filled up the whole area
of the cave to such a degree that its depth cannot
be ascertained without digging: but the pavement
must have been nearly on a level with the surface
of the sea. Its length is at least sixty feet, and its
breadth exceeds thirty. The sides have been hewn
and rendered perpendicular with some labour. It
is close to the sea, being only separated by that
portion of rock which served to support the roof
when it was entire. On the left of the entrance from
the south, at which commences the sandy beach, is
a niche, which, on being cleared from the soil and
stones, presented a species of basin resembling those
which are usually found in the walls of old churches
in England. There is another of similar construction
near the centre of the same side, and above both
are certain small channels cut in the rock which
have served for the passage of water into the basins,
and some are in consequence encrusted with stalactites, while others, where the water no longer trickles,
are tenanted by bees.

" The cave has been entered from the north as well
as from the southern extremity; the former was, however, smaller than the latter, and must have afforded

rather an inconvenient descent to the cavern. It is now called by the people of the island της Δεξιας το σπηλαῖον, or the Cave of Dexia. They are entirely unable to account for its formation, and the destruction of its roof by the Greeks, who entertain the most profound veneration even for the vestiges of a church, is a most decisive proof that it never served for the celebration of Christian ceremonies."

I have quoted this extract from the valuable little treatise of Sir W. Gell, because, at the present day, another cavern, much higher up on the hill side and much less accessible, is shown as the grotto of the nymphs alluded to in the Odyssey.

Ulysses, exhausted with fatigue and in profound sleep, is brought by the Phæacians at dawn of day to the sandy shore of a port in Ithaca. Being impelled with force by the rowers, the ship grounded on the sand, and the hero, reposing on a kind of carpet in the boat such as is commonly used to this day, was lifted and carried into the cave without being awakened. The treasures given to Ulysses by his father-in-law Alcinöus, consisting of tripods and other articles of metal, certainly of considerable weight, were also hidden in the recesses of the cavern. The following is the description of the port and cavern as given by the poet:—

"There is a port sacred in Ithaca.
To Phorcys, hoary ancient of the deep,
Formed by converging shores, prominent both
And both abrupt, which from the spacious bay
Exclude all boist'rous winds; within it, ships
(The port once gain'd) uncabled ride secure.

An olive, at the haven's head, expands
Her branches wide, near to a pleasant cave
Umbrageous, to the nymphs devoted named
The Naiads. In that cave beakers of stone
And jars are seen; bees lodge their honey there;
And there, on slender spindles of the rock
The nymphs of rivers weave their wond'rous robes.
Perennial springs water it, and it shows .
A twofold entrance; ingress one affords
To mortal man, which northward looks direct,
But holier is the southern face; by that
No mortal enters, but the gods alone.
Familiar with that port before, they pushed
The vessel in; she, rapid, plough'd the sands
With half her keel, such rowers urged her on.
Descending from the well-bench'd bark ashore,
They lifted forth Ulysses first, with all
His splendid couch complete, then laid him down
Still wrapt in balmy slumber on the sands.
His treasures next, by the Phæacian chiefs
At his departure given him as the meed
Due to his wisdom, at the olive's foot
They heap'd, without the road, lest, while he slept,
Some passing traveller should rifle them."

COWPER'S *Odyssey*, xiii., l. 111, *et seq.*

Although the existing cavern was, half a century ago, several yards from the sea, it is more than probable that since the time of Homer the natural wearing away of the rock and accumulation of detritus in a small land-locked cove would tend to remove the water-line to a little distance, as well as modify the interior of the cavern, which in other respects seems to have answered admirably to the description.

The modern grotto of the Naiads opens from the hill-side above the head of the little cove of Dexia at a height of nearly 180 feet above the sea, being accessible only by a rough and very steep and rocky path among the vineyards. It could not at any time, or by any conceivable change of circumstances, have been more accessible in the days of Homer; nor can one imagine how any one in a sleep short of that of death could be transported up these paths without being awakened. This cavern has one very small opening only large enough for a man to creep through, and a much smaller opening, or chimney, above. The principal opening faces the west north-west, and the other is almost vertical; adapted, it may be, for the gods, but not when they adopted the trammels of mortal form. The interior is partly natural and partly artificial. It measures about forty feet by thirty, and is about ten or twelve feet high. The walls and part of the roof are coated with stalagmite, and there is also a small quantity of stalactite; but there is nothing beautiful in their forms. The cave has probably been used as a receptacle of treasure and valuables of various kinds at the time when Ithaca was the resort of pirates; and for this purpose it is well adapted, as nothing could be easier than to conceal the entry by loose stones in such a way that no one who had not the clue could discover it. It is clear that the account of this cavern in no way agrees with that given by Homer, while the shore cavern, now destroyed, seems to have done so in all essential points.

I was amused to find that the Prince of Wales, during his very short visit to Ithaca, had been taken to this cavern, as one of the most convenient and most quickly visited of the lions of the island. He had ridden up on a horse, whose reputation in the island was thus for ever secured. I had the honour of mounting the same pony on several of my excursions, and certainly found him both docile and sure-footed. The owner was very proud of his achievements, and told sundry tales of rapid journeys performed by him. It occurred to me that, considering the size of Ithaca, the speed was rather thrown away; but the temper at any rate is useful.

There are but two valleys in Ithaca. One, that I have already alluded to, runs up from Frikis towards Oxoi, and the school of Homer. The other opens from the head of Bathi bay, behind the town, and runs nearly south till closed in by the high, rocky hills, that form the continuation of Mount Stephanos, and terminate in the cliff and rock of Corax, beneath which is the fountain of Arethusa. This is the most romantic and beautiful part of the island; and at every turn it presents something fresh, interesting and delightful. It can hardly be said to be watered by any stream, though a small rill traverses a part of it, supplied partly by a spring and partly by rain water from the neighbouring hills, when any rain falls. But the chief interest is concentrated on the fountain at the extremity, and in the narrow but most picturesque gorge, opening to the sea from beneath a vertical cliff. The hill top, in the time of Homer, was doubtless covered thickly with oak forests, which would still grow and add much to the resources of the island, if, as anciently, swine were encouraged and goats checked. There cannot be a doubt, that the multiplication of goats and the corresponding destruction of forests, have been in the highest degree injurious to Ithaca and others of the islands. The goat, of all domesticated animals, is the one that is most mischievous to growing wood; and indeed, in small districts, where they are encouraged and allowed to multiply, they end by entirely destroying timber and reducing it to brushwood.

But to return to the fountain of Arethusa and the rock Corax, which are beyond the extremity of the valley, south of Bathi. It was to this spot that Ulysses was instructed by Minerva to repair, on his return to his country, when he desired to unmask the numerous and troublesome suitors of Penelope. Disguised, and rendered unrecognisable by the goddess, the hero is told—

> "First and foremost go thou to the swine herd,
> Him who is chief custodian of thy hogs,
> And has at once for thee all kindly thoughts,
> And loves thy son and shrewd Penelope.
> Him shalt thou find abiding with the swine.
> Along the cliff of Corax unto the spring
> Of Arethusa are they driven for pasture."
>
> ODYSS. xiii. 403, *et seq.*

Without being transformed as Ulysses required to be, or "cloth'd with the hide deform'd of wrinkled age," but seeking the spot where the respectable and trusty Eumæus once dwelt, the progress is so accurately marked by the poet that no difficulty will be experienced. Proceeding from Bathi, however, it now involves only an hour's easy ride over a tolerable road, instead of the

> "Rugged path, which, over hills
> Mantled with trees, led him to the abode,
> By Pallas mentioned, of his noble friend
> The swine herd."

Once arrived at the top of the hill, near the fountain, the path soon becomes rugged and troublesome enough, and winding round over rough ground offers nothing worthy of remark till the fountain is reached. A transverse crevice, produced either by some dislocation or by a natural crack enlarged by water, crosses the direction of some thinly laminated limestones with a considerable dip, and a little stream coming out from the rock into a small niche, perhaps artificial, is first received into a small rock basin, and the overplus, once collected into a second basin, runs now into the gorge. Nothing can be more simple in description—few things are more charming in reality. The quantity of water is small, but constant. As soon as the water enters the gorge below, it produces a vegetation so luxuriant, that it is impossible to trace more than the result. Down the narrow cleft, the eye is guided by this exuberant growth to the sea; and just opposite are the beautiful and finely-situated islands, which so wonderfully improve the scenery of the Ionian archipelago. Like gems set in the blue sea, the islands positively sparkle in the sunshine; and one of the headlands of Ithaca projects boldly in front of them, looking almost detached. Parepagada, the

name of a rocky islet close to the narrow ravine, ;
Atoko, a larger island, much more distant, app
near. Ilex and ferns, and innumerable beautiful ev
greens, overhang the walls of the ravine.

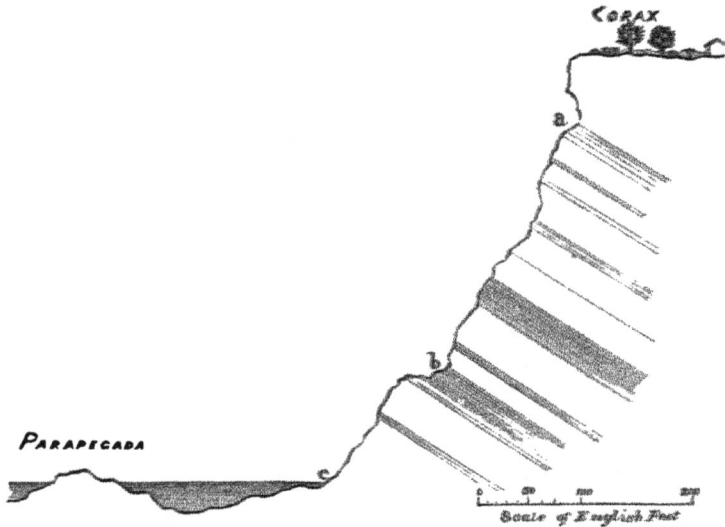

SECTION OF THE CLIFF AT ARETHUSA'S FOUNTAIN.

a. The scooped rock immediately above the shales.
b. Position of the fountains of Arethusa.
c. Sea line.

While the view towards the sea is thus beautiful
view, very little inferior in beauty or grandeur,
obtained by looking upwards and behind to the c
of Corax above. The annexed diagrammatic ske
may help the reader to understand the reason of tl
though all attempt at picturesque effect is hopele
The curious prominent and overhanging cliff of comp
limestone, capping the fissile beds of which the grea
part is made up, cannot be seen without a long a
rather troublesome climb through the shrubs, tre

and thick brushwood that cover the cliff wherever there is foothold. This climb accomplished, however, the task is fully repaid both by the peculiar appearance of the scooped-out rock, the increased extent of the landscape, and the observation of a singular echo, the reflection of sound from the shell-like surface of the water-worn rock which is there covered with stalagmite. Small springs burst forth near the bottom of this rock. Many of them are so exceedingly small that they merely fill little hollows in the limestone, holding less than a pint of water, and escaping so gently over the edge that one hardly notices them, except as keeping moist the surface of the rock below. Several of these occur, and they greatly help the vegetation on the face of the steep cliff.

A magnificent tree of ivy covers a large space of the rock above the fountain. The trunk rises twelve or fourteen feet, clinging quite closely to the vertical face of the rock by the aid of a small crack, and then it branches out, and is covered with leaves of the most intense and brilliant green. The trunk of this tree is larger than the thigh of a powerful man. The position of the tree is almost vertically above the fountain, and it is by no means easy of access.

The total height of the cliff in this part of the coast of Ithaca is about 800 feet. A huge detached fragment of rock stands ready to fall near the foot of the vertical part, and to this, perhaps, the name of "the rock Corax" may fairly be given. It has certainly fallen from above.

There was no quantity of water falling from the higher ground, over or near the fountain of Arethusa at the time of my visit (shortly after heavy spring rains), nor could I learn that a cascade was often formed. It is certainly possible, but cannot be frequent, as the wear and destruction of the cliff above would have been much greater than it has been if this additional cause of disturbance had existed. The fountain itself is so simple in its construction and in everything belonging to it, that it might be of any age. There is nothing to mark either antiquity or modern change; but the place is so little accessible, any reason for making alteration is so wanting, and the population is so little interested in the whole matter, that one cannot imagine much to have been done. There are on a small artificial terrace in front of the fountain the ruins of a small building— possibly a mill—overhanging the precipitous gorge that goes down to the sea.

The little recess into which the water is ever falling from the rock above, and which is believed to be the ancient fountain, is entirely lined with a rich covering of maiden-hair ferns. It is curious to watch and pleasant to listen to the perpetual drip. The memory wanders back in spite of all that has crowded it for years; it will sun itself once more with those old stories that are as pleasant now to our schoolboys as they were once to the unlettered and child-like people of the classic times, and we almost see the nymph Arethusa on the rocky crags of the Acro-

ceraunian mountains, "shepherding her bright fountains," pursued by Alpheus, the river god, and only
saved by being swallowed up by old Ocean.

Deep scientific as well as moral truth is involved,
too, in this and in so many of the beautiful legends
and stories of early days. This is alluded to by our
own great poet, Shelley, with that wealth of imagery
and fine taste which is so characteristic of many of
his smaller works. He tells us how the rough, dark,
mountain torrent rushes after the pure little rill into
the ocean, whence, under the bowers of coral and over
the unvalued stones—through the dark caves and beneath the ocean foam—the united streams rose

> "Up through the rifts
> Of the mountain clifts,
> And passed to their Dorian home."

The conclusion of this poem, "The fountain of
Arethusa," gives so admirable a picture of the whole
matter, that it would be as difficult to be more accurate as to find language and imagery more exquisite.

> "And now from their fountains
> In Enna's mountains,
> Down one vale where the morning basks
> Like friends once parted
> Grown single-hearted
> They ply their watery tasks.
> At sunrise they leap
> From their cradles steep
> In the cave of the shelving hill;
> At noontide they flow
> Through the woods below

And the meadows of Asphodel;
And at night they sleep
In the rocking deep
Beneath the Ortygian shore;—
Like spirits that lie
In the azure sky
When they love but live no more."

There seems little doubt that the detached rock already alluded to, and the small caverns adjacent, as well as the peculiar scooped-out condition of the rock, affording admirable shelter from the noonday and afternoon sun (the rock facing the east), are alluded to in Homer's description of the meeting of Ulysses and Eumæus. The rock is less than a hundred feet from the top of the cliff, and the path to it is one that swineherds and swine would find perfectly easy. All around, in ancient time, there were, no doubt, extensive forests of ilex, affording both food and shelter for the herd, and the position was one of great security; for, except by the narrow gorge, there is hardly access from the sea. So complete is the evidence on this head that there exists at this day a pastoral fold, or rather the stones of which such a shelter was built, on the summit of the hill adjacent. These ruins correspond well with the account of the stathmos, or dwelling, of Eumæus, and they include an ancient cistern and some ancient habitations.

From the entrance to the little harbour of Bathi, and the yet smaller and more retired port of Dexia immediately beyond, there is a noble view of the monastery of Cathara and the summit of Neritos.

"This (Dexia) is the port of Phorcys,
That, the huge olive at the haven's head;
Fast by it, thou behold'st the pleasant cove
Umbrageous, to the nymphs devoted, named
The Naiads;—this the broad-arched cavern is
Where thou wast wont to offer to the nymphs
Many a whole hecatomb; and yonder stands
The mountain Neritus with forests cloth'd."

It is impossible to mistake the description. The forests of Neritos are indeed sadly diminished in grandeur and extent, but parts of them still remain; goats, however, are now encouraged instead of swine, and there is no present prospect of increase or improvement in the timber. This is greatly to be regretted, and not very likely to be remedied, as no other animal than the goat is so convenient to supply milk, butter, and cheese, and these have become necessities of all classes.

One cannot look at Neritos without desiring to reach the summit, and it is a wish not difficult to gratify, for a very good mule path conducts to the monastery of Cathara, a height of about 1,250 feet, and thence it is a walk of less than an hour enables us to reach the summit, nearly 800 feet higher. Not thus was it in the time of Sir W. Gell, who describes the ascent as commencing from the west coast of the island, and as being "most laborious and difficult," even to the monastery. He also speaks of the mountain-side as being then covered with thick forest of arbutus and ilex. Little of this now remains, but a good road has been constructed all the way from Bathi chiefly round the shore of the Gulf of Molo, and then rising gradually, and cut in zigzag, on the mountain side. The views are very fine, and range over the whole of the channel of Cephalonia and the eastern shore of that large island.

As a visitor of distinction, whose coming had been announced, I was received by the superior at the gate with the greatest courtesy. At the present time, owing to the long-continued bad management of his predecessors, the estates of the monastery hardly yield enough to support an establishment; but they are improving rapidly. The present superior is a Wallachian, and has been for some time at Mount Athos. He is remarkably intelligent, very handsome, extremely active, and in the prime of life. He was very strongly recommended to the government, and has fully answered to his reputation. The monastery is not large, but it is well-built and in good condition. It contains a guest chamber, thoroughly comfortable and well furnished. The chapel is handsome, and abounds with votive offerings, many of them of considerable value. All the lamps (and they are numerous) are of silver and handsomely chased, and the floor is paved with Spanish tiles.

Immediately on entering the walls of the convent, I and the gentlemen who had been kind enough to accompany and take charge of me from Bathi, were served with delicious quince jelly, coffee, and biscuits, with lemonade. After partaking of this preliminary refreshment, the monk and I, but not my companions, went out to visit the neighbourhood of the monastery, and climb to the top of the mountain. This is some distance to the north. Gell does not seem to have reached the summit; but it is well worthy of a visit. The path lies along the east slope of the mountain, which is very steep, and continues for more than a mile, rising gradually over very rough ground. There is little cultivation or vegetation on this side; but the natural growth of scented herbs affords pasture for goats, of which there are large flocks belonging to the monastery. There is also a cistern and spring of water, a matter of no small importance in such a locality.

My companion, the good abbot, or 'Hegumenos,' rivalled the goats in his activity, and leaped from rock to rock in a singularly excited state. Our communication was scanty, for he knew but one word of Italian, *buono*, and I almost as little of the modern Greek, or Romaic, which is the universal language of the country. Pausing every now and then at the most beautiful points of view, he uttered a tremendous Ha! and, rubbing his hands, shouted at the full pitch of his voice, Buono! Buono! This happened several times, both during the ascent and on our return.

On the ascent all the views are towards the east, and include the marvellously beautiful archipelago comprising the islands Calamos, Meganisi, Arkudi, Atoko, the Echinades, and a number of other groups that leave but narrow slips of blue water between Ithaca and Greece, and are backed by lofty snow-covered mountains. Every fresh elevation gives a better and clearer view of these high and picturesque

islands. They are indeed like the spines of the
hedgehog (Echinus) bristling through the clear sea
waves.

Once at the top, which is marked by a small cairn,
the view includes the furthest extremities of Ithaca
and Cephalonia and the fine mountain of Stavrota in
Santa Maura. The latter closes in the landscape to
the north. The channel of Cephalonia and the gulf
of Samos are well seen, and the cloud-capped summit
of the Black Mountain of Cephalonia was sufficiently
bared to exhibit a large surface of snow at the end
of March.

A curious instance of the rapid growth of tradition
in a country like Ithaca is exemplified on the summit
of Neritos. A small fragment of a tower of stones,
not remarkably large and not cemented, is seen at the
highest point, and I was informed that at this place
the mother of Ulysses is supposed to have repaired,
and that owing to some fright or sudden accident she
was here delivered of her wise son. Subsequently,
I met a person who had himself been present when
some engineers, engaged in surveying the island for
the French Government, had erected the little tower
as a shelter and landmark. Still, although there may
be much of this kind of growth, there is a reality
about most of the traditions of Ithaca that connect
them with Homer, if not with his hero.

The highest part of Neritos is a ridge of some
length, from which I descended rapidly enough to
the plateau on the western side, jumping from rock
to rock. By degrees the clouds lifted, and the Black

Mountain became clear, but I was disappointed with its effect. As seen from Ithaca it is a meaningless and unpicturesque mountain.

Once more at the monastery, we found that a noble luncheon was awaiting us. The table was already laid, and soon a whole kid, served like a sucking pig with head and legs not removed, was seen smoking before us. This kid was twenty days old and disappeared rapidly under the attacks of my two companions and myself. Being travellers, they were at liberty to eat meat, and on me, as a heretic, there was of course no obligation to refrain; but as we were in the middle of the great fast of Lent, neither the priest nor any of the attendants would touch it. Our host fed on a kind of vegetable soup and bread with caviare; but he must have looked with longing eyes, and his mouth must have watered at the scene before him. The kid was admirably roasted, and was exceedingly succulent and delicious. It was served with wild asparagus, of which large quantities are picked on the mountains, and which, though bitter, is an excellent vegetable.

After the meat came cheese, of which three kinds were offered, all made from goats' milk. One was salted and in a state for keeping some time; but this was not particularly good. Of the others, one was pressed curds from milk, and the other from cream, both fresh. They were delicious; the latter being very rich and high-flavoured, and the other also good, though less rich. They had evidently been simply squeezed in a cloth, as they were round, like puddings, and the marks and folds of the cloth in which they had been squeezed were still to be seen.

When we had done justice to this repast, washed down by a pleasant and not very light wine made on the hill-side, we had our horses saddled, and soon found our way again down the hill to Bathi. The air was clearer than on our ascent, and the whole range of the Cephalonian coast lay stretched out before us. It looked black, and bare, and sombre.

An excursion to Aitos, the Eagle's Cliff, and the site of the ancient castle of Ulysses completes the cycle of Ithaca events. It is also in some respects the most interesting of all, for it brings one face to face with some of the earliest results of a peculiar and very incomprehensible exercise of human labour and ingenuity. Certainly, whether the remains of walls and foundations here traceable really belonged to Ulysses or not, whether such a chief as Ulysses, or such a blind poet as we call Homer, really existed, there cannot be a doubt that we have before us in this place the accumulated labour of some intelligent inhabitants of Ithaca at a time when civilization was advanced enough to render stout walls necessary to perceive some cherished property, or a still dearer liberty, and when habitations were so colossal and so massive as to require an exercise of strength and ingenuity to construct that seems utterly beyond the degree of civilization we are in the habit of attributing to such ancient races.

The so-called Castle of Ulysses is probably the building that Homer had in his eye when he imagined his character Penelope, and pictured the place where she was subject to the annoyance of her suitors, and from which his hero drove his enemies. It has certainly been a very strong place, too large for an ordinary habitation, and too small for a town. The space enclosed is a triangular area on a steep hill-side, the horizontal base being about 600 paces in length, and the length of the walls, from the extremities of this base to the Acropolis at the top of the hill, about 800. The whole space enclosed may amount to about forty acres; but the whole area, with the exception only of some terraces artificially cut near the base and at the Acropolis, is now one confused mass of huge blocks of stone, between which, overgrown as they are with brushwood, it is exceedingly difficult to make one's way.

The ruins are situated on the south face of the mountain of Aitos, "the Eagle's cliff," a hill of moderate elevation, to the north of the narrow and comparatively low neck of land that separates the head of the Gulf of Molo from the Channel of Cephalonia. It is detached from Neritos by a low and not very accessible neck of rocky ground. A few tombs, some wells, and a surface spring, are to be seen near the road which crosses the valley to the ferry that connects Ithaca with the gulf and modern village of Samos, in Cephalonia. At and near Samos are the remains, on a greatly enlarged scale, of another ancient city. The citadel and Acropolis of Aitos are so placed as to watch every movement in the Bay of Samos opposite; and, according to the practice of ancient warfare, the enclosure must have been absolutely impregnable when

the walls were in a good state. It may be that the
greater part of the space enclosed was a refuge for the
inhabitants of a town below, for the soil is there mixed
with great quantities of broken tiles and pottery, and
this method was quite consonant with the habits of the
ancient Greeks. It is the more likely that such was the
case, because a well and fountain exist at least three hundred yards below the principal line of the fortress, and
both appear to be very ancient. A tower and ancient
wall, not of the oldest construction, are also indicated
near the sources of water, as if the outer enclosure
had also been to some extent defensible.

The principal walls commence about half way up
the hill, and are continued, rising on rocky crests, to
the summit. As is so often the case in the Ionian
islands, they present in different parts styles of building
so different, that many ages probably elapsed during
which they were from time to time repaired in the
gradually improving methods of the day. Thus there
is real Cyclopean work in some parts, consisting of
huge blocks, partly fitted but not shaped, and with
small stones in the interstices.* Elsewhere the stones

---

* I have retained, as convenient and as expressing something of a
historical fact, the distinction usually drawn between Cyclopean, Polygonal and Hellenic architecture. That the former is generally the
most ancient, there can be little doubt :—that it is the work of a people
with the fewest resources is also highly probable ; but it should not be
forgotten, that great need may have induced the adoption of a similar
style at a much later period. Cyclopean walls are those in which all
shapes and sizes of material are worked in as well as circumstances
admit, only those blocks being chiselled that require fitting. Polygonal
work includes the specimens in which each stone is accurately cut and

are cut, though into the most convenient form their original shape and dimensions suggested; while here and there are portions of which the stones are equally gigantic, but as perfectly squared and regular as it would be possible to obtain at the present day with all kinds of modern appliances. All agree, however, in the stones being as large and heavy as possible. None seem to have been too large to work or too heavy to lift.

What struck me as most interesting in the ruins now under consideration, was the distinct outline of a house of large size, which seems to have occupied the whole length of the frontage. Narrow, but very regular, terraces have here been prepared, evidently with a view to the construction of the dwelling; and in many cases the foundations and parts of the inner walls or partitions are to be recognised. The various apartments as marked out by the remains of the walls still *in situ*, seem to have formed a continuous line of about 130 feet, occupying irregular terraces about 10 feet wide. One space is clear for 60 feet in length. Adjacent to this, on one side, is a kind of apartment, 20 feet by 9 feet; and on the other side a passage, 10 feet wide. Beyond the latter are the walls of a room,

fitted, but the angles are not all right angles, nor are the stones all six-sided. The latest work is called Hellenic, as introducing Greek symmetry. In the walls of this construction each stone is perfectly squared and generally bevelled. The ground is prepared so that the lowest course is laid horizontally; and of the upper courses, each stone rests partly on two that are below, and is covered by parts of two above. All the surfaces in contact are so perfectly fitted that nothing could be introduced between them.

measuring 27 feet by 12 feet, and then, after an in
terval of 12 feet, an outer wall.   The hinder apart
ments are generally on a level, 5 feet or more belov
the others; but the hill side being naturally very steep
and entirely covered with large stones, the cleare
terraces are easily distinguishable and would seen
never to have been disturbed.   The details of thes
curious and interesting ruins have been carefully give
by Sir W. Gell, and a comparison established by hir
with the castle of Ulysses, as described by Homer
Perhaps it may be considered that he carries th
identification somewhat further than circumstance
warrant; but it is difficult, in spite of German scep
ticism on the subject, to doubt that Homer at leas
must have been familiar with these ruins, when he no
only selected an island like Ithaca as the home of hi
hero, but described minutely a structure so closel
represented here.   Allowing that all details of th
hero were derived from legendary traditions, hande
down in ballads, except when for the sake of harmon
or completeness he drew upon the resources of hi
own imagination;—assuming, also, which is very pro
bable, that the account of Ulysses' habitation is bu
the magniloquent and poetical exaggeration of the ap
pearance of the much inferior ruins with which alon
the poet was probably acquainted,—there yet stand
this great ruin unaccounted for.   The descriptio
is hardly exaggerated, so far as dimensions are con
cerned; the place is alluded to in language hardly ob
scure; and the remains are such as must, so far as w
can tell, be far more ancient than the time of Homer.

For the walls of this defended hill of Aitos are partly of the earliest type, though mixed with various samples of the later and even most modern forms of that gigantesque construction, called Cyclopean. Of the Cyclops we know nothing, except from poetry; of the Pelasgi, to whom it is the fashion to attribute much of this gigantic architecture, we know hardly more. But we do know that, in various places in Greece and the islands adjacent, there are works that must have required great skill and ingenuity to design, and an amount of mechanical force to carry into execution, that would be inconceivable, were not the evidence before our eyes. Let no one judge of Cyclopean architecture without having seen and studied it. The specimens in Ithaca are not to be compared in grandeur and difficulty of execution with those of the cities of Cephalonia, of which I shall speak in another chapter, but they are quite enough to challenge attention and inquiry, and they are stubborn facts; proving the occupation of Ithaca by the earliest civilised races of whom we have any records.

Another matter is worthy of recollection. In the far west of Europe, as well in our own island as in the smaller islands adjacent, and in Britany, are numerous examples of a similar style of architecture: similar, at least, as indicating the power of lifting gigantic blocks of stone, and placing them in some way or other so as to form enclosures, and even afford shelter. It is true these stones are not chiselled; they are for the most part of a material so unmanageable, that even the perseverance of these indefatigable tribes was unable to accomplish this. They also belong, however, to races of whom there is no record, and perhaps indicate a part of human history undescribed in any other way.

Besides the foundation stones of the main buildings of the Castle of Ulysses, two grand fragments of Cyclopean wall run up to meet at the top of the hill, where they form an Acropolis of the recognised kind, the ground being levelled, and large cisterns and stores excavated in the solid rock. A tower in the Acropolis is apparently of later work, though certainly very ancient; but the outer wall of the Aeropolis is in the coarsest and least artificial style of Cyclopean architecture, though some of the stones even in the upper courses are not less than seven feet in length, and between three and four feet across. They are, however, less regularly placed than is usual, and in many cases are set one above another without bonding, so that the strength is very inferior to that of the better and later built walls. The height, however, is great, and it is clear that the walls, when in good condition, would have been absolutely inaccessible without scaling ladders.

The slope of the hill is very steep, but the walls follow the slope even when steepest. No doubt, at present, the parts that have fallen down and decayed greatly increase the difficulty of getting over the ground; but it is difficult to conceive that it could ever have been an easy task. Perhaps, however, the space between the Acropolis and the buildings at the bottom of the wall was partly under cultivation, and was terraced for this purpose. The destruction of terraces once carefully formed on a large scale, on a steep hill, would no doubt obliterate and confuse every mark of former occupation more completely than any other cause, and perhaps render the hill less accessible than it would otherwise have been.

The levelled space at the top occupies about an acre, and has evidently been very strong. It has probably served an important purpose as a look-out, up to a much later period than that at which the rest of the building remained defensible. No account seems to exist of it, and as the whole island of Ithaca has certainly been depopulated and re-peopled many times, and as the re-peopling has taken place some-times from Cephalonia and sometimes from the opposite shores of the main land, there cannot exist any particle of evidence in legends or traditions on the spot. Such things, or the semblances of them, exist in abundance; but if taken at their value, they can only be regarded as counterparts of the ingenious modern antiques so commonly sold at Athens and Corinth. Of these it is well known that there exists a manufactory at Rome large enough to supply all the private collections in Europe and America with false antiquities.

Within the Acropolis are two large rock cisterns, both still in tolerable condition. The larger appears to be cylindrical, and is probably deep. It is, however, partly filled up with rock and soil, and a large tree has grown out of the rubbish thus accumulated. The other cistern is of the shape so often seen else-where in the old Greek cities. It is pear-shaped, swelling out rapidly as it descends, and is certainly deep, though also partly filled up with rubbish.

The view from this crowning point of Aitos is exceedingly fine. Though very much below Neritos, and even far below the convent of Cathara, it commands the whole of the west coast of Ithaca, and the east coast of Cephalonia, hardly a nook being concealed. There is, however, but little cultivation, for the mountain sides are steep quite down to the water's edge, and are only covered at present with brushwood. That they would bear a growth of forest trees is more than probable, for both the ilex and the pine flourish in all this district if encouraged.

On the Ithaca side the view includes the village of Leuca, consisting of a few houses on a little plain, richly cultivated with corn, and well supplied with water. Gell ingeniously suggests that it represents the garden of Laërtes, to which the father of Ulysses retired during the absence of his heroic son.

> " The delightful farm,
> Which old Laërtes had with strenuous toil
> Himself long since acquired. There stood his house,
> Encircled by a line of huts, in which the hinds
> Who served and pleased him, ate, and sat, and slept."
>   ODYSS. xxiv. 204.

However this may be, there are not only rock cisterns, but some remains of ancient dwellings in the neighbourhood.

But whilst the exact identification of these subordinate localities is more than doubtful, and there is certainly no assistance given by any local traditions, it must not be forgotten how important and suggestive must be the careful study of all objects of antiquity on the spot, and how valuable impressions. thus made on intelligent persons really is. No one will certainly trouble himself to imitate Cyclopean architecture, and Ithaca is far too rarely visited to make the office of cicerone a paying one. One may find by chance a lad who will drag the unlucky traveller through the thickest brushwood and over the sharpest and largest blocks of loose stone to a *castro*, but of anything else he knows nothing. The stones, once the foundation-stones of large buildings—the wide terraces—the fields recently turned up, showing more fragments of brick and tile than of the common limestone of the district—these are facts that cannot be contradicted. They speak of former inhabitants, of inhabitants who required strong places to protect themselves and their treasure; of men who built houses, and con-structed walls to surround and defend them, so diffi-cult to put together that it would need all our me-chanical appliances to produce the like, and we feel sure that such men had an early civilization, of which it is equally certain that there are no written records.

It is, no doubt, of great value to obtain the careful opinion of the verbal critic and untravelled classical scholar as to the exact words and literal meaning of ancient writers; but this is not the only problem to be solved. The poet probably aimed only at pro-ducing general impressions, and provided his descrip-tions agree reasonably well with the actual appear-ances of the localities described, no one is justified in denying that they are intentional. But there is also the ethnological problem, and that is more difficult, because far more obscure. The Cyclopean work was old in Homer's time, and we must conclude as we began that the Ithaca of the last two thousand years was also in its day the Ithaca of Homer; that Homer knew the island well from actual personal experience, and that in describing the history of Ulysses he had special reference to this particular island, and the remains of very ancient but suggestive buildings existing upon it even at that distant time. He exercised the privilege of the poet, rendering subservient to his purpose all that he saw, and all that his mental vision suggested, not allowing himself to be tied down by a slavish adherence to detail in his descriptions of places and scenery, but still so far making use of the facts as to enable the traveller after the lapse of ages to follow his descriptions, and recognise not only the same natural features but the artistic modification of them.

CALAMOS.

This large island, situated on the western coast of Acarnania, and several smaller islands between the coast and Santa Maura, or Ithaca, are politically united to the latter government in order to average in some measure the populations of the various divisions of the republic. Calamos, formerly Carnus, is lofty, and is a prominent and picturesque object from the heights both of Santa Maura and Ithaca. It was in ancient times inhabited by a piratical race, described by Homer, and called Taphians, or Teleboœ; and even so lately as the middle of this century the tendency remained, until finally put a stop to by Sir Thomas Maitland and Ali Pasha of Joannina. Calamos contains about a hundred families, who grow chiefly corn. During the Greek war of independence, Calamos was a favourite resort for the families of those who had made themselves too notorious to be safe away from British protection.

Castus, Atoko, Arcudi, and the Echinades, are other insular appendages of Ithaca. They are of little value, and many of them mere rocks; but they add greatly to the picturesque beauty of this part of the Ionian sea. Petalá, one of the Echinades, the largest of the group, and having two harbours, is identified with the ancient Dulichium. It is true that Homer alludes to Dulichium as cultivated, whereas now it is barren; but this may be merely another of the many examples of permissible poetical licence in a small matter of detail.

CEPHALONIA.

———◆———

Stern Cephalonia braves
The beating storm and ever restless waves;
In awful state erects her rugged brow,
Where mountain plants in wild profusion grow.
    *   *   *   *
Samè, that long the Roman power defied,
In ruin'd state o'erhangs the western tide.
On the eastern shore
We mark the cliffs where distant Cranea stood,
Or nearer, Proni overlook'd the flood.

WRIGHT'S HORÆ IONICÆ, p. 35.

CHAPTER X.

CEPHALONIA, the Κεφαλληνη of Herodotus, derives its
name from Cephalus, who is said to have fled there
for refuge after the death of his wife Procris, acci-
dentally slain by an arrow from his bow. It is called
Σαμη, or Samos, by Homer; but the people are called
Κεφαλλῆνες. It is the largest island of the Ionian
group, having a greater area than Corfu, though a
shorter coast line. Parts of it are within five miles
of Ithaca; other parts within six miles from Santa
Maura. Others, again, are within eight miles of

Zante.   It contains a loftier mountain chain and more
perfect and interesting antiquities than have elsewhere been met with.   Not less than four ancient
fortified cities are recorded to have belonged to it,
and of these the remains of two, Samos and Cranea,
are of extraordinary interest.   Homer describes it as
subject to his hero, Ulysses.   The early inhabitants
were of the race of Taphians, the piratical inhabitants of the Echinades.   Later it joined Athens, but
was ultimately Corinthian.

This large island, though more compact than Corfu,
is indented by several very deep and open bays, and
has also several very prominent headlands.   The gulf
of Samos on the east side and the bay of Argostoli
on the west (the latter entering from the south) are
noble and striking natural basins.   There are in this
island fewer of those singular kettle-shaped valleys
than have been described as common in adjacent
islands, but the scenery is not wanting in characteristic features.   On the flanks of Mount Enos, or the
Black Mountain, as well as in other parts of the
island, there are fine points of view.

Cephalonia is a large rocky island, well placed for
trade and conquest, and tolerably supplied with navi-
gators; its ancient history and early growth have
been lost sight of in some measure of late years,
comparatively modern events having attracted more
attention; but there is no doubt that the inhabitants have frequently fallen under foreign dominion
in spite of their fenced cities.

Between Ithaca and Cephalonia there is regular com-

munication by a ferry-boat, the distance from port to
port being about nine miles. I was fortunate enough
to have a very rapid and pleasant run; but this is by
no means always the case, for the winds are generally
either violent or calm, and blow, if at all, either up
or down the narrow channel. They are also accompanied by powerful currents, so that the crossing is
often tedious and disagreeable. Half the distance,
however, is within the Gulf of Samos. The views of
Ithaca, looking back from the water, are interesting;
and Aitos, especially, seems to lift itself like a pyramid
of rock, almost detached from the water, the Acropolis
crowning the hill.

The Gulf of Samos is the only deep inlet on the eastern coast of Cephalonia. It is a noble sheet of water,
sheltered from almost every quarter. Its breadth,
from Pilaro to Port Kelia is more than three miles;
and the distance from Port Kelia to Samos, being the
length of the gulf, is four miles. Samos at present
consists of a few modern houses built close to a mole,
and provided with a small but convenient harbour,
near a stream coming down from the interior of the
island. By the exertions of the late resident, the
Baron d'Everton, now stationed at Santa Maura, the
marshy land near the mole, formerly undrained, and
the source of much malaria, has been greatly improved,
and the place, though small, is tolerably healthy.

Neither the scenery, on approaching nor on landing,
is very remarkable; and the little port of Pilaros opposite has more appearance of beauty than the head of
the gulf.

The whole interest of Samos is derived from the ancient city of the same name on the hills adjacent. The position of this city is well marked, and the remains are marvellously interesting. The chief ruins occupy two hills to the east of the present village, and part of the low ground close to the sea. The latter part is chiefly the Roman city, founded on, and partly constructed of, the material of an early Corinthian city. The date of the oldest part cannot be determined,— that of the Corinthian colony is probably a thousand years before Christ; and that of the Roman establishment is between two and three centuries before Christ.

The remains of the old city consist almost exclusively of broken pottery in the soil, and walls of Cyclopean architecture running up from the sea to meet at the Acropolis on the hill top. The adjoining hill presents remains of monumental works, and the contents of tombs. Over the whole of the hill, within the walls, and also between the west wall and the cemetery, the surface of the ground is so thickly strewn with fragments of brick tile and coarse pottery, that in many parts these are actually more abundant than the stones. When it is considered, that in all this part of the country the surface is almost exclusively composed of loose fragments of limestone, with a thin sprinkling of soil, the vast abundance of these indications of the ancient population will be duly appreciated.

It is a serious and impressive thing to stroll among these remains of the mighty past. It is the more so, when we endeavour to trace back any accurate history, and endeavour to define the state of our knowledge of the people,—Pelasgians, or by whatever name we call them who built these walls. We ask in vain for such knowledge, and know neither the habits nor resources of this people. Nor can we guess what influence they exerted on their contemporaries—what effect they had on those who came after them—who were the enemies against whom these mighty walls were intended to act as a defence—who were the recipients of that accurate practical engineering knowledge they possessed. We know only that they used vast blocks of solid and weighty stone as the Romans used bricks, and handled them with as much freedom as we now, in the plenitude of our strength and by a combination of various mechanical powers, manage to move our heaviest weights, whether of stone, metal or machinery.

For it is no light problem that is presented for our solution in Samos and the other ancient cities of Cephalonia. The bare facts are apparently few and simple; but both the facts and the inferences are really very important. We know what the Greeks did in their day; and we know, that before them there were ancient people who they superseded. We have a few names and a few doubtful dates; but really we have no clear evidence of any history that can at all include the original construction of these monuments;—little that explains even the latest modifications of the structure of these walls. That it must have been necessary to construct them at all in localities naturally very strong and not very accessible, is one fact;—that they should be so large and numerous, is another ;— that they should exhibit successive systems, gradually advancing towards a more finished style, but all equally efficacious against certain attacks, is a third. It would be unreasonable in the highest degree, to suppose that protection would have been secured at such enormous cost of labour, if there were not something valuable to protect, and some powerful and ever-watchful enemies to attack. Such work as the construction of the great walls of Samos and the other towns, must have taken, under any circumstances, a number of years to execute, even if we assume, which is probable, that the original work was comparatively rough, and that a really large population could be collected, employed and fed, for the required time, in such a place, on labour so utterly unproductive. However this may be, the works are there still standing to speak for themselves; they were certainly constructed with an object, and we cannot but conclude that there were enemies of corresponding strength who would at least try to overthrow them. These enemies, if they came from the main land, must have had powerful means of transport. Let me endeavour to communicate to the reader who has not visited Greece, and who is not familiar with the accounts of similar works by other writers, a notion of the state of the ruins of ancient Samos.

From the present clump of modern houses by the mole towards the east, a narrow space of level land from the sea to the foot of the hills, is covered almost entirely with remains of Roman houses and other buildings. These are constructed of flat bricks, and often yield fragments of pottery, coins, household utensils in metal, mosaic pavements, and works of

art of poor and inferior style. Several common mo-
saics have been laid bare, and some of them cover a
large area. The sea appears to have encroached and
carried away many of the houses; those that remain
being often cut in half by the same agency. Thus
are laid bare some curious points of .detail in the
construction. . Drain pipes conducting, perhaps, from
a bath, open out downwards from some of the houses;
and in one case I noticed that a perfectly good drain
of about one and a-half inch diameter had been
built into a stout wall :. not in this case the outer
wall of the house. Many other curious illustrations
of the habits of the people might easily be discovered by a little search. All these houses, however, are quite without the walls of the more modern of the ancient cities, and they mark the occu-
patiou of the Roman colony during a period commencing about two hundred years before Christ.
Compared with the walls, these parts are exceedingly
modern; for the walls were in existence as permanent
defences when the Romans besieged and took the city.
We have no evidence as to their condition of repair,
beyond the intimation by Livy, that they were very
troublesome obstacles. They must then have presented the same mixed state of very ancient with
more modern style, that they do now.

Besides the Roman remains now visible, the foundations of some of the old buildings have been traced
under water to some distance, and they are easily
followed to positions to where the sea now has permanent access. It would seem, then, probable that

there has been a depression of the land within the last two thousand years; but it would not be easy to estimate the amount; nor is it certain that the effect is greater than the natural action of the waves on an exposed coast line.

The date of the Roman occupation of Samos is fixed by Livy, and the description he gives sufficiently corresponds with the present state of the surrounding country. He describes the attack of M. Fulvius on the southern side of the city in the following terms:—" Quatuor menses obsidionem Same sustinuit, quum ex paucis quotidie aliqui eorum caderent, aut vulnerarentur, et qui superarent, fessi et corporibus, et animis essent; Romani nocte per arcem, quam Cyatidem vocant, (nam urbi, in mare devesa, in occidentem vergit) muro superato, in forum supervenerunt. Samæi, post quam captam urbis partim ab hostibus senserunt, cum conjugibus ac liberis in majorem refugerunt arcem, inde postero die dediti, direpta urbe, sub corona omnes venerunt·"—[T. Liv., l. 38, c. 29.]

"Samos supported a siege of four months. At last, as some of their small number were daily killed or wounded, and the survivors were, through continual fatigues, greatly reduced both in strength and spirits, the Romans, one night, scaling the walls of the citadel which they call Cyatides, made their way into the forum. The Samians, on discovering that a part of the city was taken, fled, with their wives and children, into the greater citadel; but submitting next day, they were all sold as slaves, and their city was plundered."

Two hills and a considerable tract of ground are
included within the walls; and there is a large outer
space that has been occupied, but was apparently un-
protected. The whole, where not now under cultivation, is one mass of broken stones, the fragments of
wall rising here and there out of the ruins. At the
highest point of ground is the Acropolis, a wide,
smooth space, evidently left without much building,
though surrounded by strong fortifications. There
are some few indications of Roman work in some
of the towers, proving that they repaired parts of
the wall.

The old walls commenced from the sea near the
first rise of the hill, and were continued in a perfectly
straight line up the steep face of the nearly detached
hills, towards the keep or Acropolis, at the summit.
There, as I have just said, they were made to enclose
a citadel. In this respect the description exactly
agrees with that of all fortified cities, constructed by
the earlier races in this part of the world, both on the
main land of Greece, and in the islands. It is the
Castle of Ulysses repeated over again, but on a larger
scale, and in a more perfect state.

The walls vary extremely in their style. Some
parts are so rough and so imperfectly fitted, that they
are evidently of very early date. These are truly
Cyclopean, and rarely include many of the largest
blocks. Of this most ancient style little remains, and
it has no doubt been gradually replaced by work of a
later period, where it was least effective, or where it
had fallen down after the lapse of ages. Thus, on the

rise of the hill, on the side nearest the village, we have a part of the wall formed with the most perfect regularity, as shown in the subjoined diagram. This is one of the best specimens in the whole ruin, and is no doubt late. Every stone is most carefully squared and bevelled, and is perfectly smooth. The foundation stones are not seen, owing to the accumulation of fallen stones and rubbish on the hill side; but the rest is bonded, and the sizes of the stones correspond much more regularly than is usual even in Hellenic work.

Scale of Feet. 10 Feet = 1 Inch.

ELEVATION OF PART OF THE GREAT WALL OF SAMOS, IN CEPHALONIA.
[Hellenic Architecture—Later Period.]

In this wall, if it were of moderate sized stones, there would be nothing whatever to remark; but when we find that each stone measures at least two cubic yards,* that not one is chipped or injured, that they lie one on the other so closely, that though there is no mortar

* Limestone, of the kind these blocks are built of, weighs about 150 lbs. the cubic foot. Each block, therefore, weighs in its finished state at least 3¼ tons.

it would be impossible to pass a long thin blade between them, and that during the two thousand years that have elapsed since the town was attacked and taken by the Romans, vegetation has failed to penetrate the narrow crevices in those parts that are still perfect:—when we further see that water has failed to injure them, and that they remain as they always were, we almost doubt whether they will ever change.

We shall see in another page, while considering another specimen of similar kind, what change they do undergo; but there is something strange and solemn in contemplating these works. The specimen of Hellenic architecture at Samos, to which I am now more especially alluding, is in no way remarkable for the large size of the blocks, but rather for their extreme regularity. It belongs, no doubt, to the very latest period at which work of this kind was constructed, and was a partial restoration made in a weak place of the old wall. In this wall it is decidedly the outsides of the stones that are the most perfectly worked. Their faces are all carefully bevelled, and the planes in contact smoothed. The insides of the block are left roughly hewn, and it is clear that what we see was only the facing, the wall being very much thicker than the thickness of one stone, and having an inside face, generally of smaller but smoothed stones. The interspace was filled up with rubbish, or roughly built.

But these delicate and finished portions of the wall are not of great length, and seem to have been interpolated only where absolutely necessary, and the great labour required to prepare and place the stones, will fully account for this. We often come to an isolated fragment of this finished work which has been scarcely injured, while the rougher and less perfect joints left by the older people have given way, and the stones lie on the ground a mass of confused blocks.

It is not easy to estimate, and it would take much time and trouble to measure the actual dimensions of the enclosure at Samos, nor would such measurement give an idea of the size and population of the town, for there is no doubt that a large part of the inhabited portion was outside the enclosure. This is evident, because all over the hill, and on the ground adjacent, to some distance, are the red fragments of brick and tile, and pottery, which so clearly mark the place as the habitation of the ancient people. Except a very few coins, little in the way of antiquities has here been obtained; nor is it, perhaps, very likely that there will be much found at any future period.

Near the Acropolis, on a broad and large terrace artificially cut, not much below the top of the hill, a small tower may be seen in the wall overlooking the adjacent valley. It is higher than the rest of the wall, and is evidently part of the Roman additions to the defence built during their occupation. It is constructed partly of moderately large stones, and partly of alternate courses of brick and stone. It is very clear from it that the Romans, during the time they held possession, did not imitate their predecessors in the construction of public works involving the expenditure of so much labour. Here, as elsewhere, they built with bricks and mortar, and trusted more to their own activity than to the mere dimensions of their walls.

An interesting gate is seen on the side of the hill, facing about due east. At this part the walls are in indifferent preservation, and consist largely of the intermediate or polygonal work, much of which has fallen. They are built of huge blocks, cut into a definite shape, with smooth surfaces; but the angles are not made right angles. The ingenious fitting of stones to make a compact wall of this kind, with such huge blocks, is a very interesting study. The gate in question is of the simplest kind. It is composed of a cap stone, measuring not less than seven feet square, and thirty inches thick (weighing, therefore, about eight tons), carefully supported on columns, each consisting of two four feet cubes. The support stones, and the under surface of the slab, are perfectly smooth. The width of the entry is about three feet six, and the whole thickness of the wall at this part was at least twelve feet. The ground has here risen about four feet, owing to the accumulation of fallen and broken stones, and thus the gate is now nearly buried. Immediately beyond the gate is a noble specimen of wall of squared blocks of a late period, but of gigantic dimensions. Parts of this wall that remain tolerably perfect are at least twenty feet in height, and are composed of regular courses from the foundation. Many of these stones are eight or nine feet long.

The top of the hill is levelled, and consists of a large, irregular, oval space, measuring about a hundred paces by fifty. Fine soft turf covers this surface, from which all stones have been removed; and there are no marks on it of buildings or constructions of any kind. At the extremities there are fragments of walls, and many squared stones of various dimensions lying about. It is chiefly on the north side that these are seen. The strength of this part was no doubt very great, owing to the great difficulty of access up the precipitous form of the rock, which has been carefully scarped to add to its natural strength. A rock cistern, of large size, occurs on the east side, and there are indications of other similar cisterns.

At the south end of the level summit there is a lower terrace, covered with blocks of stone. Ancient towers or other defences, and the entry to the Acropolis, were probably here.

A large and magnificent specimen of Hellenic wall, consisting of perfectly squared stones, of variable but gigantic proportions, and in courses absolutely regular, is still to be seen on the north side of the hill, below the Acropolis. This wall consists of eight courses, each of blocks of various length, but all about 3 feet in thickness. The wall was thus about 24 feet in height. Of the single blocks, one has originally been about 16 feet in length, and could not possibly have contained less than 6 cubic yards of stone when, after being perfectly squared, it was lifted into its place. To move this vast and cumbrous weight of about twelve tons without injury, over ground so rough as that which must always have characterised these hills;—to place it so carefully on two other stones that it should bear the dead pressure of a heavy wall of almost equally massive stones above it;—that there should be no chipping, no injury of any kind, to the equally well-chiselled blocks below;—and that all this should have been done to form part of a wall of defence, cannot be too often pointed out as a miracle of ingenuity and industry on the part of any people; and as a feat fully equalling, if not altogether exceeding, anything recorded in Egypt, or gigantic works in other countries, where human labour has been ruthlessly employed to accomplish useless objects.

Certainly, the pyramids have long stood, and still remain; but they are monuments of folly and tyranny. These walls involve at least equal ingenuity in their construction, greater power of combination, and had a much more definite object than the pyramids; and thus the Pelasgians, or whoever else invented and kept them up, were at least as intelligent, and probably a more practical people, than the Egyptians, if we are to judge of them by such of their works as are handed down to us in a perfect state.

The gigantic stone just alluded to is not alone, nor is it on the bottom course,—there are several others almost as large close by, and in the second or third course from the bottom. Some are partially broken by the heavy, crushing weight, to which they have so long been exposed; nor is this surprising, when the extreme difficulty is considered, of obtaining a perfectly level surface for the two or more underlying stones on which the large block is to be placed, and the necessity of a foundation that shall be precisely the same for each of these two. Without this perfect foundation, one of the stones would sink and the over-lying block be imperfectly supported. It needs some thought to perceive the mechanical difficulties that must have been met and overcome in bringing to per-fection the art of constructing massive walls,—a perfec-tion which had certainly been attained at least 2500 years ago, and which had probably been very nearly reached a thousand years earlier.

Since the time of the Romans the island of Cepha-lonia, and especially this part of it, has been often and severely shaken by earthquakes. It does not appear, however, that the earthquakes, though destroying cities, have been sufficient to shake the foundations, or even overthrow any important part, of these walls. The destruction that has fallen upon them is from another less paroxysmal, but more constant and insidious an enemy, to which I shall allude more particularly in another chapter.

The history of the construction of Cyclopean walls has long interested and puzzled the antiquary, the historian and the traveller. And it is not alone the modern historian who finds this difficulty. Thuey-dides, in describing the walling of the Piræus, alludes to its appearance in his day, as indicating haste in con-struction; but he also speaks of the inner lining wall as being formed of squared stones. "Within, there was neither rubble nor clay" (no small stones thrown in to fill up space); "but the stones were large and hewn square" (ἐν τομῇ ἐγγώνιοι, *square in the cutting*), "fitted together in building, and those on the outside ·

bound together with iron and lead."—THUCYD. i. 93. Now, this construction of squared stones is beyond all question the very latest form of the defending wall; and the lining of the wall is a luxury also of modern date. The walls of the Piræus, therefore, are of late construction, and refer to a period long subsequent to that in which Cyclopean or polygonal work was common. It is true, as Mr. W. G. Clark observes, that neither Pausanias, writing seventeen centuries ago on the subject of Mycenæ, nor those authors from whom he quoted—writing six centuries earlier—recognised the distinction now made between Cyclopean, polygonal, and Hellenic styles; but this only proves that the whole question had ceased to attract much attention, that it was a familiar antiquity, and was accepted without discussion.

Mycenæ I have not myself seen. It includes, according to Mr. W. G. Clark, both Cyclopean and polygonal styles, and is certainly of great age. Euripides alludes to it, as in his time already fabulous. In the play, "Hercules furens," the messenger, threatening to go to Mycenæ, remarks, that all the known appliances of that day of the nature of siege apparatus would be required for the attack; and he adds—

τὰ κυκλώπων βάθρα
Φοίνικι κανόνι καὶ τύκοις ἡρμοσμένα.

[HER. FUR. l. 944.]

From their deep base I'll heave
The well compacted ramparts, though by hands
Cyclopean built.

This reference to Cyclopean power is at least a sure sign, that five hundred years before the Christian era there existed as much mystery concerning this remarkable style of building as there does now; and that, in the utter inability to suggest any means of construction, the works were then referred to a fabulous race. It is not surprising that, at the present day, we are now obliged to leave the inquiry incomplete.

There is no place for a stranger to resort to for a night's lodging at Samos without taking advantage of private hospitality. The Health Officer, who is an official of considerable importance in all ports of the Ionian islands, was kind enough to admit me to his house. So much has been suffered from plague and cholera, and such extreme inconveniences would ensue from any carelessness in carrying out the regular and prescribed forms of inquiry in the event of contagious diseases, that every one acknowledges the necessity of a staff of careful, intelligent men to occupy the post of deputy of health. I was fortunate enough to find an excellent specimen at Samos. Provided with letters from Ithaca, I presented myself at his house. He was absent taking an afternoon walk, but his wife was at home, and she spoke admirable English, having associated much a few years before with the family of the late Resident at Argostoli. Nothing could exceed the friendly attention paid me. Every effort was made to obtain a meal suited to the appetite of a man who had had a hard day's work on the hills since breakfast; but such efforts were in vain, as nothing but a few eggs could be found in the whole place.

With these and bread I managed to get on, and a bed was made up for me on the sofa of the sitting-room, where I slept very comfortably. The Christian name of my hostess was Diamantina, and I think she really deserved it.

Besides the ruins of the ancient city, several tombs have been opened in the adjacent hill, and some objects of considerable interest obtained from them. These are all more or less monumental, except a few coins. Some glass lachrymatories and a few vases are worthy of notice. One of them is represented in the annexed cut. It is broken at the lip and the side. It is somewhat coarsely made, but is coloured red, and partly glazed. The form is good, but not in any way uncommon.

EARTHENWARE VASE from Samos. (Height 4 inches.)

The hill where it was found appears to have been systematically made use of as a cemetery, and whenever one tomb is opened, it is certain that others may be found immediately adjacent. Various small objects in metal have been found in the same spot.

Very few inscriptions of ancient date have been discovered at or near Samos; nor are any of those that have been deciphered of much interest. The history of the earlier city is very imperfectly given; nor is there anything by which we can determine the exact date of any epoch in the history of the town until its final capture by Fulvius as already described.

From Samos I went on the back of a mule to Argostoli, a morning's ride that would. be pleasant enough on horseback, or in a carriage, and a distance (about fifteen miles)' that one might walk without inconvenience, but not a pleasant excursion seated sideways on an obstinate brute with one's bag as a cushion and a piece of cord as a stirrup.   However, without sending a messenger to the town for a conveyance, by which a day would have been lost, there was nothing better to be got than the mule, and I took it accordingly.   My animal was not one of those that would steadily and actively do its work for the love of work; there are such mules, but I have rarely fallen in with them, and my experience of the race is not pleasant.   A stimulus was required in the present case that could only be given by the muleteer, a young lad, chiefly communicative to his animal, and fond of amusing himself, wandering from the path to cut a twig, or merely to loiter.   Immediately the mule would obey the signal, and not hearing his master's footstep would stop, munch at some of the hedges by the wayside, or go in search of water. Soon a loud *Hé* would be heard; the mule would prick up her ears; but move no further.   Then would come a heavy thwack on the back.   This was understood, and the animal would go on for a few yards to be treated again presently to a repetition of the same argument. It may be supposed that the journey was tiresome enough, and the more so as, from the omnibus fashion in which I was seated, one-half of the landscape was always hidden, and I was constantly twisting my neck and straining myself to find out the unknown beauties of the concealed moiety.

The road lies at first up the valley of the Samos, which is watered by a considerable and perennial stream. At intervals, however, parts of the stream are swallowed up, so that little, if any, water reaches the sea. This swallowing up is a phenomenon not very rare in limestone districts, especially where caverns abound, as is the case here. The quantity of water that comes down is very considerable, being supplied during the spring and summer months, and, indeed, during a great part of the year, by the melting of the snows on the east and north sides of the Black Mountain. The stream runs between this mountain and a much lower coast range to the vale of Samos, passing through part of the vale of Rakli. All along these valleys there is much fine scenery. The land is tolerably cultivated, and the climate appears to be warm, for in the opening of the valley may be observed numerous aloes and other plants which are comparatively rare in Corfu and even in Santa Maura, though common enough in the south of Spain, Sicily, and other Mediterranean coasts and islands. In this part of Cephalonia the climate seems indeed milder, and more fitted for sub-tropical vegetation than on the other side of the same island.

After crossing the valley, the road to Argostoli winds up the sides of the high central mountain range and crosses a pass probably about 2000 feet above the sea. This range is the continuation northward of the great chain which culminates in the Black Mountain,

the highest point of land in any of the islands off the
coast of Greece, and not much inferior to some of
the flanks of Pindus. The road over the mountain is
one of those for which the island of Cephalonia is
indebted to Sir C. Napier, who, with all his eccen-
tricity and in spite of his peculiar temper, did great
good, and was thoroughly appreciated in this island.
He has the credit of having originated all useful
measures, and there can be no doubt that his energy
and great talent were fully exercised during his government of the island. That he ruled with a rod
of iron, acknowledging no law but that which seemed
to him good for the occasion; that he went about
armed with a walking-stick, which he freely used on
the backs of those who offended him, though probably
never without reason; all these anomalies were rather
reasons for popularity than the contrary with a people
like the Greeks, and at a time like that during which
he was chief. The anecdotes about him are very numerous, and all smack of the same peculiarity. He
was a tyrant; but he was strictly just even against
himself as well as against all evil doers. He insisted
on every one about him doing his will, but his will
rarely exceeded that which ought also to have been
the desire and intention of every one.

Of all things road-making seems to have been his
hobby, and his chief employment while in the island.
Quarrelling with the Lord High Commissioner was an
amusing relaxation he allowed himself in large measure. The road-making, however, he attended to
thoroughly and unceasingly. Employing forced la-

bour, raising such funds as he thought fit, and seeing after their expenditure with his own eyes, he succeeded thoroughly, and managed to construct about an hundred and thirty miles of carriageable road over extremely difficult ground. So well was his work done that it still remains, and must long remain available, although since his time almost every kind of carelessness and wanton mischief has been allowed to go on, while nothing has been attempted in the way of preservation and renovation. As an example of the habits of the people, and their appreciation of these roads, it may be enough to say that for a long while it was the custom in descending one of the steep zigzags across the mountains, to employ as the drag or slipper of the country carts, part of the trunk of a tree trailing on the road. Wherever by this treatment, or by torrents rushing over them, the road is injured, it is simply let alone, and naturally tends to become rapidly worse. A fine is now imposed on this shameful and wilful destruction; but constant watchfulness and severe punishment are necessary to prevent those for whom the roads were made from destroying them by wilful mischief and neglect.

The road from Samos to Argostoli, after winding up through a deep and enclosed valley, with barren limestone rock on each side, descends again into a wider and more broken valley, cultivated in every part, from one end to the other, from the bottom of the valley to the summit of the hills. Here the currant vine flourishes remarkably well. The grape vine also grows very freely. The latter occupies the low grounds and hollows, and the former is planted quite up to the tops of the hills, generally in loose stones, and on the barest limestone rock. In the early spring, before the leaves are out, the country thus looks very naked; but no doubt the effect is greatly improved as summer advances. Even then the drought is generally so great as to parch up all vegetation, except the vines, so that there is only a transfer; half the country still looking desolate, though all yields crops.

The view of the Gulf and town of Argostoli, obtained from the high ground, after passing the crest of the mountain chain is very fine, and the form of the country decidedly picturesque. A deep and wide inlet, not unlike the Gulf of Molo in Ithaca, penetrates the land for a distance of more than ten miles, having a width of two and a-half miles. A small harbour, opening from the east side of the gulf, contains the town of Argostoli, and nearly opposite the opening of this inlet is the town of Lixuri. These two are the towns of Cephalonia. Both are large; but Argostoli is the principal one, and is the reputed capital. The road down to it is pleasant, and in good condition, and passes entirely through cultivated land, till the final descent through a rocky hill brings us opposite the town, at a point where the head of the harbour is crossed, partly by a long causeway, and partly by a bridge. The water is here shallow, and there is no room for shipping above the bridge. A little below, however, there is water enough to float large ships.

The head of the harbour has been, and must remain

marshy and malarious; but much has been done of late years by the present Resident to diminish the evil, and great success has been the result. There cannot be a doubt that the whole of the shallow part of the harbour will ultimately be filled up, and that during the process great care will be required to drain the part occasionally flooded. This being done, the danger from malaria is greatly diminished.

The causeway and bridge form one curved line of carriage road across the harbour, and lead into the upper part of the town. There are here some good streets; one especially, that was commenced by Sir C. Napier, and unluckily stopped, because of the determination of the landowners not to sell their sites, except at prices utterly unreasonable. This street, if completed, would have been a great improvement.

Argostoli is a long town, consisting of several pretty good streets, parallel to the quay, and a multitude of others of all kinds crossing them at right angles. The chief street is the Strada Marina, which extends from the commencement of the town at the bridge, and is nearly a mile long, facing the harbour for the whole distance, and terminating with the parade ground. An excellent quay has been constructed here, of course by Sir Charles Napier, whose residence was originally a small house in the terrace. The present Residence is a little behind, and out of sight, but is roomy and convenient. All along the Strada Marina are open shops or stalls, and the market is held there every day. The scene is very lively, but the variety of food during Lent I found very small. Long rows of small loaves, of many shades of colour, were undergoing a second baking in the sun from morning till night. Vast heaps of oranges, like so many golden cannon balls covered the pavement, and the usual admixture of slippers and old iron, linen and books, arms and figs, so common in markets, were displayed in every direction.

Arriving in Argostoli in the morning, before I had breakfasted, and having had but a few eggs for dinner the day before, I naturally hoped to find shelter and a meal at a place apparently so promising. I was the more led to expect accommodation, as I had been told at Samos that there were two *Locandas*, to one of which I was specially recommended. After marching past half the stalls on the quay, we—my mule driver, mule, and I—turned down an exceedingly narrow passage, barely allowing the mule and a man to pass each other, and presently stopped at a doorway, fully occupied by a cobbler's stall, at which sat the owner at full work. This I found was the model locanda— the Hotel of Argostoli. There was nothing for it but to get off the mule, and mount in search of accommodation. In a small hole on the third floor I found two old women sitting and spinning. When informed that rooms were wanted, one of them preceded me up another flight of rickety steps, and showed me a small apartment, nearly filled with a bed, one chair, and a minute washing apparatus. This was the nature of the accommodation, and certainly it promised more fleas, and fewer comforts, than I had been led to anti- cipate. However, I was too anxious to be settled to make much objection, and wanted to know if I could breakfast. This was out of the question; and, in fact, the locanda was merely a lodging house; but I was directed to a place at some distance for a meal. Moreover, nobody could speak more than a few words of Italian, and I could speak no Romaic. My wants, few as they were, would hardly have been much attended to.

Under these circumstances I thought it the best thing to appeal to the Resident. Inquiring my way to his house, I found when I reached it that my troubles were over. A room was at my service immediately; my luggage was sent for, a meal was provided, and before half an hour had elapsed I was comfortably and luxuriously established, and ready to set out on my explorations of the lions of Argostoli.

Besides the Strada Marina there are several good streets and some very respectable buildings in this town. It is also well paved, and the newer streets are wide and even handsome. The parade ground at the end of the town is a large open space, admirably adapted for its purpose; and there are convenient barracks and hospitals at no great distance. Among the public buildings is a respectable theatre, where operatic performances take place in the season to crowded audiences.

Just outside the town a handsome building is now rising, intended as the store of a French company, established to manufacture and export wines from the Cephalonian grapes. The wines hitherto made are varied in quality, and some of them are very good, though generally heady. It is proposed, by improving the treatment, to bring out the higher qualities, and it is hoped that a large and profitable trade may be formed. There is no doubt that the climate and soil are well adapted to the culture of the grape; but it is equally certain that the quality will be peculiar. A mistake was at first made by the Company, who pretended to identify the wines they made with familiar qualities—as port, sherry, claret and Burgundy. It would be simply impossible to produce imitative wines of the smallest value, whereas, if contented to work with and develope the full quality of the grapes grown, new varieties might be introduced that would be valued. Wines are made occasionally of the currant grape, and some of them are much liked. The currant contains a large quantity of saccharine matter; but up to the present time it has been better worth while to dry and export the currants than convert them into wine. Should the threatened supplies from Patras and other parts of the Greek mainland completely glut the market, and carry the price too low, or should the Greek Government after annexation be foolish enough to lay on currants an export duty large enough to affect the price in Europe, it is not unlikely that wine-making from this fruit may assume importance. The climate of the islands is, however, peculiar, and fine weather is by no means to be depended on at ripening time. This and the fact that the currant ripens much earlier than the grape, so that the fermentation would have to be conducted in hotter weather, would certainly influence the result.

It is fortunate that capital is employed in the business, and that intelligent and instructed labour may be obtained when needed.

It is only within the last two or three years that the market for currants in England has been in any sense in a normal state, for till then it had been interfered with partly by a heavy import duty and partly by the terrible results of the disease. It is, therefore, not easy to say what will be the result of the large increase of imports that we may now look for. Judging from experience and from the nature of the case, it may be concluded that the demand will increase with the supply of good, cheap fruit; and it is impossible to limit the increase, provided England remains in its state of rapidly-advancing prosperity. Thus, the time when the currant will be used for manufacturing wine to any large extent is probably far distant.

CHAPTER XI.

A CURIOUS natural phenomenon occurs, and is taken
advantage of, in the neighbourhood of Argostoli. At
four points on the coast the sea, at its ordinary level,
enters a very narrow creek, or broken, rocky channel;
and after running somewhat rapidly through this channel and among broken fragments of rock for a short
distance, it gradually becomes sucked into the earth
and disappears. By conducting the water through an

artificial canal for a few yards, and so regulating its course, and forcing all the water that enters to pass in a single stream beneath an undershot wheel, power enough is obtained in two cases to drive a mill. Mills have in fact been placed there by an enterprising Englishman, and are constantly at work. The stream, after being utilized, is allowed to take to its natural channel, and is lost among the rocks.

It is common enough to drive a wheel by a current of water going from the land towards the sea; but it is certainly rare, and, as far as I am aware, peculiar to this locality, to find mills driven by a current of sea water, acting quite independently of tide, the water constantly and steadily rushing in over the earth's surface and finally disappearing. It is not the river god pursuing the nymph, but the great Neptune himself invading the domain of Tellus. No wonder the Cephalonians are proud of their mystery; and it will be interesting to consider the circumstances connected with it.

Apart from the facts that the water sucked into the earth is sea water, and that it enters below the sea level, there is nothing extraordinary or unusual; for numerous instauces occur in every limestone country of streams, often of very considerable dimensions, entering into open fissures and disappearing. In England there are two or three cases of this kind; and in the Ionian islands absorption of water into the earth is so rapid, that there is hardly an instance of any appreciable quantity of the rain-fall being retained long enough on the surface to form streams and carry off the water to the sea. Almost all the rain is there absorbed; and this is certainly the result of the cracked and broken nature of the limestone rock—of the numerous natural caverns penetrating every part—of the constant enlargement of fissures into caverns in one place, and the choking up of caverns by stalagmite and stalactite in another—and of the especially fissured and cavernous nature of certain kinds of limestone, of which the rocks found in the Ionian islands and Greece afford notable examples.

But it is certainly very seldom that we are able to satisfy ourselves of the empty state of the limestone caverns close to the sea and below the sea level, as we can at Argostoli; and for this reason, if for no other, the phenomena are worthy of particular notice.

The general condition of the surface is as follows. The small harbour of Argostoli is enclosed on both sides by the hard, broken limestone rock, so common in the islands. On the east side it rises immediately into hills of moderate elevation; and on the west side, behind the town, there is a plateau, scarcely above the usual level of the water, rising about two or three hundred yards from the shore into a low ridge, which in fact, by its projection into the gulf, makes the harbour. Between the shore line and this low ridge there is an evident depression of the surface in all that part over which the sea, when it enters, is sucked in. There is evidently, beneath this part, an extensive cavernous tract, which may well hold much more water than during any ordinary season or succession of seasons can drain naturally into it, in consequence of the rain-fall at the surface. .

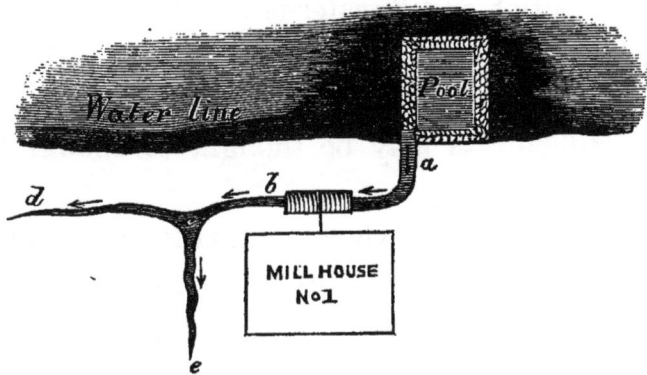

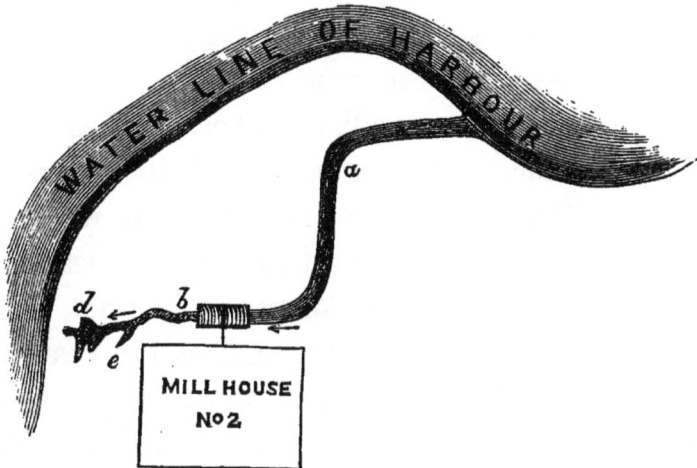

GROUND-PLAN
OF THE COURSE OF THE CURRENT OF SEA-WATER DRIVING
THE ARGOSTOLI MILLS.

References.

a.—The course of the entering current.
b.—The water-wheel.
c.—The bifurcation of the clefts.
d, e.—The points at which the water disappears in the earth.

But what, it will be asked, becomes of the waters of
the sea thus pouring in continually to fill the cavern?
Certainly, in time, any cavity must be filled, if it has

no natural outlet, and if water is constantly entering it. How, also, can the water run off, if its level in the cavern is already below the sea level? It is not, perhaps, so difficult as may be thought to answer these queries.

The water that everywhere enters the earth is always circulating. It not only passes down, into, and amongst all rocks, but it is afterwards lifted, and the level of these subterranean stores is greatly lowered by operations going on at the surface, often at a great distance above.

The cause of this is evaporation, which proceeds incessantly from the surface of all rocks, but especially from limestones. The narrow crevices, common in limestone rocks, act as capillary tubes. When water falls on the surface of such rock, it finds its way down readily, and this seems quite natural; but when, in hot countries, where there is a long summer season of great drought, the surface becomes dry and hot, moisture rises in steam from below; and, as the heat and dryness increase, the accumulated stores become more and more exhausted. All this goes on without reference to the actual level of the water line within the earth, which may be far beneath the level of the sea.

That this is the case in the softer limestone rocks, even when not cracked, has been proved by actual experiment. That it takes place to an enormous extent in the limestones of the eastern Mediterranean, is proved, if in no other way, by the fact, that vines, planted among bare stones, without soil, obtain an ample supply of moisture from the earth, and ripen their fruit to perfection in the hottest and driest

seasons.   No doubt the earth and rocks are hot, and
appear dry; but so long as there remains any water
below that has passed down during the rainy season,
so long will a part of that water be given back to the
dry and thirsty soil above.

If, then, as is probably the case, there is so large an
evaporation from the part of the surface of the island
of Cephalonia, within range of this district, as to keep
the water level of the year below the sea level, in spite
of the joint supply of rain and sea water, it is clear
that the water may run in for ever at the same rate
without filling up the space.   And this, I believe, to
be the correct explanation of the phenomenon.

The influx of water, however, is not small.   It
amounts; as far as I could make out, to more than half
a million of gallons per diem, for the two mills together.   The fall of water from the sea level into the
cavities, where it disappears, seems to be little more
than a foot or eighteen inches.

There appears to be something like a lunar tide in
the harbour and gulf of Argostoli, the water entering
and flowing out twice a day, and the level of the water
varying about six inches in ordinary weather, and
when there are no disturbing influences.   Any wind
blowing steadily for some time, and all storms, whether
at a moderate distance or near, affect the water level
in a marked degree, and complicate the apparent tide.
In one of the cavities where the water disappears
from the surface, the level of the surface of water
below may always be reached, and it is said to rise and
fall with that of the sea, even when the influx of the

water is stopped. This is quite possible, without assuming a free communication, which would of course at once fill the cavern to the sea level.

There is a constant tendency to choke up the crevices through which the water disappears, by a seaweed very common on this coast. This and the silt would probably soon interfere greatly with the current that enters the crevices, if the channel were not kept artificially clear. The water, however, is greedily and rapidly absorbed by the whole surface of broken ground near the sea, between the two mills.

It will be evident that if sea water finds its way into any large natural cavity, from which it is afterwards evaporated, a deposit of salt must be taking place in this cavity, or in the rocks adjacent and connected with it. Assuming the influx to be at the rate already mentioned, this may be estimated roughly as about equivalent to an area of ten or twelve acres of solid matter, one foot thick, accumulated each year. It is an interesting question to consider where this deposit is going on, and whether saline springs may not be thus fed. There are no known springs in the island of Cephalonia that present any large quantity of saline matter.*

Situated on a hill, placed, in reference to the shore, somewhat like that on which the ancient city of Samos was built, and a little behind and to the south east

* Not having the means of accurate measurement, and not being able to learn that the quantity of water entering the land has ever even been estimated by the mill owners, I can only give these quantities as rough approximations to the truth.

of the harbour, was the old fortified city of Cranea,* larger in dimensions than Samos, and containing finer and more perfect specimens of Cyclopean work, but little noticed by travellers. It is, indeed, well known, that in this important island of Cephalonia, there were from the earliest times not less than four fortified cities,—Samos, Cranea, Pronos, and Palæ. Of these, the remains of the two latter—one near the vale of Rakli and the other near Lixuri—are inconsiderable; but the others are equal in many respects to the best specimens of early constructive art.

Much of the work of Cranea is polygonal, and the rest Hellenic. There is very little of the older or strictly Cyclopean style. The walls would seem to have been commenced therefore at a later date than those of Samos and the Castle of Ulysses, in both of which there are specimens of the latter. It is, however, possible that the older work may have been replaced. In Cranea the most perfect remains are those that run down the side of one hill, and up another, on the east side; and of these, the walls at the southern end are the most modern, and in best condition. All this wall is very remarkable for the number of projeetions or towers with which it is defended. The foundations of many

* Herodotus, in describing the early history of the Athenians, describes them as a Pelasgian race, which had been settled in Attica from the earliest times, and had undergone no change, except in name and language. "The Athenians," he says, "when the Pelasgians were in possession of the country now called Hellas, were Pelasgians named *Cranai.*—See Thirlwall's History of Greece, vol. i. p. 37. What the Pelasgians were no one knows; but this notice by the Father of History is interesting in reference to the name of Cranea.

of these are in good condition, and they seem to show that the line of fortification consisted of a number of towers, about eight yards square, connected by a strong wall, and was not merely a continuous wall. It is also clear that this part of the wall was extremely thick.

0 1 2 3 4 5ft
Scale of Feet.

PORTION OF A WALL OF POLYGONAL MASONRY AT CRANEA,
NEAR ARGOSTOLI.

The polygonal work in Cranea is, perhaps, more perfect and more gigantic than in any part of the Ionian Islands. I noticed, especially, one group of particularly well-fitted stones, of which I took a rough sketch. The annexed wood-cut is drawn to scale, to exhibit the singular proportions and forms of some of the stones; but the figure represented on the wall is much too small, except for a young lad. Another single stone, not very far from this part of the wall, was much larger than any of those represented. It

GROUND PLAN

OF PART OF THE ANCIENT WALLS OF
CRANEA,

SHOWING ONE OF THE GATES, AND PART OF A
SMALL TOWER.

TOWER

OUTER WALL

→ ENTRY

GATE TOWER

→ ENTRY

OUTER WALL

0   10   20   30   40   50   100 ft

SCALE OF FEET.   50 F.ᵗ = 1 INCH

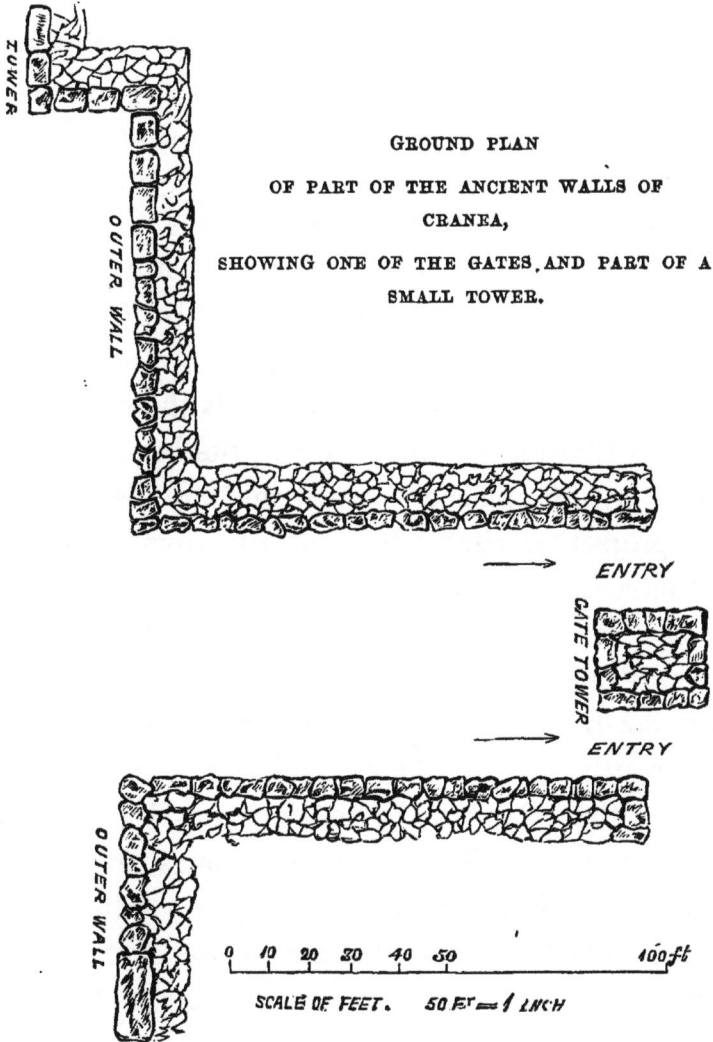

was certainly upwards of sixteen feet long, and measured six feet in height as it stood in the wall. The
thickness was irregular, but could not have averaged
less than a yard, and was probably much more. The
weight of this block, which was admirably smoothed
and squared to a right angle, could not have been less
than twenty tons. The old question recurs, when and
how have these vast works been executed?

A remarkable and most interesting gateway, entirely of polygonal work, but probably late, may be
seen in the hollow between the two hills on which the
city stood.   I give a sketch plan of this gateway,
which is somewhat different in principle from those of
the Greek cities.   A deep recess, consisting of a rectangular space measuring forty yards by twenty, and
therefore an exact double square, has been formed by
a return of the walls inwards towards the city; where
these end there is a massive tower, the base measuring
24 feet by 16, placed exactly midway between the
walls, projecting partly towards the town and partly
into the recess.   The actual entry is thus narrow and
strongly defended.   All the stones of the walls are
large and carefully fitted.

Not far from the city, and a little way up the hill
to the south, there is a good and very marked transi-
tion from the polygonal to the late, or Hellenic, style
of wall building.   The polygonal stones are remarkably fine, but have evidently been in a falling state.
During the latter period of Hellenic wall architecture,
the old work has been replaced by some of the finest
rectangular blocks, finished with bevelled edges, that
could anywhere be found.   This continues to the
Acropolis, which is, however, very imperfectly preserved.

The state of preservation of these walls was to me a
subject of great interest.   Of all hard limestones, I
know none that more readily show the action of vegetation and the change produced by weathering than
those of the Greek islands.   Very hard and brittle,

they are often almost like imperfect marble in everything but the texture; and the surface, if not the
whole of the rock, is naturally split up, and abounds
with almost innumerable crevices.   Wherever there is
a crevice and where moisture can be sucked in, there
is sure to be some kind of vegetation, and each growth
enlarges the space, and leaves fresh material for a
future plant.   Thus it is that over a wide space the
actual rock *in situ* is never seen at the surface, which
is covered with a great thickness of loose angular
stones.   But these stones are only the unbroken rock
of a few years ago; the largest have been the most
recently detached, and by degrees each large block is
converted by the same process of destruction first into
smaller fragments and so into small stones, which
ultimately pass into mere powder and mud.

The peculiar physical features of Greece and the
Ionian islands are not a little due to this condition,
and even the habits of the people are connected with
it.   Thus there is at all times at hand, an ample
supply of ammunition of angular stones, which are so
useful against the dogs: and, on a larger scale, these
stones have been found available in time of war.
On the one side, as related by Livy, in his account of
the siege of Samos, the attack was greatly facilitated
by the slingers, who kept up a ceaseless shower of
stones—no doubt of large size and very destructive;
and on the other side the defence was prolonged by
the rapidity with which inner walls were run up as
soon as the battering machines had produced a breach
at any point.   It does not appear that the city would

have been taken if it had not been for the smallness of the garrison, insufficient to defend so great a length of wall as enclosed the town.

Something of this kind no doubt goes on in most countries; but here, in the Ionian islands, the results are so curious, and have such important bearing on the habits of the people, and even on their political condition, that one is specially attracted by the pheno- menon, and more inclined to think seriously of it than elsewhere.

There is no doubt that the action of water, espe- cially of rain-water, on limestones is very great. It eats away a certain portion of the rock each time it comes in contact with an undefended surface; and in this way the direct result on every exposed surface is very great, especially where the bare rock is much exposed, and vegetation chiefly takes place in crevices.

But this direct action is trifling compared with the effect of vegetation itself. In certain parts of all the Ionian islands, out of a hundred detached stones on the surface it would hardly be possible to select a score of which the geologist could not at once read the history. A large majority would tell their own tale to any intelligent person, whether geologist or not. Riddled through and through with holes of all sizes, from the diameter of a quarter of an inch to more than a foot, there are also numerous pits, still incomplete, that help to illustrate what has been the course of procedure. In each of such pits is some vegetable matter, some plant, or even a group of plants. From the smallest lichen, or stone-crop, we pass through a long series terminating only with actual trees, for so large sometimes are the pits, and so roomy the space at the bottom, that there is abundant soil for the seeds of the ordinary forest trees of the country to germinate. The swelling roots of the plants enter the minute cracks and doubtless help to split up the stone; but the actual drilling performed in the course of time, is often completed without other help than moisture and the natural growth of small plants.

To this slow, but incessant destruction, must be attributed much of the decay of the Cyclopean, polygonal, and Hellenic walls. Far too massive and too regularly built to have suffered from any ordinary decay, it would seem that nothing but an earthquake would disturb them. Doubtless, earthquakes, which have been very common in the islands, may occasionally have thrown down portions of these massive walls, though the style of building is such as to keep them pretty well together. Doubtless, also, the hand of man has attempted, not always without success, to destroy what must have cost so much human labour to construct; for it is certain that in all cases they have served as quarries to succeeding generations. But I am quite satisfied, from the results of my own observation in Cephalonia and Ithaca, that vegetation has had much more to do in oversetting these gigantic blocks than either man or accident. Their foundations may often be traced now, much below the surface; and the line of wall is clearly marked along its whole extent. But even where the wall itself is hardly traceable, it is rare to find uninjured squared stones on the ground adjacent. Whatever cause has tended to destroy the large blocks, and break them up into shapeless fragments, has clearly acted first on the uppermost stones, and least on those covered with regular squared blocks,—only, in fact, affecting them when they became exposed. Foundations below the actual surface of the rock are clearly unnecessary, nor are they likely to have been attempted; but the rock must have been very carefully squared to receive the first course of blocks, which are by no means always the largest. That all exposed stones have been subject to the destruction caused by vegetation, is certain; and that so many have escaped, while others adjacent have been penetrated, may be owing partly to the harder nature and closer texture of such stones, partly to the absence of cracks on the exposed surface, and partly, to the newer and compact work of the Hellenic type being better adapted to resist than the old polygonal, or still more, the Cyclopean.

The vegetation, that destroys the stones by piercing holes through them, makes its way in almost every direction. The holes are never found commencing on the under side of horizontal stones, but they are very frequently slanting, and often nearly horizontal. I have even seen roots working their way upwards, though of course commencing sideways.

Besides this drilling method, adopted by vegetation to overthrow the walls of these ancient cities, a very effective leverage has been exerted by growing trees. A wild olive tree, or an ilex, planting itself in some cavity or recess, near a large block, will soon throw its roots into every crevice and convenient corner. Should there be the slightest space between two stones, a root will inevitably pass in. In the course of years, the root constantly expanding, this force is capable of uplifting, and even overthrowing, a weight of many tons. Numerous instances of this might be quoted; and there cannot be a doubt that stones have been pushed over in this manner, although so large that no ordinary combined efforts of any number of the human beings in the neighbourhood could move them. I have noticed stones moved by the roots of trees and placed in such a position by this cause, that the slightest shake must upset them; and where earthquakes are so common, it is impossible that they should not, in the course of many centuries, produce some result. At any rate, it may be regarded as more extraordinary that there yet remain indications of walls after so long an interval, than that so much of them has been thrown down and destroyed.

The ground, within the walls of Cranea, is not so thickly strewn with broken brick and pottery as that of ancient Samos. Neither have the tombs that have been rifled yielded results so important. There are not wanting, however, some jars and vases; and, on

A CUP, OF COARSE POTTERY, FROM THE CEMETERY NEAR CRANEA.

one occasion, a few coins and medals, and some pieces

z

of metal were found. It is worthy of remark, that the ground within the walls is higher than that outside; and that the large stones bearing the marks of the tool are almost entirely beyond, and not within, the walls. It is clear that the walls were very thick and were faced within the city by stones of comparatively small dimensions; and it is probable that they were only built of finished and perfectly-fitting gigantic stones for a portion of their height, the rest being of lighter and easier construction.

It is a pleasant but fatiguing walk from Argostoli to the walls of ancient Cranea; and among these most ancient and singular works of a lost people, one is struck by the contrast between a people who were capable of constructing such vast works in defence of their altars and hearths, and the race who, for centuries past, have dwelt in Cephalonia. These latter, indeed, under guidance, and with the help of that civilisation which belongs to the west rather than the east, have obtained good roads in the place of unassailable walls, but having got them, they hardly can be said to know their value; and certainly they show no great inclination to keep them in repair.

A modern, or at least, a mediæval fortress was constructed by the Venetians, on a hill behind that of Cranea. It is a picturesque object enough, and is tolerably extensive, but offers nothing worthy of special remark. For many reasons Cephalonia seems always to have been appreciated as a convenient resort, and Argostoli as a good neighbourhood, till the use of heavy artillery rendered all its strong places untenable. It possesses now a comparatively large maritime population, and a small labouring class. But the people are active and energetic, and repair to their homes when the state of the crops requires it.

From Argostoli, the roads to the principal valleys of the island on the west side of the Black Mountains are good, but beyond that they are only indicated; with the exception, indeed, of that one which connects the capital with Samos, and so by the ferry with Ithaca. That portion of the carriage road which is completed towards the vale of Rakli, reaches the summit of the pass through the principal mountain range of the island, and there stops; there being no access at present except for mules and horses, without making a very long detour. This is much to be regretted, as the vale in question is rich and cultivated.

Cephalonia contains the principal mountain chain of the Ionian Islands, culminating in the Mount Enos of antiquity. The chain extends for a distance of nearly fifteen miles, in a line nearly straight, and very narrow, running from north west to south east. It presents a long succession of lofty ridges, nearly of the same height, and all more than five thousand feet above the sea. The summit is near the south eastern extremity of the range, and appears, when seen from a distance, very little above the general ridge.

The mountain chain rises very rapidly, both from east and west; commencing on the west side from the valley of St. Gerosimo, about 1,400 feet above the sea, and on the east side from the vale of Rakli, whose elevation is even less considerable. It is possible to reach the top of the mountain by a very steep path, a little beyond the convent of St. Gerosimo, the rise, which is there nearly four thousand feet, being made without a single important terrace or break of any kind.

The most usual way of visiting the Black Mountain is by taking the carriageable road from Argostoli, across the hill and plateau of Rasata, rich in currant and grape vines, and so to the first ridge separating Rasata from the valley of San Gerosimo. The whole of this hill, which rises more than a thousand feet above the plateau, is well cultivated, and from it there is a descent to a picturesque valley, the mountain rising beyond. After a descent to Frangata (about four hundred feet below the hill top), we enter this valley, which receives its name from the convent of San Gerosimo. The valley is wide and long, and like most other level tracts, is richly cultivated, though not very beautiful. A steep zigzag road, still carriageable, but daily becoming more and more dangerous, conducts up the mountain side to the pass of Liberale, the lowest gap in the Black Mountain chain, and about 2,200 feet above the sea. From this point there is a branch road towards the mountain top, and here the real ascent may be said to begin.

At first, and for a long distance, the road winds along, rising slowly but steadily, until we reach a region of pines, where in the early part of March in this year (1863) I found the snow still recent and thick, at a height of about 3,800 feet. A little beyond, buried among the pine trees, is a comfortable cottage, built by the late Resident, the Baron d'Everton, and adapted to the requirements of summer visitors, besides giving permanent shelter to the forest guardians.

The whole of the western face of the Black Mountain, from the valley of San Gerosimo to the summit, is interesting. In the valley is the convent, also dedicated to San Gerosimo, and not long ago the scene of events scandalous enough to all concerned. Miracles —more especially miraculous cures of maniacs and persons supposed to suffer from demoniacal possession, were here so common, that the place became in the highest degree attractive. Lazy scoundrels, simulating madness, were allowed to come and feed for awhile at the expense of the establishment, and when tired of this kind of life, they would pretend to become cured by the interposition of the saint. Women also took up their abode in the principal apartments, and there separated from their husbands and friends, received some favoured suitor, either lay or clerical. At length the affair became notorious, and the Resident thought it necessary to interfere. He paid a visit one day unexpectedly, performed a series of unexpected miracles on the sham maniacs, and made a clearance of the whole establishment. It is now respectable enough.

The Greek convents and monasteries, like those of Roman Catholic countries, are liable to occasional abuses, and they necessarily act as inducements to an idle, useless life; but, as far as I could learn, these cases of open and notorious scandal are rare, and indeed, generally, the properties of the religious houses are too small, and their position too little accessible, to admit of much mischief originating in them. The women are hardly more locked up than the men, and for the most part they are not young, and are more devoted to charitable deeds than to the bad habits induced by idleness.

The western slopes of the Black Mountain, dotted over as they still are with the remains of the magnificent pine forests that once covered them, afford many fine views. They seem also to be connected with the legends and superstitions of the people, although, as the population of the island is comparatively modern, these do not date back very far. Thus the time of Venetian occupation may almost be regarded as belonging to the antiquity of the country, and a reference to it is equivalent to giving no definite date for the event alluded to. Among the current legends of the country is one relating to two brothers named Lucchesi, who in those old times acquired a large property on the mountain side. A fierce dragon then occupied a cavern in the mountains, and, as is usual with dragons, prowled about at night, retiring by day to his den. Each night he required some wretched victim to satisfy his horrible appetite. No village was safe from the attacks of this monster; but he was too powerful and too cunning to be laid hold of. No ordinary person dared undertake to meet him in the open field, or beard him in his cavern; for, according to all experience in similar cases, it needed a hero, and a clever one, to outwit and master him. At length two brothers named Lucchesi, at that time

charcoal burners, or following some similar occupation, undertook, on certain terms, to destroy him.
The brothers, after discovering the direct path from
his den, prepared during the day two pits, each large
enough and deep enough to hold a man and allow him
to conceal his presence by heaping boughs and twigs
over him. These pits were some distance apart,
though within call. When all was ready, and the
plan agreed on, the brothers stoutly prepared for the
encounter. Each being armed with such weapon as
he could use, they entered the pits they had dug, and,
covering themselves carefully up out of sight, waited
patiently till sunset. Soon the dragon came out for
his evening walk and dinner, and on passing near the
pits, one of the brothers, as agreed, made a noise.
The dragon, pricking up his ears, believing that his
prey is at hand and his necessity for a walk already
at an end, proceeds at once in the direction of the
sound. As he approaches the place whence it came,
and is looking about for the victim, the other brother
makes a similar noise. Oho! says Mr. Draco, to himself, I've made a mistake, and my dinner is over
there instead of here. Off he trots towards the other
pit, the tenant of which keeps still after making the
signal. By the time he has got towards this new
attraction, our friend in pit number one gives the
signal again; and so the poor beast was inveigled
backwards and forwards, like the ass between two
bundles of hay, or like the lover who exclaimed,

> "How happy could I be with either,
> Were t' other dear charmer away."

until he was so exhausted with the exercise, taken, too, on an empty stomach, that he lay down fairly beaten. Then out came the two brothers, and attacking him together at this disadvantage, he fell a victim to the trick, and the victory was secured. There is no record of his having left any issue, and the country has since been quiet, the brothers Lucchesi receiving for their reward a valuable tract of land on the mountain side.

A fitting place for legendary lore is the great pine forest on the Black Mountain. Glorious old trees shoot up their straight stems to the clouds, and the rich foliage covers the ground with its shadow and rustles sadly in the air as the winds, which are rarely absent, sweep across the ridges. Often broken near the mountain-top by the weight of snow that accumulates on their broad, flat branches and spreading tops, these trees yet attain admirable proportions where they have not been injured by the goats during their early growth. These animals, however, are very mischievous, and interfere with the increase of the forest. They are kept away as much as possible, and their owners are subject to a penalty if any of them are caught trespassing, or are even within half a mile of the nearest trees; but it is very difficult to prevent encroachment on so large a boundary, particularly when there are no fences to keep out any kind of cattle.

The Cephalonian pine is a noble tree, and though apparently only indigenous in the island, it grows freely in England from the seed. It is rather a quick-growing but very serviceable timber, and is valuable for ship's spars, sticks of almost any size and perfectly straight being very plentiful.

Through a couple of miles of forest of these noble trees, through two or three miles also of hard, granulated snow and some snow recently fallen and very soft, I made my way from the cottage to the top of the mountain. The path is long, but nowhere steep. It conducts by a succession of slopes and terraces to the culminating ridge, which is itself of considerable length, and comprises at least half a dozen points of rock, all within twenty feet of the highest point. There is a cairn of stones at the last of these, and the remains of an altar dedicated to Jupiter Enos. Numerous fragments of calcined bones have been taken from the ground at the foot of the altar, where there seems to be a large deposit. This point is not really the highest, being a little to the east of it and ten or fifteen feet lower; the culminating point is about 5,400 feet above the sea.

The view from this summit when everything is favourable must be exceedingly grand, as, except the Pindus range which is distant, there is nothing to intercept the view. All around is a rich panorama of islands: Zante at one's feet in all its elegant beauty of form; Ithaca to the east; beyond it a silver strip of ocean, and then the gulf of Patras, which is seen in all its length to the bay of Lepanto, in the vicinity of Corinth. Athens is not much further in the same direction. A noble chain of snówy mountains shuts in this view towards the south east. Looking down in the direction of Argostoli a minute speck is seen in the water. On the island called Διος (Thios), that looks so small, was once a temple to the father of the gods, and when sacrifice was offered and the smoke was seen by the priests stationed at the altar on this summit, another sacrifice was here made, and the curling incense rising from this lofty point in the thin air was a sign, far and wide, of the completion of the offering. Here above remain the stones of the altar and the burnt bones of the bulls and the goats; there below, at a distance of several miles, the more solid and beautiful temple is gone—not one stone remains upon another, and there is nothing but the story, probable enough for that matter, to connect the two localities. The permanent construction, carefully built to last for ever, has vanished! the few rough stones heaped together for a temporary purpose remain. So it often will be in this world of ours.

It is a pleasant though fatiguing trip to the summit of the Black mountains; but the descent to the Cottage, especially over the snow, I found rapid enough. The quantity of snow was unusually large, considering the advanced state of the season; but it seemed to me still more remarkable that the snow should be so hard and granular. A few mules and their drivers, both men and women, were on the mountain, removing the snow to the ice houses for the benefit of the Resident and the mess. Cephalonia supplies all the neighbouring islands, especially Zante, with this substance. There are some natural and some artificial ice caverns, where there is always a supply till very late in autumn.

The first heavy snows rarely fall before November; but after that the mountain is never uncovered till towards April.

There are gloomy passages of history connected with this part of Cephalonia, for the inhabitants of the district are a wild race, having little respect for law, and none for human life. There has long been a contest between the government and the neighbouring villagers, the former naturally desiring that so valuable a property should be preserved and its growth encouraged, and having also some regard to the game, of which there is a good supply. The forest was partly burnt, and large parts of it destroyed, some years ago, whether mischievously or by accident, did not seem quite clear; but afterwards officers were appointed to watch over the remains, and see that the trees were not wilfully destroyed. The punishment inflicted, either for destruction of trees or permitting the goats to approach them, was a fine—small for a first offence, but increasing in amount after a first conviction. At that time, also, the whole of the fine was given to the informer. The forest ranger was an active, intelligent man, and not a native, and very properly took advantage of this law. He rapidly became rich, and was buying land and preparing for a settlement, either in the island or at his own place, when, on one occasion, being out at night, he never returned; and his body was found after a time with a ball through the lungs.

A still more sad tragedy was performed some years afterwards. The ranger then was an English gentleman, who had previously been in the army. He lived

with his wife, a Greek woman of the island, in the
Resident's cottage, and was active and earnest in the
performance of his duties. He was not otherwise unpopular; but the repressive measures thought necessary with regard to the forest, interfered with what
the people around chose to consider their right of obtaining fuel. After several years, during which he
continued to perform the duties of his office, he was
on one occasion walking out in the evening after dinner, his wife by his side, along the road leading down
from the cottage to the outskirts of the forest. A few
hundred yards from the cottage is a large, detached
rock, that has fallen down from above. This rock is
as large as a small house, and is partly covered with
trees and thick vegetation. Behind it crouched half-a-
dozen murderers, with guns loaded. As soon as the
poor man had passed the rock a shot was fired, which
broke his leg at the knee. The wife, with one loud
scream, ran down the mountain side at full speed, and
is said not to have stopped till she arrived at the convent of St. Gerosimo, in the valley below. The brigands emerging from their shelter when their victim
was disabled, rushed at him and beat out his brains
with the ends of their guns. They then decamped;
but most of them were afterwards taken and executed.

Since that time the forest has been quiet enough;
but there is still a good deal of difficulty in preventing
damage. The fines are no longer paid to the informer;
but there are two excellent guardians, who do not
allow the goats to come too near. For this, some ingenuity is required; for goats are clever animals, and

are trained by their goat herds to return rapidly, or escape pursuit in some direction or other at the sounding of a certain peculiar note—a kind of half shout, half whistle—which may, perhaps, have some proper use when wolves are in the neighbourhood, but at any rate enables them to escape from the guardians. Not long ago one of the forest guards saw a flock of goats, certainly within the prohibited distance. Knowing his game, he rushed at once towards the goat herd, and with one blow threw him on the ground, and there nearly strangled him, to prevent his making the well known call. During this time the brother guardian was quietly counting the goats and making arrangements to secure the fine. The fine is still heavy, amounting to sixpence per head for the first offence, and a shilling for the second. The number of goats in a flock being large and the value of the animals not very great, this is sufficient, and even ruinous, if the flock is either neglected, as is generally the case, or is left in charge of children whose eye is not accustomed to measure distances. No doubt it would be much better that the forest lands belonging to the municipality should be enclosed; but there is little chance of this being effected, public money being more frequently and more readily granted for jobbing than for good practical improvements, or for preserving public property. There should be no complaint now about the want of fuel, as the present Resident has arranged that the thinnings of the forest should be sold for the cost of cutting. This supply, for years to come, will be large, as there is a vast quantity of young, growing

wood, that ought to be removed; and as the wood is collected and has only to be carried away by the peasants,
they certainly ought to be satisfied. If they are
not, or if in any way the management of the forest
is unpopular, this great source of national wealth
will almost to a certainty be destroyed once more by
fire.

There cannot be a doubt that the encouragement of
goats in the Ionian Islands has been the cause of great
injury to all kinds of tree vegetation, and that nothing short of destroying the race, will bring back the
ancient, and probably much more profitable, condition
of the country.

With the removal of the tree vegetation the climate
must inevitably have undergone great change, and the
dryness of the surface, now so remarkable, has increased very considerably. It takes away much from
the picturesque beauty of the islands also, to see large
tracts of country naked during the greater part of the
year, and burnt up by the hot summer sun. At the
same time it is only fair to say, that though for many
crops, important elsewhere, the climate must have
changed for the worse; yet for the present staples,
the grape vine and the currant vine, it is more likely
to have been improved. The effect of large forests on
the mountains, would probably be to increase the permanent supply of water in the rock by checking
evaporation, and to attract clouds and increase the
rain fall during the season of autumn, when the grapes
are being sun-dried, or require the full rays of the
sun to develope their flavour. Much heat, and great

dryness, in July and August, are necessary for the vines.

The goats are at present the only sources of the supply of milk and cheese used in the islands. No doubt a few cows would yield enough for the towns, and could be kept without difficulty in the swampy tracts. But in the country this would be impossible. The ground is too hopelessly arid during summer to enable them to live.

The Black Mountain, near the top, rises in successive steps, there being on the mountain side an alternation of steep faces, and slopes which are almost gentle. This is, however, especially remarkable towards the north-west, where the terraces are very narrow, and the descent precipitous. The cottage is placed on one of the slopes, at between three and four thousand feet elevation, and near it there are several hollows or small kettle-shaped valleys, containing water immediately after rain, but losing it afterwards by evaporation. These are no doubt connected with natural caverns, whose roofs have fallen in, and they are interesting, as connecting Cephalonia in this respect with the other islands. The larger valleys are not of this kind; the vale of Rakli for example, which is one of the richest and most important, being connected with Samos on the north, and with the sea, with little interruption on the south. It contains, however, some natural curiosities, and amongst them are deep pools always filled with water. Some of these pools are of considerable size; and the following description of one of them, from Dr. Davy's account of the Ionian Islands, will be read with pleasure. I was not myself able to visit the spot.

" In a wild valley, contiguous to that of Samos, at a higher level, is a small lake, known by the name of Abatho, signifying bottomless, which it is supposed to be by the natives. It is circular, about two hundred yards in circumference, and is surrounded by rugged hills, composed chiefly of clay, conglomerate, and sandstone. A small stream constantly flows from it, most copious in winter, which joins another small stream, flowing from a similar little lake, separated by an intervening hill, and these two streams joining form the river of Rakli, the principal perennial stream of Cephalonia."—Vol. i. p. 162.

I heard of another of these lakes about forty yards across, and there appear to be several on the hills on the east side of Rakli valley. This valley itself is well worthy of a visit, and may be conveniently reached from Samos. The upper part of the valley of Samos is very richly cultivated, belonging chiefly to small, but not impoverished farmers. Much fruit of various kinds is grown there, including, of course, grapes and currants. Beyond the valley of Samos the scenery becomes wild, shut in by mural precipices, but still luxuriously wooded. The distant views, too, are superb, and the Black Mountain rises rapidly at a very short distance, producing a fine contrast between its wild grandeur, and the soft verdure of the low grounds. In the early months of spring, when snow still covers a large part of the Black Mountain, this part of the island is especially interesting.

The return from the Black Mountain to Argostoli is an easy task, and is very rapidly performed. We soon reach the valley of San Gerosimo, and then on rising to the hill beyond, the harbour lies at our feet. The whole trip is a very pleasant one, especially when the traveller is fortunate enough to secure for his travelling companion so intelligent a man, and so good a mountaineer as the present Resident, who was kind enough to accompany me on the occasion of my visit.

AN EARTHEN VESSEL, WITH HANDLE AND SPOUT, FROM THE CEMETERY BEHIND CRANIA.

CHAPTER XII.

ALTHOUGH the inhabitants of Cephalonia devote themselves greatly to the sea, and make excellent sailors
and boatmen, they are also good cultivators of the
soil; and the island is not without some few manufactures that should not be passed over without notice,
since they seem capable of expansion. The country,
like that in all the islands, is thinly peopled, and does
not increase rapidly. It is in this respect somewhat
superior to Corfu, but not much. Thus the country

population of Corfu in 1857 was 42,576, and that of Cephalonia 55,770, the area of the islands being respectively 227 and 311 square miles.

The chief manufacture of Cephalonia at present may be said to be wine, and I employ the term *manufactured* instead of *grown* with intention, inasmuch as there is at Argostoli a company, chiefly of French shareholders, who established themselves with the view of manufacturing all kinds of wines in the island, and exporting them as representing the various growths of France, Spain, Portugal, and the Rhine. This first intention has been, I believe, modified, and an effort will be made to create a taste for the genuine produce of the vines of the country. There is no reason why this should not succeed, for the soil and climate are certainly not unfavourable. Being very different, however, from those of any of the great wine-growing countries, it is in the highest degree unlikely that the quality of the produce should be the same.

A large breadth of land is under vine cultivation in this island, and the returns do not seriously vary, though since the öidium established itself, there has been always more or less disease. The process of sulphuring is largely adopted, and the success is said to be complete. I observed that the grape vine generally occupies the higher parts of the hills and the less favourable soils, the better aspects and richer soils being retained for the currant crop. Probably the want of a south aspect may prevent either grapes from attaining full flavour; but, at any rate, there is no want of saccharine matter in the ripened fruit if one may judge by the body and flavour of the wine that is made for common drinking in the country. This wine is heady, and the better kinds mix well with water as a table wine. By improved methods of manufacture and attending carefully to the fermentation, it is quite possible that the peculiar and slightly disagreeable flavour the Ionian wines generally possess may be avoided; and if so, they would perhaps suit the English market better than some of the French wines, owing to their greater body.

The culture of the grape vine in Cephalonia, and generally in the Ionian islands, is good and sensible, well adapted to the climate and soil, and on the whole successful. The vines are pruned in February and March, at which time, or a little later, the ground or the stones around them is moved with the hoe, and raised in heaps; sometimes the heaps are round the roots and trunk of the vine, sometimes between the vines, leaving the roots bare: this is according to circumstances. In May the ground is once more levelled, when the leaves are out. In June, the extremities of the young shoots are broken off, and the trees are then left to fruit. When the fruit is ripening, the branches are lightly powdered over with sulphur. The grape vintage takes place in September, generally in the third week.

The vines are kept very low, and the lower in proportion as the ground is more rocky. In some places only two or three buds of one or two of the last year's branches are allowed to remain, the pruning being carried as far as possible to check the tendency of these almost rootless plants to branch unduly, in which case the plant will be weakly and the fruit poor. There can be little doubt that this rigorous pruning is absolutely essential, and is the result of long experience. It is strange, however, to ride over the country when the vines have been prepared, for in many cases one sees nothing but the merest stumps, and the turned up ground looks like small gravel heaps strewed over the country.

Although the culture of the vine is good, the management of the ripe grape for wine is generally very faulty. The grapes are roughly and carelessly gathered by women and children, and carried in baskets to the press. They are left heaped together for many days, and are then squeezed with the skins, at first by the feet of men, and afterwards by a screw. The must is fermented with the old husks of black grapes to deepen the colour. Black and white grapes are mixed together; and little care is taken in any part of the manufacture. Systematic treatment seems quite unknown.

The must, when obtained, is put into pig skins, and carried on the backs of mules and donkeys to the towns, where the fermentation is completed, either in casks or in vats of masonry. The better wines are, no doubt, somewhat more carefully made, and without the mixture of white and purple grapes; and some of these superior kinds are really very good. Only very small quantities, however, are made, and of some kinds, of which samples were sent to London to the Exhibition of 1863, not a cask could be found for sale when

ordered.   A few years may see a great improvement
in this manufacture; and it would certainly be to the
advantage of the islands if wine could become an important article of export.   Dr. Davy, in speaking of
these wines, compares them with Marsala in its early
stages; and it is not unlikely that the analogy is chiefly
with that growth.   They do not seem to be connected
by any points of resemblance either with north Italian
or Spanish wines; and still less do they resemble
French and Ĝerman.

Another product of Cephalonian industry is a very
pretty fabric, manufactured by the people in some of
the country villages out of the fibre of the aloe.   This
is worked up into a kind of lace; and various articles
of ladies' dress, as collars, sleeves, &c., are the most
common and least costly manufactures.   Larger objects
of dress, such as the kind of cloak called burnous,
elegant table or toilet covers, anti-macassars, and a
few other things, can also be obtained; but there is
no place in the town of Argostoli where this lace is
sold, and in order to obtain specimens, notice must be
sent to the villages in which it is made.   Many very
beautiful specimens were sent to the International
Exhibition of 1862, and were greatly admired, and
readily purchased at high prices.   No impulse seems
as yet given to the production; but this, like many
things, may come in time.   At present, there is generally a simple and oriental taste in the designs, which
adds to the beauty of these specimens of native lace.
So far as I am aware, the manufacture is confined to
Cephalonia, and does not there extend beyond a few

villages not far from Argostoli. The aloe is not much
encouraged in any of the islands; but I observed more
in Cephalonia than elsewhere.

An ornamental kind of basket-work, and a considerable variety of basket-work for common purposes, are
made in many parts of this island; but I was unable
to procure specimens of the finer work, as the demand
is too small to justify its being offered in the shops of
Argostoli. A carpet, not unlike Turkey carpet, is
also among the productions of the island. It is made
in narrow strips, of a peculiarly complicated pattern,
and is a useful material for various purposes. Like
the baskets, the better specimens of this weaving can
only be obtained by ordering them beforehand. They
are not particularly cheap.

A considerable number of boats are built both at
Argostoli, and also at Lixuri, on the opposite side of
the harbour. The larger ships, however, that navigate
these waters, although belonging to and manned by
Cephalonians, are built in Dalmatia. On the whole,
Argostoli is a busy place, and prosperous. The streets
and marine parade are gay and lively; but the shops
are very poor, and exhibit little that has the smallest
interest.

The communication between Argostoli and Lixuri
is carried on chiefly by ferry boats of large size, which
are generally crowded with people, coming and going.
My own trip across was performed in the health boat,
which the Resident was kind enough to place at my
disposal during my visit. When the wind is favourable, the transit does not take more than half an hour,

the distance being between four and five miles. It is a pretty sail enough, the country being pleasing, though not strikingly beautiful. The harbour of Argostoli is closed on the east side by hills, which extend round to the gulf; and on the opposite the hills, though lower, are prettily broken. After passing the low ground, where the water of the sea enters the earth and is utilised at the mills, we soon enter the main gulf, and Lixuri is seen just opposite. It is a picturesque looking town enough, with a mole and quay, and several respectable public buildings. One principal stack of buildings includes the courts of justice, the town hall, and the exchange, and is handsomely built. It is a sort of square bungalow, with a very wide balcony all round, and a large, central staircase, leading to the various offices. Stairs and balcony I found crowded with people of all classes, elbowing each other in a friendly manner. The back of this building forms one side of the market place, which, on the day of my visit, was crowded with people buying and selling. Although in the middle of Lent, I was surprised to see a fair show of meat. All kinds of vegetable food, both in season and out of season, was abundant; and caviare was equally so. The caviare used in the islands is generally from the Black Sea, and is not very good, being carelessly preserved. It is, however, a main source of nourishment at this season, and is very freely eaten. It always strikes me as curiously characteristic of the lower tendencies of human nature, this endeavour to cheat one's-self in the performance of a religious ordinance. The injunctions and instructions on the subject seem clear enough, and simply deny the use of animal food at certain seasons. It does not at first seem a very difficult task to define animal food; but, practically, it proves to be so. And as wholesome food in warm climates is insufficient in cold climates, and all constitutions are not alike in·this matter of food, a church interpretation has become necessary. In fact, it has been found in practice, that Europeans, at least, who have been accustomed to work on regular nourishing food, cannot and will not work without it. To escape, then, in some measure, from the dilemma, the order is held not to be binding on travellers; so that a certain quantity of animal food is always in the market. But this is not enough. Thus it has happened that eggs are exempt; and in Greece caviare is an allowed food, enormous quantities of it being eaten. Sometimes fish is permitted,—sometimes forbidden. In Greece, some kinds of shell fish, and those not very tempting animals, the sea urchins, are regarded as vegetable food. It is difficult to say where the line is drawn. Certainly, on the whole, the Greeks try to be conscientious in this matter; but the tendency to self-deception is as strong with them as with other people; and the determination as to what is animal food must be a sore subject for consideration.

The streets of Lixuri are inferior to those of Argostoli, and the population is much smaller. There seems, however, a good deal of business doing, and the people look active and industrious. The shipping indicates a considerable amount of traffic, which must be chiefly confined to the productions of the island. The mole, which is of recent construction, has converted a mere open roadstead into a good port, and rendered Lixuri independent of Argostoli, which it formerly was not. As the country around Lixuri affords some of the best crops of the island, and is highly cultivated, this is a matter of no small importance; for ships are able to come and go where formerly boats only could approach. In conjunction with the mole is the custom house and sanitary establishment.

About a mile to the north of Lixuri are a few indications of the ancient Pelasgian and Greek city of Palé, one of those that surrendered to Marcus Fulvius when he attacked the island of Cephalonia and besieged Samos. The modern town has perhaps been partly constructed of the stones used in the walls of this old city, and thus the fragments remaining are now only a few scattered blocks. Palé once successfully resisted an attack made by the Macedonians, and some coins are known which were coined there. Except by the examination of these few antiquities nothing more can be discovered of this place than may be gleaned by studying the works of Livy, Polybius, and Strabo; and neither of these seems to do more than allude to its existence.

Not far from Lixuri, on the coast, is a moving rock, of which the people are very proud. I did not go to visit it, as the trip would have required more time than I had to spare; but I learned the particulars by inquiry. It is a mass of rock no doubt fallen from a cliff and balanced in the water, so that it rocks slightly with the motion of the water. Except being partly under water, it probably differs little from the logan stones elsewhere.

The country near Lixuri consists chiefly of gypsum and gypseous marls, with much soft clay easily acted on by the water. It is intersected very deeply by the rains, and retains a grotesque appearance during the incessant and rapid change that is going on. At two points, one to the north and another to the south of Lixuri, there are sulphur springs. The former is strong, and has been celebrated for a long time for its curative properties. The other is less important; but is occasionally resorted to by the Greeks after excesses at table. In addition to sulphuretted hydrogen gas, of which the per-centage is small, it contains sulphate of magnesia and a little carbonate of magnesia, which will help to account for its reputation.

The other sulphur spring might be made much more important than it now is. It rises in a marly hill through highly inclined strata of gypsum mixed with black shales in large quantities, alternating with the marl. The spring is not strong, and no bubbles of gas escape; but the smell and taste of sulphuretted hydrogen in the water oozing out of the earth are very powerful. The colour of the water is pale-yellow, and films of sulphur float on its surface, covering everything that the water has been long in contact with. Dr. Davy found in specimens of the water as much as 17 cubic inches of sulphuretted hydrogen gas in each 100 cubic inches of water, and sulphur was also suspended in it to a marked extent. It contains also a little carbonic acid, and both sulphate of magnesia and sulphate of lime. At present the water is suffered to mix with the rain and is weakened; but if collected in a basin under shelter, it might probably be bottled and exported with advantage.

So strongly impregnated is this water with sulphur, that its curative powers are well known to the natives; and a church was formerly on the spot, where many miracles have been performed. This church is now in ruins. It is to be regretted that measures are not taken to make it available for cutaneous diseases, for which it is especially adapted.

A large quantity of gypsum, generally crystalline, is found throughout the country near Lixuri, and for the most part harder rocks are absent. Some of the hills are capped with plates of re-cemented shingle, which are hard and much cracked, and in many cases these cracks have become filled with stalagmitic gypsum.

Further to the north, about five miles from the town, are some quarries of a peculiarly soft limestone used for some of the public buildings in Argostoli, and very easily and cheaply worked. A vertical face, at least 25 feet in height, is laid bare along a length of several hundred yards. It is evident that blocks of almost any required size could be obtained very cheaply. It much resembles the Malta freestone, but is rather harder.

A little further north than this quarry, at the monastery of Jaffeo, on the west coast of the island, is a somewhat remarkable cavern opening from the sea. It is not very accessible, and is the more talked about perhaps because it is rarely visited. What is most remarkable about this cavern, which is merely a recess in inclined strata of limestone, about thirty feet high and of the same width, entering about forty feet, is the singularly high temperature of the air in the interior. This is, however, probably only a result of its sheltered position, and the fact that it serves as a sort of permanent barrack for goats and cattle. Its only opening is to the south-west and south.

The southern part of the promontory of Lixuri is a constant repetition of low hills of gypsum alternating with soft shale and marl. All this district is richly cultivated, and is said to yield very fine crops of currants, for although mere gypsum is poor enough in itself, the gypseous marls and shales decompose into rich soils, and are constantly disturbed by every shower. In some places a good pottery clay alternates with these marls, but this of course does not help to produce a picturesque effect. On the whole, this part of the island is wanting in general interest.

The climate of Cephalonia differs from that of Zante, and it is worthy of notice, that although in the larger island the mountain chain is so lofty as to be covered with snow always more than half the year, there is no appearance of the general temperature being much affected by it. The currant-grape is said always to ripen earlier in Cephalonia than Zante by at least a week; the aloe flourishes and flowers very early, and the prickly pear, when cultivated as a hedge, is very rapid in its growth. The neighbourhood of Argostoli is celebrated for its melons, which grow to enormous size, and possess a rich flavour. When kept suspended in a cool place, they will keep from the month of August (the time of ripening) to the following March, or even April, without injury.

On the other hand, the first snows that fall on the Black Mountain chill the air in Zante, and affect the climate of that island; and the cold of winter is said to be more trying and disagreeable in the smaller than in the larger island.

Cephalonia is not an unhealthy island. In the neighbourhood of Samos, the drainage that has already been effected under the superintendence of the late Resident, has so far improved the climate, that agues and marsh fevers are comparatively rare. At Argostoli, the large tracts of flat marsh land at the extremity of the harbour, which at one time must have seriously affected the salubrity of the climate, have also been greatly improved; being now converted into pastures, separated by deep drains that are not left stagnant. No complaints are made of any want of health among the troops; but as they are stationed outside the town, on the side furthest from these swamps, it might easily be that they would not suffer. Lixuri is also free from swamps in the immediate neighbourhood, though the villages at the extreme end of the gulf may probably be less fortunate. There are few swamps in the principal valleys parallel to the Black Mountain.

The summer temperature in Cephalonia is certainly high. According to observations taken probably with imperfect instruments in the year 1830, the mean summer heat is said to have been as much as 84° Fah. in the plains; but in the cottage on the mountains, and even in the valleys at the foot of the mountain, the air is much cooler. In the year quoted, the difference of temperature between the cottage and the hospital of Argostoli, averaged 16°. In all the islands there is a great difference between the towns and the country villages, and the latter, when not rendered poisonous by miasma, must be more healthy, as well as much more convenient.

Cephalonia is subject occasionally to severe storms, especially about the time of the equinox. Shortly before my visit, and while I was in Santa Maura, there had been a hurricane of the nature of a cyclone, which had swept over a part of the town and suburbs of Argostoli, doing great damage. One of the barracks was so shaken and injured, that it was necessary to pull down the front wall; many roofs had been blown away, and upwards of a hundred olive trees had been rooted up and destroyed. Fortunately the path of the storm was very narrow, and the duration short. On the same day were several shocks of earthquake, but they were not serious. Storms of this kind are not common; but the position of the town, near the extremity of a cul-de-sac, with hills on all sides, and a lofty mountain-range quite close, must be apt to bring high winds occasionally.

The island also suffers from earthquakes; though it is generally said that in this respect it is intermediate between Zante and Corfu. As an illustration of

the partial and local nature of the propagation of
earthquake wave from island to island, I may ment
that a sharp earthquake felt in the western part
Santa Maura, about $5\frac{1}{2}$ A.M., on the morning of
21st March, 1863, and at the town of Santa Ma
about the same time, was represented at Argostoli
two or three shocks at various times during the d
not one of which could be distinctly identified
that of Santa Maura.

Generally, as far as I could learn, all earthquak
and not only those of comparatively small importan
are propagated in an exceedingly capricious m:
between the different islands. For a long time Z:
and Santa Maura were much more remarkable
earthquakes than Cephalonia; but latterly Cephalo
seems enjoying its share.

There are several interesting observations on reco
which clearly show that the earthquakes in the Ion
Islands are not usually coincident in the differ
islands; but that each island is, to a great exte
independent of the others in this respect. So l
ago as in the year 1818, in the Hospital journals k
at Cephalonia and Zante, all the sensible shocks w
tabulated, and this record extends over two compl
years and a quarter. During this time thirty dist¹
and well-marked shocks were recorded in Cephalo
but in no case did the shocks in Zante, although nea
contemporaneous, absolutely coincide with them.
most cases an interval of some days, and almost alw
more than twenty-four hours, seems to have elap
between the times of the disturbances in the ¹

although they are so near, that in these days of long range, a cannon shot fired from the one might reach to the other.

It has been observed, too, that the same want of correspondence between earthquakes occurs on the mainland of Greece and Albania, where similar phenomena are also common. It is indeed evident that whereas a large area may be so far connected underground that a very important shock originating at great depths shall be communicated rapidly in every direction, there may be smaller pulsations. These are not without some obscure relation, but are so far independent that each one only affects the ground directly above, and extends no farther at the time, though the same cause which produced one pulsation in one place is able to produce other similar pulsations at a little distance after a short interval.

One other point is indicated by the small stock of statistical information I have been able to procure in reference to the distribution of earthquake shocks in this island. It is that the greatest number of shocks do not seem to have taken place there in the winter, and that the barometer has not been affected during even a considerable shock. The evidence, though too small to be worth laying stress on, would also seem to show that more shocks have been noticed in calm than in rough weather.

Besides the earthquakes, there are other points of the physical geography of Cephalonia worthy of more careful attention than they have yet received, and many of them are clearly connected with the geological structure of the island. The existence of the main central chain of the Black Mountains and the nearly parallel coast ranges, each continuous for some distance, though comparatively low, are beyond a doubt the causes of the principal phenomena of drainage; but it is clear that the nature of the rock influences the result. Thus there are no rivers properly so called, and indeed hardly any streams of any kind in Cephalonia, with the exception of that which runs through the vale of Samos, and this, as I have said, almost diappears before it enters the gulf. This stream takes its origin in the small lake of Abatho, or bottomless, which I have mentioned as an example of those curious circular pits so common in all the islands. This pit is full of water. It is about two hundred yards in circumference, and surrounded by rugged hills of clay, conglomerate, and sandstone.

A short distance from this curious lake are the remains of the ancient city of Pronos, little visited, but showing some fine Cyclopean walls. Pronos was the fourth of the ancient walled cities of Cephalonia, and, according to Polybius, must have been the smallest. It is situated amongst beautiful wooded scenery, and in a rich profusion of orchards, villages, and vineyards. The valley above Pronos, and leading to it, is described by Dr. Davy as not unlike Roslin, combining beauty with a certain wildness and grandeur, walled in by mural precipices luxuriantly wooded. The views of Greece and Ithaca are also

very charming. Not far from Pronos a colony of
Maltese was founded by Sir Charles Napier, but it
does not seem to have led to any important result.

Among the remarkable physical phenomena connected with Cephalonia are occasional sudden risings
of the sea on its coast, apparently not connected with
any near earthquake action, and confined to the
narrow waters in which they originate. One of these
took place in the year 1827, when the sea rose ten
feet, without any warning, on a fine calm night,
moving heavy masses of stone recently brought for
the construction of the mole, and alarming the people
greatly. Others, on various parts of the coast, are
recorded. They are not easily explained, and, until
more detailed particulars are known, it would be useless to speculate on the cause. Among the permanent
curiosities of the gulf of Samos (in which the sudden
rise of the water just alluded to took place) is the
outburst of a spring of fresh water in the sea at a
point about half way across from Samos to Pilaro.
This goes on constantly; but can only be observed
in calm weather, when the water is seen to rise a
foot above the mean level. This is the more interesting, as the bay is crowded with fish, who do not
seem disturbed by this intrusion.

On the same side of the island, but at the other
extremity of the valleys of Samos and Rakli, is the
district of Scala, with its village of the same name.
This portion of the island extends from the southern
foot of the Black mountain to the sea, and is not
much cultivated. "The soil is poor, the surface being

sandy, upon a stiff, clayey bottom. The whole is
nearly overrun with fern, and the scenery is beautiful, owing to the profusion of shrubs and evergreens,
amongst which, in July, the rhododendron, with its
beautiful and brilliant scarlet blossoms, makes a delightful contrast. The remains of an ancient city are
marked out here, by several ruins and by the foundations
and scattered fragments of a temple. There are also
stone tombs cut in the rocks, and portions of Roman
baths, with a little temple adjoining, built of brick.
The baths are situated upon the left bank of the bed
of a little stream that formerly ran into the sea close
by, but is now dried up and its mouth choked with
sand. Tesselated pavement is found all around. A
considerable city seems once to have existed at Scala;
and a tradition is current of a city, said to be sunk
under water, about three miles distant from the shore.
There is a shoal at this point, called κακαβω, or the
bad cape, on which vessels have often been wrecked."
As it is probable that the ruins of the old city of
Samos extended at one time much further seaward
than they do now, it has been suggested that the
whole of the south-eastern part of the island has been
subject to depression on a large scale. However, it
seems to have been proved, by an expedition, made
for the express purpose of determining the fact, that
the shoal is nothing more than a ledge of sandstone
rock, with no appearance whatever of ruins or ancient
buildings.

The proportion of land under cultivation in Cephalonia is very small, probably not one-sixth part of the

whole. There is no reason for this but the smallness of the population; for the people are not idle and communication is tolerable. I have said that the olive is better looked after than in Corfu; and I may add, that both grape and currant vines are cultivated with care and success in the valleys and on the sides of the lower hills. It is chiefly in the larger valleys and flats near the sea that there is opportunity for an important growth of other crops, and at these points there is generally more or less stagnant water during some part of the year; though on the whole the land must be regarded as exceedingly dry.

The cultivation of the lower parts of Cephalonia, especially of those tracts gained from the water, and still existing as half swamps, is a matter that admits of improvement. The present Resident has suggested that the district lately recovered near Argostoli, at the head of the harbour, which is already large, and is steadily increasing, might be devoted partly to grass lands for the feeding of cows to replace goats, and partly to the growth of cotton. Samples of the finer kinds of cotton grown in the island from American seed, were sent to the International Exhibition, and very favourably reported on. It does not seem that the cultivation of cotton here involves any unhealthy exposure; and though the quantity of land adapted for the purpose is not very large, the climate appears particularly well fitted for ripening it. Further experiments on a larger scale may be necessary; but the question clearly involves considerations that ought not to be neglected. There should be no practical difficulty in introducing a new 'article of profitable trade, and it might be hoped that such an innovation would be met at least half-way; but the Greeks, and especially the Ionian islanders claiming to be Greeks, are not a people much given to new methods, and nothing but experiment can decide as to whether they will take to the novelty, or refuse to have anything to do with it.*

Of the corn crops cultivated in Cephalonia, maize takes the precedence of wheat, as it especially suits those numerous hollows—half swamps at one period of the year—into which the rain must soak, since it cannot run off. The maize crop does not fully ripen till towards the end of September; but the produce is large, more than two heads on each stalk not being uncommon. Besides the fruit, the leafy envelope of the head is much in use for mattrasses. For this purpose it is well adapted; being elastic, very clean, and free from smell. The valley of Samos is the richest in the island for the growth of corn.

The country population of Cephalonia is at present quiet enough, and apparently under good regulation; but it has not always been so, and when excited, the people have frequently shown symptoms of great insubordination. They are more independant than the

---

* I may mention here that most of the Ionian islands have entered, to some extent, on the cultivation of cotton. In the year 1860 the following were the quantities grown, according to returns made to the House of Commons, and published in 1862. Zante, 8,721 lbs.; Cerigo, 8,000 lbs.; Cephalonia, 4,250 lbs.; Corfu, 2,730 lbs.; Santa Maura, 1,600 lbs. Cephalonia has since then increased much more in proportion than the other islands.

people of Corfu, but not at all less ignorant. In political matters they have shown a tendency to oppose the existing authorities, even without a shadow of reason; and during the unfortunate disturbances of 1848, when the Lord High Commissioner of the day, Lord Seaton, had in some measure yielded to the wishes of the people, and had granted more self-government than had previously been enjoyed, he was rewarded by a mad attempt at insurrection, which had it succeeded even for the moment, might have had serious results. On this occasion the villagers had been inoculated with the republican fever then raging in Europe, and armed with a great variety of weapons a number of them determined to attack the capital. The state of feeling was well known to the Resident (the Baron d'Everton), and the troops were kept in readiness during the night preceding the attack. In the morning, when it was thought the danger had passed, and whilst some of the men were taking rest, and others preparing their food in the different barracks, a message came to the Resident to say, that a large body of rioters were actually on the road, and then close to the town. Knowing the vital importance of checking the movement before it should become very serious, the Resident sent for the soldiers, and found them dispersed, so that probably half an hour would elapse before they were ready to act. Fortunately, the only access to the town from the east, without making a very long detour, involves crossing the causeway and bridge, the approach to which is defensible by a few men. Collecting therefore, at the instant, the armed police and the guard, he marched off with them to keep the bridge, and thus prevent access to the town.   He made the appeal, so vigorously expressed by Macaulay in his well-known ballad :—

> " I, with two more to help me,
>   Will hold the foe in play :—
> In yon strait path a thousand
>   May well be stopped by three.
> Now who will stand on either hand,
>   And keep the bridge with me ?"

There was no lack of replies to this summons; and the brave, though small body, reached the narrow way before the rioters.   Their advance, thus met by a small body of disciplined and determined men, did indeed make an attack, but was easily beaten back without much loss, and time was thus given for the troops to form.   Many prisoners were taken, and several of the ringleaders were punished.   Unluckily, Lord Seaton was soon afterwards removed, and was replaced by a governor, who was more fond of personal popularity than careful to understand the real state of society, and distinguish political feeling from mere brigandage. The movement in question was much more one of brigands than of political victims. He allowed the prisoners to escape without punishment; and the result of this ill-timed leniency induced other troubles, during which several of the native residents, living in remote parts of the island, were murdered by the peasants, instigated by some of the demagogues who pretended to desire union with Greece.   The Lord High Commissioner himself foolishly and quite needlessly proceeded to the spot where the troubles had taken place, and was fired upon by the rabble. He was forced to admit, that "the only body of men known to be in arms against the government was a gang of robbers and assassins, whom it was impossible to·dignify by the name of insurgents." Even after this, the real originators of these disgraceful scenes were allowed to escape; and the result was seen in the first assembly elected after this event, when all the demagogues and the most infamous of the libellers, who had been punished by his predecessor, were sent to Corfu to beard the Lord High Commissioner in his very palace.

This little episode of Cephalonian politics may be a useful indication of the state of popular feeling—of the facility with which disturbances and misunderstandings arise—of the absence of harmony that has long existed between the peasant population and the institutions by which they are governed—and the difficulty there would be in permanently settling a people subject to such outbursts. At present, it may be said that the islanders are perfectly quiet, and have no causes of complaint; but the smallest unpopular act of the protecting government would inevitably light a spark which would rapidly be fanned into a flame of rebellion by some of those troublesome and dangerous characters to be found in every community. Even so slight a matter as the endeavour strictly to carry out the law for the preservation of the public property in forests, might, and probably would, bring about a small rebellion.

And although at present even-handed justice is dealt to all (and this is fully appreciated), it must be admitted, to the disgrace of our country, that such has not always been the case. Giving too much power into the hands of the old oligarchy, and shutting their eyes to the almost inevitable consequences, the authorities for a long time chose to govern indirectly by this oligarchy instead of looking out for the right men to fill important posts. A great deal of injustice has certainly been committed by the nominees of the English government that no Englishman at head quarters had the smallest idea of. Still less has the English public been aware of the details of proceedings carried on here in the name and with the power of the law.

MAP

OF

CEPHALONIA AND ITHACA.

0 1 2 3 4 5   10 MILES

Scale of English Miles 69 1-1°

M & N Hanhart. li

ZANTE.

———◆———

"Fair is Zacynthus; lovely ever shone
 To the bright east, up-heaved Lacinion."

THEOCRITUS' Idylls, iv.

Welcome, Zacynthus, welcome are thy shades
Thy vine-clad hills, and deep sequester'd glades!

         *   *   *   *

Sure 'tis enchantment bids the prospect rise,
Like some bright fairy vision, to my eyes:
On every side what varied beauty charms!
Here the throng'd city spreads her crescent arms;
To her white bosom woos the swelling tide,
And rises on the mountain's shelvy side.
  "Tow'ring far above their little state
Scopò with conscious majesty elate
Lifts to the skies his consecrated head.

         *   *   *

Hard by his foot, where rolls the turbid main,
Cheri unfolds her wild and marshy plain;
High rugged cliffs the barren spot surround,
And steams sulphureous issue from the ground;
And pitchy springs, that quickly seek to hide ﹅
In subterranean course their murky tide,
Till distant from the shore again they rise
And tinge the billow with their varying dyes."

Horæ Ionicæ.

CHAPTER XIII.

FROM Argostoli to Zante city is about forty miles;
but from Cape Scala, the southerly point of Cephalonia to Cape Skinari, the northernmost point of the
island of Zante is only eight miles; so that the trip
from one island to the other is always within view of
the island, and generally quite close to the coast.

The views of Cephalonia, obtained while sailing
down the Gulf of Argostoli, and crossing the channel

that separates the two islands, are generally fine, owing to the vicinity of the Black Mountain, which rises in frowning majesty almost from the coast, with extreme abruptness, capped with snow, and streaked here and there with broad white vertical lines, marking the course of torrents. This is by far the best point of view of the mountain, which from almost every other direction, is comparatively tame, owing to its great length compared with its height, and the absence of a prominent peak at the summit.

The south coast of Cephalonia is not very bold or picturesque. Three quaint looking rocks, shaped like cheeses, rise out of the water near its southern extremity, and the shore, seen from a distance, is studded with cultivated patches. This part of the island, though thinly peopled, and much of it left without any kind of cultivation, is apparently very fertile.

The steamers that run down from Corfu, touching at the Ionian Islands, proceed on beyond Zante, touching also at several of the Greek islands, and finishing their voyage at Constantinople. The number of first class passengers is small, for the fares are very high; but the deck is generally crowded, and one thus obtains an insight into Greek life, that would elsewhere require a good deal of trouble and inconvenience to secure. Looking down from the elevation of the quarter deck, on the mass of human beings and rags below, one is apt to fancy at first that they must all be in miserable plight, and one wonders how they can have obtained funds for the long journey some, at least, are taking. In fact, however, many of them have pockets well lined with gold, and are rich enough to carry on a considerable traffic. They come on board with many bundles tied up in bedding, large outlandish boxes painted with all the colours of the rainbow, and such arms as they can obtain, or are allowed to wear. There seems to be some mutual understanding amongst them, and it is only the better classes that occupy the comfortable warm corners and the soft planks near the chimney; the rest herd towards the fore part of the ship, and only creep round now and then to look about them. Women and children are very rare. Travelling seldom involves the removal of his family to a Greek; and, indeed, there would be no object to be obtained by incurring such an expense as indulging the roving propensities of the female part of the population, if they were allowed to possess such feelings.

My trip from Argostoli to Zante was amusing enough in the scenes of life it presented. One stout and rather handsome middle-aged man, has taken up his quarters close to the steps leading down from the quarter deck to the main deck. He has packed round him his bedding, and some carpet bags—the lighter part of his baggage—and sits on the ground, surrounded by his wealth on three sides, and having a comfortable place for his back. He is evidently a fellow who studies what is good for his own comfort, and means to make the best of his position. Squatted cross-legged, with his knees far apart, he is just thinking of dinner, for it is past eleven, and no doubt his appetite is sharpened by the sea air. By his side are several passengers; some in Greek costume, others in very shabby and unsatisfactory imitations of the ugly western fashions of dress. One next him is fast asleep; but in a dignified Turkish way; and I don't think anybody will disturb him after looking at his face. A third is doubled up in a singular fashion, and has packed himself into a kind of box-shaped recess, a great deal shorter than himself. If he stays there long enough he will be hardly able to move; but I suppose he likes it. Another is stretched out, arms and legs all flying, and covers the boiler case, close to the funnel. He looks exhausted, and seems also asleep. I should think that between the sun which shines fiercely upon him, and the boiler, which has made the iron plates so hot that one hardly likes to touch them with the hand, he will be sufficiently dried before long to take his place as a mummy. Each of these good fellows is happy in his way; but certainly his way would not be mine; for the deck is by no means clean, and the prospect of fleas and other companions is too lively to justify me in carrying on my researches any nearer. But I am well placed, looking over the rail on the group below me.

My friend, the hungry Greek, attracts me again. He has begun to dine. Between his widely-expanded knees is a large saucer full of very thick, muddy-looking oil, such as one sees flowing from the press in the last stages of oil-making. It is yellow, and very unsightly; but he approves of its flavour. In one hand he has a large piece of black bread, and by his side are about a dozen small onions, besides one particular onion of the most gigantic dimensions. I have never seen a Spanish or Portuguese onion so large, and, if one might judge by appearances, it was of far higher flavour than those delicate luxuries. My friend thrusts a piece of bread into his mouth, and, while masticating it, he breaks off part of the large onion, dips it and rolls it well about in the saucer with his finger and thumb, and then carefully introduces that also, not soiling his beard and moustache more than can be helped. Presently, one of the small onions, after being exposed to a similar preparation, is devoured, stalk and all, and is followed by another lump of bread. But it is not eaten hurriedly. The white root of the onion well dipped goes down first; then a part of the stalk, and lastly the extremity; all being oiled beforehand. Occasionally the bread is dipped in oil to heighten the flavour. Presently, the first lump of bread having disappeared, he takes out his knife, cuts off another large slice, and begins again.

There is no doubt that this man is bound for Constantinople, and has a large proportion of his temporalities with him. There is a huge basket of bread and onions by his side that will look very small before he arrives, and, unless the weather is very unfavourable, he will enjoy himself greatly, and perhaps not rise from his corner a dozen times. He will eat, and sleep, and be happy.

Shall I attempt to describe his dress as far as I can discover it from his appearance? I will do so conscientiously. Be it remembered that the month is

March, and the weather remarkably fine. The air coming down from the mountains is a little fresh, but the sun is very hot. No one on the quarter-deck could bear an over-coat or cloak.

The inner garment, which I can detect by unmistakable evidences at the wrists and neck, must be a thickly knitted cotton under-shirt—a kind of jersey, closely fitting. It is very brown indeed where visible, but I do not imagine that to be its natural colour. Over it is a sailor's pale blue check shirt, one shade less filthy. The trousers, terminating at the knee, are of the usual baggy sort, and of the usual blue material, but so marvellously patched that I don't suppose one particle of the original material remains. Even the patches have long since lost all colour; but they are recognised by their different shades, the results of age and wear. My friend's legs are encased in coarse woollen stockings, over which warm socks are drawn, and his feet are covered with the usual Greek slipper. He has a thick woollen under-waist-coat, and a second waistcoat or jacket with long sleeves braided and ornamented round the edges. Of course he has a broad and long silken sash twisted round his middle, for this is necessary to hold his knife and all sorts of treasures; it is, in fact, his pocket. Over all he has a coat lined with sheep-skin; and by his side I see a brown capote with a hood intended to throw off any amount of rain to which a man may be exposed. On his head is the usual tight-fitting red cap and tassel.

All this time, while I have been jotting down the

particulars of his dress, dinner goes on, slowly, as if
he _ felt that there was ample time for everything,
and with manifest gusto. As he advances with his
meal he finds that he can afford to be luxurious,
and instead of merely dipping the onion, he dips his
bread into the saucer more frequently than at first,
and allows the crumbs to accumulate there. Presently he rolls up all these well-soaked crumbs into
a little ball and neatly inserts them within his lips
with his finger and thumb. This is done with an
air, as if he felt that he has a right to enjoy this
small extravagance. But now the time has come
to wash down the meal. He dives into the recesses
of his large and well-stored bag, and slowly brings
out a gigantic black bottle, shaped like a wine-bottle,
but holding at least a gallon. With a small rag
greatly worn, and much torn, but which is probably
well accustomed to its work, he wipes carefully his
moustache and his hands, and then the bottle slowly
rises into the air. Large as the bottle is, the neck
is very narrow, and the wine gurgles slowly and
pleasantly over his palate and down his throat for
a considerable time. He then gathers up the fragments, takes a small fragment more of bread to soak
up the oil in the saucer, pours carefully into his
mouth the few drops that remain, and puts back into
his bag part of the large onion that he had not
eaten. He picks up a few straggling bits of root of
the onion, rises slowly, and throws them over the
bulwarks into the sea as a sacrifice to Neptune, then
blows his nose grandly, in a primitive fashion; also

for the benefit of Neptune, takes a turn round his
part of the ship as if to start digestion, but soon
returns and re-seats himself on his mattrass to enjoy
the repose he ha so well earned. · A cigarette wafts
him slowly into the realms of bliss, and he has no
more to think of till the time comes round for the
next meal.

It must not be supposed that all the Greeks are
fat, well fed, and warmly clothed. This was the
Dives, and close by was a Lazarus also, as, indeed,
is generally the case in this world. He was a poor-
looking wretch, thin, blue, and cold, with only a
scanty covering of the coarsest canvas and a capote.
The latter he constantly wears, because he has nothing else to keep off the sun or rain; but in it he
resembles a most melancholy Robinson Crusoe. Many
such poor fellows go about from island to island.
They certainly manage to live and travel, but the
living must be of the coarsest kind; and I suppose
the travelling does not cost much.

The appearance of Zante from the north is that of a
low island enclosed in a semi-circle of high hills richly
covered with wood, the plains also being richly cultivated. And this is a correct general account of the
island. The hills are of very different elevation, many
of them loftier than one at first imagines, and they
are not really monotonous, as they include more than
one range. Practically, the whole of the western
part of Zante is hilly, and even mountainous; the
western slopes are not cultivated, and there is not
much cultivation even on the eastern slopes of the

higher hills. All the lower hills, however, on the east of the island are covered with growing crops from top to bottom, and the whole of the lower ground is under tillage, and yields large and very valuable agricultural results.

There is only one important hill on the east side of the island. It is Mount Scopos, at the south-eastern extremity. The smaller hills, such as that behind the town of Zante on which is the castle, and some others at various points, are very distinct in all respects from the western mountain chain. The highest point in the island is towards the northern end. It is called Mount Vrachiona, and is considered to be 2,300 feet above the sea. Scopos is about 1,500 feet.

The coast of Zante, from Cape Skinari almost to Crionero Point where Zante Bay commences, is bold and fine, though the cliffs are not lofty. About four miles from the cape is a curious phenomenon not very easily visited, and known in the island as the grease well. It is a spring of a peculiar fluid mineral, apparently issuing from below a considerable depth of water in a small cavern about two miles from a flat part of the coast called the Salines. This spring can only be visited from the sea, and when the weather is perfectly calm. During my stay in the island I had no opportunity of investigating the conditions, and as I found no one who could give me much information on the subject, I think it worth while to give the minute and careful statement of Dr. Davy rather than either pass by so singular a phenomenon

without notice, or give a less complete statement from
the results of imperfect observations and inquiry.
Dr. Davy's visit took place in August, 1824. From
time to time since then various persons have examined the phenomena in a general way, but I know
of none who have given a more detailed account,
or more satisfactory explanation. I was, indeed, informed by Count Nicholas Roma, who is very familiar with the natural history of his island, that, in
his opinion, the issuing fluid was a kind of naphtha.
Certainly, judging by Dr. Davy's own statement,
it would seem much more likely that some mineral
oil is the exuding fluid than that it should be derived from sea-weed or animal matter.

Dr. Davy says, "the morning was very favourable for the boating excursion, the sea but slightly
ruffled by a very gentle north-west breeze. We em-
barked at the Salines, and when we had approached
within about a quarter of a mile of the cliff from
whence the spring issues, we perceived the smell of
sulphuretted hydrogen, and very soon after we saw
white flakes and particles floating in the sea which
thickened so much in nearing the source as to render
the water quite white. The odour and the whiteness of the sea guided us to the principal spring,
which is situated in a small cave formed by limestone cliffs of moderate height. The cave is skirted
on each side by projecting perpendicular rocks; its
roof is shelving, pretty lofty at its mouth, but rapidly declining, so that a boat can only enter a few
yards—cannot reach its extremity, which may be

about twenty-four yards. About the middle of the cavern, or rather, I should say, as far as the boat could enter, the depth of the water was about 12 feet. This was ascertained by letting down the anchor. The water felt very cold where we sounded; its temperature was 62 degrees, the sea at a distance was 78 degrees, and the air under the awning of the boat 81 degrees. To explore the innermost part of the cave it was necessary to leave the boat, and have recourse to swimming. It proved a very disagreeable task, partly from the coldness of the water, and still more from its stench. I was induced to undertake it with the hope of discovering something interesting, but my observations were chiefly negative. I could observe no appearance of air-bubbles ascending, and no distinct gush of water; and the temperature of the water inwards did not increase. It was fortunate in this rash attempt that the sulphuretted hydrogen was not more freely disengaged; if it had been, in all probability it would have proved fatal. As it was, I returned to the boat with very disagreeable sensations, and was presently seized with purging and vomiting, which I mention as a caution to others. The walls of the cavern were either covered with green sea-weed, or with a dead-white incrustation, the latter predominant. The current of water proceeding from the cavern was well marked by the outward movement of the flakes and particles of white matter suspended in it.

" With some difficulty, owing to the specific gravity of the white matter differing very little from that of

salt water, I collected sufficient for examination.
The following are the results of my experiments on
it, made after my return to the town of Zante, and
also on the incrustation on the rock and on the water
itself. These experiments were not so minute as I
could have wished, owing to my limited means;
the results, however, were very distinct. I shall
commence with the matter which gives a peculiar
character to the water, and which has been improperly considered as a kind of mineral grease. It is
nearly milk-white, tasteless, and after exposure for a
short time to the air it loses the odour of sulphuretted
hydrogen, and has no smell. It is of a gelatinous
consistence; examined with a lens, it has the appearance of a delicate semi-transparent membrane, studded
with white particles. It is heavier than water, as it
is indicated by its sinking readily, when perfectly
quiet. It is, however, even more readily suspended,
when agitated, showing that its specific gravity is not
much greater. Exposed to the air till dry, it appears
in the form of a thin, light, yellow pellicle, of some
toughness. This pellicle before the blow-pipe partially fuses; it burns with a blue flame, emitting a
strong smell of sulphureous acid, and leaves a coal
of its own form, which is easily reduced to an ash,
white, very small in quantity, and consisting chiefly
of lime. Dilute acetic acid does not dissolve the
peculiar matter: it renders it, however, more trans-
parent. Strong nitric acid imparts to it a yellow
tinge; when heated it dissolves it slowly, and sulphuric
acid is formed. Concentrated sulphuric acid appears

to dissolve it rapidly; a little white powder remains, which is chiefly sulphur. A solution of acetate of lead renders it more opaque and heavier, judging from its sinking more rapidly in water. Subjected to heat in a retort, connected with a pneumatic apparatus, the products were a fat that had an offensive empyreumatic smell, unmixed with that of sulphuretted hydrogen; a yellowish fluid, in which sulphur was suspended; and a residue of coal. The fluid had an empyreumatic smell, similar to that of the gas; and tested by a strong solution of caustic soda, it afforded indications of the presence of ammonia.

" From these results, it appears that the matter in question consists of two substances,—of sulphur, and of another akin to animal mucus, or to animal albumen, and very analogous to Barégine, or that matter which exists in the sulphureous water of Barèges, which I have submitted to a few experiments, the results of which tolerably accord with the preceding. The specimens of rock which I brought from the interior of the cave were of two kinds; both were varieties of limestone; one resembling indurated chalk, the other crystalline, and more resembling marble. They were both composed of carbonate of lime, and contained a very minute portion of alumine. I could not detect in them any sulphur, nor did they emit any smell of sulphuretted hydrogen, when in the act of solution. These remarks do not apply to their surface; for they were superficially incrusted with a light yellowish matter, which, on examination was found similar to the peculiar substances in the water; the only difference noticed was, that when subjected to distillation, the gas disengaged was not free from the odour of sulphuretted hydrogen.

" A specimen of water taken from the cave was of considerably less specific gravity than that of the water of the sea adjoining; its specific gravity was 101·103.   Besides the animal-like matter and sulphur suspended in it, and the sulphuretted hydrogen dissolved in it, it contained pretty much carbonate and sulphate of lime.   As the sulphureous spring rose in the sea, and its waters were mixed with those of the sea, it necessarily contained the common ingredients of sea-water.

" Besides the cavern I have described, there are one or two more in the neighbourhood, similarly situated in the cliffs, yielding the same kind of water.

" These springs have been long known to the inhabitants; and it is stated by F. Sauveur, in his account of the Ionian Islands, that the natives of Zante are in the habit of collecting the peculiar product of them, when thrown up on the shore, and applying it as a remedy to the cutaneous diseases of their cattle. This was not confirmed by those I had an opportunity of questioning on the spot.   If it has ever been collected, as F. Sauveur states, it was probably in a moist state, and when entangled and suspended, as it were, in the froth and foam of the waves.

" The origin of the animal-like substance is not a little mysterious.   M. Longchamp, in his Memoir on Barèges, read before the Academy of Sciences, in 1833, does not even offer a conjecture respecting it.   Various conjectures, no doubt, may be entertained on the subject. To me it appears most probable that it is of a vegetable nature, a species of mucor, or perhaps of tremella, somewhat analogous to those found in the sulphureous springs of Aix, in Savoy, and described by Saussure. There they grow on the basin and rocky channels of the waters; their mucous filaments are impregnated with sulphur, and are liable to be detached. Perhaps the Zante springs flow through concealed caverns, to which air may have access in sufficient quantity to allow of the growth of such plants; and they may be destitute of colour, from the exclusion of light; and in favour of this notion, I may mention that, on the rocks in the neighbourhood under water, I observed what appeared to be a species of tremella, growing abundantly. In my notes, taken at the time, I have called it a soft velvetty species of sea-weed, perhaps an ulva, to which adhered slightly, and might easily be detached, a kind of gelatinous matter, not unlike that accompanying the sulphur from the cavern. I collected a portion of it with the intention of examining it, but neglected to do so. If the gelatinous matter just alluded to were found to afford azote or ammonia, and to have the principal properties of the animal-like substance in question, strong confirmation would be obtained that the origin of both is similar." *

Leaving this curious spring and its history at some distance, we approach the Bay of Zante. It is small,

* Davy's Ionian Islands and Malta, vol. i. p. 147.

and not very sheltered, but wonderfully picturesque.
It lies at the foot of a steep hill, which is crowned
with the castle, and broken off in the most singular
manner by a chasm, said to have been produced by
an earthquake ; but of which the fracture is constantly kept fresh and clean by the rain.   It stretches
far away on each side, having an appearance of greater
magnitude even than Corfu, and far exceeding in style
and variety of its public buildings, any of the island
capitals.   There is a mole and small harbour, and
near the landing-place a large square.   The streets
are numerous, wide, decently paved, and full of shops;
they are covered with arcades, as in Italy, and built
in tolerably regular style.   The Strada Marina is not
very extensive; but is really handsome in its noble
quay, its wide road, and its beautiful churches.   The
market place is handsome, and well filled; the people
cheerful and lively, and crowding the streets.

Zante contrasts favourably with all the other cities
of the Ionian Islands.   It is more uniform, and has
more characteristic features than Corfu, and if we
except the Palace, it is quite equal to that city in its
public buildings.   Not being enclosed or fortified, it
has expanded more naturally than Corfu, and has not
the poor suburbs of the metropolis.   There are in it
many fine old Venetian houses still inhabited by the
families in whose possession they have been for centuries, and these give it an air of solidity and respecta-
bility that is not felt elsewhere.   The native population
of Zante in 1860 was returned as amounting to 38,183,
of whom more than half are resident in the town.

Although the Zantiots, like the other islanders, re-tain the Greek church as their national religion, and there are no churches or priests of other persuasions in the country villages, the number of Roman Catholics in the town is considerable. They have several churches, some of which are handsomely built and decorated. But the Greek churches are especially fine. Constructed as usual in the oblong form of a classical temple, and without much external or archi-tectural beauty, they are still well proportioned and lofty, and even grand in their internal proportions. The screen that separates the choir from the nave is, as in other modern Greek churches, complete to the ceiling, and this of course takes off from the effect of the interior; but the northern or women's gallery is kept comparatively low, so that the eye takes in the whole of the rest of the roof. This is usually richly decorated with much gilding and good paintings, and in good taste. The carving of the stalls is old, and very good. The chief pictures on the screen are well painted, and offer nothing ridiculous or offensive to good taste, and the paving of the floor is rich. On the whole, these churches afford a far more pleasing notion of the so-called orthodox church than any I have seen. It must, indeed, be said, with reference to this creed, which is adopted by so large a section of Christians, that although like all systems that involve priestly tyranny, and teach what is practically the worship of created beings, there is a door open by which the mass of the people may be enslaved; still in the Greek church there is, if sought for, a sound basis of religious principle, and a presentable reason for most of the anomalies produced by time. The absence of any one recognised head of the church, possessed of political power, has tended, perhaps, to purify, while it has in no degree weakened priestly influence. Certainly no better reply could be given to those Roman Catholics who honestly believe in the religious superiority of their system, and yet uphold the territorial power of the Pope as necessary for the religious influence, than to point to the Patriarch of Constantinople, who since the time of Constantine has retained a mild and not injurious sway over the clerical appointments of the Greek church, and does not cease to be respected in spite of his poverty, and his total want of the smallest political influence.

It is difficult to understand why the Bishop of Rome should, so far as religion is concerned, lose any prestige, or be shorn of any of his most esteemed ecclesiastical rights and dignities, if those who take advantage of his position, and act in his name, should be prevented from misgoverning and urging to rebellion the people of Rome, who ask only to be allowed to select their own king, and are quite ready to respect and provide for the Pope as their spiritual chief.

But I have nothing to do here with the Italian question, and must apologise for a digression, which, however, seemed forced upon me on seeing the Greek church under one of its more favourable aspects. To return to the churches of Zante, I must repeat that they are on the whole the best and richest of those of the Ionian Islands.

The quantity of the precious metals, and of votive offerings, sometimes of great value, seen in some of these churches, is very large. The lamps, of which there are many, are all of silver, and are not only massive, and of enormous size, but of extremely beautiful workmanship. At least a dozen large lamps will be seen swinging in one church. The tombs of the favoured saints are also generally encased in silver plate; not very thick it is true; but thick enough to admit of embossing and engraving, in a style which is more than respectable. Slung on strings or in festoons, round the picture of a saint, are sometimes seen scores of rings, ear-rings, and other female ornaments, offered up for some supposed miracle. Miracles are, indeed, common enough among the votaries of this form of religion everywhere, and no one would venture to interfere with the public faith.

The great and most popular among the Christian saints of the Ionian islands has always been St. Spiridion, sometimes familiarly abbreviated to Spiro. His body is said to have been brought from Constantinople to Corfu in 1489; but it is supposed to have been preserved at Constantinople since the seventh century. All the islanders believe equally in his great power. He is supposed to walk the fields by night to inspect the crops as well as to superintend generally the sanitary condition of the island. After some of his expeditions his feet are exhibited to the faithful sprinkled with soil, or dust, as a proof of his peregrinations. Other saints are indeed recognised, but none is so powerful as he, and therefore it is not wonderful that churches are dedicated to him, and his picture is everywhere suspended.

In Zante, as in the other islands, the belfry, or campanile, is usually detached from the church. Some of these towers are picturesque, and most of them are Italian in style, and of comparatively modern date. The reason assigned for their being detached is, that in case of earthquake the bells, if they fall, shall not destroy the roof of the church, and involve the destruction of the church.

One of the principal churches of Zante bears the name of the *Phaneromene* (the Presentation of Christ in the Temple). It is of admirable proportions, being nearly a double cube between the narthex, or women's portion, at the west end, and the choir, separated by a lofty screen, at the east. The style of the decoration is Byzantine, and is rich and pleasing, fully equal to anything usually seen in Roman Catholic churches, and in a purer and better taste. The absence of side altars greatly simplifies and improves the appearance of the interior, and the more so as the Greek churches are rarely large. So, again, the range of stalls, not occupied as seats, but simply to give a certain relief while standing, has a good appearance, though little calculated for comfort. Most of these stalls are contrived to make seats when the service is not proceeding, but I have rarely seen them so used. In the Zante churches the women's part is closely screened off with lattice-work, and is not large.

Except the churches, there are no public buildings

in Zante of any pretence to architectural style. The Resident's house is hardly so large as many private houses, and enters from a recess in a narrow back street. There are two clubs, and one of them at least I can describe as particularly well fitted and very comfortable in comparison with the casinos usually seen in continental towns. It contains a large newspaper-room, fair billiard-rooms, a well-furnished drawing-room, and a restaurant. The number of members is very considerable. There are also in Zante two locandas of a superior kind; one of them nearly equal to the hotels of Corfu. After saying that the Corfu hotels are intermediate between those of second-class Italian and Spanish towns, it is not much praise to the Zantiot houses of entertainment to place them next in order; but they certainly deserve no higher position. At the best hotel the sleeping accommodation is very poor, and the eating much worse. With regard to the other, said to be generally frequented by the English merchants who come to the island, and kept by one Gabriel Macree, all I can say in its favour is, that my bedroom was tolerably clean and free from insects. I would, however, strongly advise any one who has occasion to put up there for a time, to bargain beforehand as to the price of everything. In my own case, on asking for the bill, I received a document in which a certain total was mentioned for food and lodging, without any details being given. The amount seemed extravagant, and the price of a horse hired for half a day was about as much as it would have been in

England. I therefore requested further particulars,
and after a long time another bill appeared, showing
a reduction of nearly twenty per cent in the price of
accommodation and food, and an increase of ten per
cent in that of the horse hire. Demurring rather to
this, I was told to pay what I liked, and I found, on
inquiry of a native, that the first price charged for the
horse was half as much again as it ought to have
been, and no doubt the same was the case with everything else.

Zante has two or three manufactures besides its
large exports of fruit, oil, and wine. The silk-worm
is cultivated, and silk made in small looms in the city.
The quality of this silk is good; but the retail price is
not low. The designs are not altogether those of the
European countries. The colours are very good.
Soap is manufactured for exportation. A large quantity of salt is also made.

Behind the city the ground rises rapidly to a range
of low hills richly wooded, and covered with well-
built country-houses occupied by the principal merchants. The road up to the ridge of this hill is
charming, abounding with beautiful little peeps of
the sea, and dotted here and there with cultivated
gardens. I entered one of the houses belonging to a
gentleman to whom I had an introduction. The
views from the terrace and balcony could not be
surpassed for a mixture of cultivated valleys and
distant hill, with the sea at no great distance, and
the town below. Another of these houses is placed
on the brow of the hill looking towards Greece in one

direction, and along the east coast of Zante to Cephalonia, the Black Mountain finely closing in the landscape. These houses are large, richly furnished, and in excellent taste. No doubt the merchants of Zante, who include many gentlemen of the best families of the island, are still able to do much very profitable business in spite of the sufferings and losses incurred by the bad crops, of which there have been so many for some years past.

At the other end of the hill, on which are these country-houses, is the Castle, a large enclosure adjoining a village constructed by the English shortly after the occupation during the French war. It is regularly but not very strongly fortified, and includes barracks, in which a considerable number of troops can be housed. The position is good, and commands the town and harbour; but there are few guns mounted, and most of these are worthless. The castle does not seem now regarded as defensible, but it is occupied by the force stationed in the island.

A good view of the island is obtained from the castle, and most of its peculiar features can be recognised. A long sweep of rich valley extends from the sea to the south-west in Chieri Bay, to the sea in the north-east, in another bay, where are the Salines and the Grease Spring. The rather lofty detached and picturesque mountain of Scopos stands out prominently opposite the town, enclosing the bay on the south side. The higher peak of Vrachiona is seen to the right among the mountains of the western and north-western district. Low hills extend along the east coast to the north, and gradually die away. Opposite, at a distance of twenty miles, are the low shores of the Morea.

The eye is soon attracted by one of those appearanecs so common and so characteristic of the Ionian Islands; a low flat tract, partly covered with water. The ever-recurring swamp is recognised, and one naturally and inevitably turns to one's companion, with an inquiry as to the salubrity of the climate. It is all that can be desired; but—there is fever. It does not seem to occur to a native of these islands, that a country is the worse for occasional but constantly recurring malarious fevers, or that it is worth while to endeavour to ward them off. In other respects Zante may be healthy enough; but as the fevers are the cause of nearly half the deaths that occur, this is not saying a great deal.

Much of the district towards the south-west near Chieri Bay is flat and swampy, and in the spring, when I saw it, was partly under water. The whole is cultivated, and good roads are constructed across the valley in various directions, to the villages and farmhouses in the plains. There are a few villages also among the mountains; but these are only reached by mule trucks, and are not always in a very pleasant state to travel over.

The character of the Zantiots is, and always has been, somewhat different from that of the other Ionians. The people are singularly lively, active, and quick tempered, and are excitable, even compared with other inhabitants of the Mediterranean shores and islands. Crimes of violence are more common among them than elsewhere in the islands; but all classes are agreeable in their manners and industrious, possessing many useful and amiable qualities. They are both more speculative, and spend money more freely than the inhabitants of the other islands, and thus it is that Zante presents so much that is favourable in agriculture and trade. Before the vine disease had attacked the currant vines, many of the proprietors were rich, and lived luxuriously. At that time they lost largely, and are only beginning to recover themselves.

Much good feeling was shown by the people of this island on the occasion of the marriage of the Prince of Wales. Besides the public illuminations, and many private entertainments, including a handsome ball given by one of the principal gentry, the people generally put on their festal dresses, appearing in the town in their costumes. This is the more worthy of remark, because there was at the time a certain amount of excitement, on account of the turn affairs had taken in Greece, and the necessity there had been to check public demonstration on the subject of annexation.

Even at the present time the ladies of the higher classes of Zante are somewhat secluded from general society; but till within the last few years they were rarely seen, especially before marriage. Mr. Goodison, writing in 1820, speaks of the windows of the houses being " defended by a thick lattice work, which projects into the street, giving them more the appearance of so many prisons, or houses of correction."

He adds, "a Greek lady is hardly visible anywhere."
This has now changed, and a number of Zantiot
ladies have intermarried with English officers and
merchants; but even now the balls and parties are
thinly attended compared with the number of young
ladies in the town, and compared also with what is
seen in the other islands.

CHAPTER XIV.

THE great lion of Zante, the phenomenon which every stranger is at once taken to see, and the site of innumerable pic-nics, from the time of Herodotus to this present year, A.D. 1863, is an excursion to the Bay of Chieri, and the pitch wells that there continue to flow.

Thither canters off as rapidly as a horse will carry him, the young middy, who has obtained a day's holiday. Thither proceed cavalcades of gay, beautiful Zantiot damsels, escorted by the officers of the garri-

son, and headed by the highest civilian authorities in
the island—thither now and then resorts the curious
islander—and thither, also, in more sober guise proceeds the rare traveller, desirous of investigating the
curious natural history of the spot. It is beyond
doubt a trip of great interest, and though often already
described, I must not pass by so important a matter
in my account of Zante.

The position of these celebrated wells is about nine
or ten miles to the south-west of Zante, in a corner
of the island, on the further side of Chieri Bay, between the high range of the west coast, and a lower
flanking range in the interior. The road crosses the
level plains and valley of Zante for about five miles.
All this is alluvial, and is no doubt rapidly increasing the swamp that stretches continually further out
into Chieri Bay. It has sometimes been considered a
great mistake that the Venetians, when they established themselves in Zante, did not take advantage of
this fine natural harbour. By running a mole from
the south-western headland, perfect shelter might have
been secured, and the space, as will be seen by the
map, is large enough to receive a fleet. Perhaps, in
this case, however, the Venetians selected the ground
for the city with more judgment than has been shown
by those who criticise them. Unless drained with
great care, and many precautions taken, a large city
in the swamp near the pitch wells would certainly not
be healthy, and sweet water might have failed in dry
seasons. At any rate, the present site of the town is
pretty enough, and pleasant enough, and far enough

from the worst of the marshes, to make it very undesirable to think of moving it. It is true that the
harbour is small, and rather open, especially to the
north and east; but there is not much lost, for the
harbour, small as it may seem, is amply sufficient for
the trade, and the trade is already larger in proportion
than in any of the islands.

After crossing the plain the path to the pitch wells
diverges from the main road, passing a small village
whose name, Lithake (λίθαξ rocky) sufficiently indicates that we have reached the rocks. Here, indeed,
the limestone begins, but the hills are low though
rugged, and are separated by valleys from each other
and from the principal mountain range. Passing then
through execrable stony paths with great mud holes,
in any of which a horse might break his leg, and
skirting the hills, we approach the coast before proceeding further west. The path crosses a rocky and
beautiful ravine, through which water was running at
the time of my visit. The ravine is water-worn and
interesting, laying bare some of the features of the
geology of the district. Its walls are vertical and
broken, and at one point they close in and almost
form an arch over a dark, deep, quiet pool, from
which issues a considerable stream of water. The
pool is shaded and entirely overhung with long tufts
of the maiden-hair fern, which also grows plentifully in
the other parts of the ravine. There is a fine rough
conglomerate, in thick bands, pretty heavily inclined
towards the north, beneath which the water comes
out. A large mass of the conglomerate rock over-

hangs and forms a roof to the pool, and the reflexion of the sun on the water, slightly rippling from the rise of the spring, dances charmingly on the under side of this flat surface. I have rarely seen anything more beautiful of its kind. One might fancy it a place for Diana and her troop, or for the Naiads to disport themselves. In the absence of such an appropriate use, it occurred to my companion that, if there were time, it would be a delicious spot for a dip, and indeed no more delightful bath could be imagined. Above the pool the ravine closes in, and is only continued at a much higher level. The rocks around are covered with myrtle and oleander, broom, and numerous flowering herbs. There are also many beautiful ferns. The water issuing from the foot flows over the rocks, and occasionally falls in a broken stream. The quantity seems, however, to diminish as it goes on, the water being lost under the large, loose blocks of stone that abound in the bed of the ravine.

The bay of Chieri is well seen from the path as we approach the valley of the pitch wells. It presents a noble sweep, enclosed by the high land of Scopos and the peninsula beyond on the one side, and by the western coast range, also projecting into the sea, on the other. Within it are a few islands: one, named Maratonisi, is high and prominent, and is nearly opposite the wells; others, flatter, are more towards the middle and eastern side of the bay. The high island is now called Goat island, from a trick played on an officer of the garrison not long ago. This gentleman being very fond of sport, sometimes indulged in it to the annoyance of the landowners. A certain Zantiot one day took an opportunity in the Club to compliment him on his shooting, and ask him if he had ever shot the wild goats on this little island. "Oh! dear no; he had no idea that there were any.". "Well," said the wily Zantiot, don't talk about it, or you will have no chance; but just take a boat over to the island one day and try." Our sportsman fell into the trap, and very soon made arrangements for a day's chamois hunt. He landed in the island, and climbing the rather steep, rocky cliff, soon saw a few goats feeding on the scanty herbage. Naturally enough, they were rather shy and endeavoured to get out of sight of the stranger. It was in vain. One of them soon fell a victim; but the others, luckily, escaped for the time. He returned with his spoil, but said nothing about his luck. A day or two afterwards, a gentleman (not the informant) stopped him in the street, and said, very politely, "Pray go and amuse yourself on my island whenever you like, but *please don't shoot the goats.*" The proprietor had put the goats there for their summer feed, and had no idea they were to be treated as *feræ naturæ*.

A little further on we came in view of the low, flat, marshy ground where are the pitch wells. It is entirely enclosed on three sides, and quite open to the sea. The whole surface is barely above the sea level, and is intersected with very numerous wide drains, rendering it difficult to cross. Without the drains it would, however, be under water. All the ground is spongy, and the water in the drains is rippled if one jumps upon the bank.

Within this space there are at present two pits that yield pitch. It is probable that many more might be opened, and a much larger quantity extracted if it were worth while. One, much larger, has probably been modified. The principal pit now is about eight feet in diameter and three feet deep, and a stream of clear, sweet water issues from it. In the pit the water is about a foot or eighteen inches deep, and is said not to change in any respect all the year round. From a part of the bottom of the pit, perhaps about half the whole area of the bottom, the bitumen appears to rise, coming up in very large black bubbles, which do not easily break. The surface of the water is covered with a thin iridescent coating of mineral oil. The bitumen is so tough and pasty that it does not rise unless disturbed. When, however, any quantity is removed, it is immediately replaced, and the fragments float. It is usual to lift out the bitumen and place it in other pits to stand for a while before putting it in barrels. The surrounding soil is made up partly of bitumen, and the air is also impregnated, especially in the early morning and towards sunset. Another pit, smaller, and not now used, lies further in amongst the tangled growth of the swamp. The water here is brackish and stagnant. There are several small pits without water at hand, into which the pitch is put.

On an examination of the gas occupying the bubbles in the pitch, Dr. Davy found that it consisted

chiefly of light carburetted hydrogen, perhaps mixed
with a little nitrogen and oxygen, and also of a small
quantity of carbonic acid gas. The bitumen was carefully examined by the same authority, and he states it
to contain 30 parts of volatile oil and naphtha, 43 parts
of petroleum, and 27 of asphalt, or bitumen, of higher
specific gravity than water. The quantity of mineral
tar yielded in the course of the year is now inconsiderable.

" Tar is occasionally observed on the surface of the
sea in the neighbourhood of the springs. In the
month of October, I saw a considerable extent of sea
between Maratonisi island and Chieri Point covered
with an iridescent pellicle of petroleum, and streaked
with lines of pitch. This was at the distance of about
three miles from the shore of the valley of the pitch
springs. The water there was very black, as if the
bottom were black (giving the idea of a stratum of
pitch); the depth was considerable, exceeding twenty
fathoms, but how much more I had not the means of
ascertaining. Similar pellicles of petroleum were seen
on other parts of the sea; but not to the same extent.
Whether they arise from springs in the bottom under
water, or are derived from land springs conveyed by
the little stream which flows from the valley into the
sea, it is not easy to decide; the first seems most
probable." *

There is no use made of this pitch at present, nor
has it ever been determined whether the supply ob-

tainable is large enough to be of economic importance. That it might be used to obtain illuminating
and lubricating oils by distillation at low temperature,
does not seem to have occurred to any one; but it is
evident that if it could be so employed, a very important manufacture might be established. It is by
no means unlikely that by carrying on operations on a
larger scale, and boring to some depth, a somewhat
different product would be obtained, although I
hardly agree with Dr. Davy as to the probability
of finding a bed of bitumen, asphalt, or coal. There
is certainly lignite in the neighbourhood, and no
doubt it may have something to do with the pitch
springs.

It is a prevalent opinion that a communication exists between the pitch springs and the sea. The existence of springs that ooze out beneath the waters
of the adjacent bay renders it probable that so far
as level is concerned, there is no reason why this
should not be the case. That foreign bodies falling
into the wells on the marsh are carried out to sea by
some under-current, requires much more proof than
has hitherto been given to render it credible. It is
true that Herodotus makes the assertion, but that
wonderful old narrator of marvels is not always an
authority in matters of fact.

It is also the opinion of those who are familiar with
the island that earthquakes affect the pitch springs.
That this is the case where a sea wave is produced,
may well happen, especially if the bitumen oozing out
under water is connected with that welling up on the

shore. Direct evidence in proof of this opinion is, however, also wanting.

As interesting for comparison with the foregoing account, I will here add the notice that appears of these wells in Herodotus. There would seem to be little difference except in the size of the wells, and it is said. that there still exist remains of circular walls at greater distance from the sea than the present walls, which agree with the dimensions given by the old Greek.

" At this place (Zacynthus) are a number of lakes, the largest of which is 70 feet in circumference, and of the depth of two *orgyiæ*. Into this water they let down a pole, at the end of which is a bunch of myrtle; the pitch attaches itself to the myrtle, and is thus procured. It has a bituminous smell, but is in other respects preferable to that of Pieria."— HERODOTUS, *Melpomene*, cxcv.—[*Beloe's Translation*].

Earthquakes in Zante are not uncommon, and are sometimes very severe. There have been none of importance very lately, and perhaps for this reason the next may be serious. It is recorded that a very great earthquake in the year 1514 rent the castle hill from top to bottom. Marks of great disruption are still evident, and they are probably preserved and yearly increased by the action of the rain on the soft marl of which the hill is composed. The last great earthquake took place so lately as 1840, and the following account by Sir Howard Douglas, the Lord High Commissioner of that date, will be read with interest.

Writing from Zante, on the 6th of November, Sir Howard Douglas states:—" I arrived on the morning of the 30th ultimo, half an hour after the occurrence of a dreadful calamity, which has irreparably injured the whole town and island. At half-past nine o'clock on that morning, when about three miles from the land, an extraordinary concussion was suddenly experienced, agitating violently the vessel and the machinery, and which it was quite evident was occasioned by an earthquake. The reality of this apprehension was immediately confirmed by the noises that were heard, and by several clouds of dust which were seen ascending from various points of the coast, and which were occasioned by the falling in of cliffs, and other effects of a violent shock. On approaching the port, the effects upon the buildings of the town were plainly visible. Several houses in the outskirts greatly injured; part of the prison unroofed, the body of the building cracked, and one of the outer walls thrown down. Onwards the ruins appeared more numerous; and, when we arrived in the port, so as to have a near view of the whole town, I perceived that a terrible and general calamity had fallen upon Zante.

" On proceeding through the streets, I found them filled or encumbered with ruins; the bulk of the population still out of doors; the tiles, and the shattered and disunited portions of houses fallen, or ready to fall; very few of the houses, not even those most solidly built, had escaped external and apparent injury; and, even where such was not visible, had suffered greatly internally, in their furniture, by the concussion.

" The consternation of the inhabitants was extreme; for I had scarcely entered the town when a considerable shock was felt, the dismay and confusion occasioned by which it is impossible for me to describe; and as I proceeded through the streets, constant successions of minor shocks were felt, which continued for many days; and here I may add, in order to show your lordship how incessant has been the alarm and consternation, that, up to the 4th instant, ninety-five shocks of earthquake, some very severe, were counted since the first great crash.

" I regret to acquaint your lordship that the devastation is still more general in the country than in the city, and that the distress is, and will be, infinitely greater; and the means of the inhabitants, whose huts and houses have so generally been destroyed or injured, afford little or no resources for them to fall back upon."

Sir Howard Douglas mentions the villages which he visited, all of them on, or bordering on the plain, and all of which he found had suffered more or less. They were the following:—Litakia, Pisimonda, Musaki, Romiri, Lagopado, Melinado, Bujato, Makiradi, Pigadakia, and Catastari, which had suffered slightly; Sottiro, St. Demetrio, Karkiesi, Draka, and Sculikado, which had suffered severely, the last-named most of all. The state in which it was found is described in the following extract.

" I then proceeded to Sculikado, and there I wit-
nessed a scene of desolation and ruin, of consternation
and misery, far exceeding any I had previously seen
in the course of these visits; and I may well add, in
the whole course of my life. This village, containing
a population of about 800 persons,. is nothing but a
heap of ruins; not a house untouched, and very few
left standing. In all the other villages, even those
most injured, there is covering left, which will enable
the more fortunate to show their hospitality and feel-
· ing for their unfortunate neighbours, by giving them
shelter; but here in Sculikado there is no shelter left.
The site of the village is on a small hill, no part of
the surface of which is free from ruins. The furniture, the beds, buried in the ruins of the houses; the
devastation is so great, that no parts of the fabric, in
the shape of planks, are in a state to form fresh cover.
I noted the cases of utter destitution; they are numerous. I intimated to those who had some resources
of property, though at present none in ready money,
that they might seek relief, in the shape of loan, out
of the sum decreed by the senate; and I acquainted
the Capo, that if they would send to the town a sufficient number of horses to carry out seven or eight
hundred planks for the use of the destitute, and to
form covering for them, I would direct that these
should be supplied gratuitously. This has been done;
small sums of money have, by my directions, been
dispensed to the most destitute for immediate necessities, and to enable them to get shelter put together,

should their fellow-townsmen either refuse to labour for them gratuitously, or be too much involved in distress themselves to assist them."

Sir Howard Douglas, referring to the amount of injury occasioned, states:—"The material injury which the island of Zante sustained is extensive, and cannot be rated at less than £300,000 sterling. No notice is taken of any damage occasioned in the mountain villages; from whence it may be inferred that, as heretofore, they escaped the destructive effect of the shock."

Except near the castle, where the effect of the earthquake is constantly renewed by the rains of every season, there is nothing now in the islands to mark any of these sad events. The houses are built for the most part much higher than in Santa Maura, and the villages certainly are not likely to show marks of injury of any kind beyond the year in which it happens.

Although the climate of Zante is pleasant, it is warmer than that of the other islands, and seems much more subject to thunderstorms. This is no doubt intimately connected with the strong contrast exhibited by the prevalent winds in respect to moisture. The north winds are exceedingly dry; the south winds loaded with moisture. The north-east, or scirocco, wind is especially damp, and affects the senses and spirits to a remarkable degree. Dr. Davy states that on one occasion, on the 8th August, 1824, at 1 p.m., he observed a difference of 32 degrees Fah. between the dry and moist thermometer exposed to

the wind. The dry thermometer stood at 99 degrees,
and the wind was west-north-west. The scirocco
rarely raises the thermometer above 84 or 85 degrees, and the difference between the dry and moist
thermometer is then seldom more than 5 degrees.
But the hot, dry wind at 99 degrees is less oppressive than the scirocco at 85 degrees, though, in the
former case, everything metallic burns, and the furniture cracks with explosive violence. With the air
in such a state the sensation of heat is not disagreeable; the skin is dry, and exercise may be
taken in the open air with pleasure and alacrity,
and with little feeling of fatigue. With the scirocco,
on the other hand, one is bathed in perspiration;
one feels as if in a vapour-bath, and life is almost
a burden.

The clearness of the air is extremely variable in
Zante; with the wind from the south-east there is
no distant view; the air is thick, hazy, and gloomy.
The change from the south-east to north-east, or
north-west, lifts the curtain and presents a glorious
panorama of the Morea, with the distant mountain
lands of northern Greece. The amount of radiation
is, of course, greatly affected by the clearness of
the air.

On the whole the climate of Zante is particularly
adapted to the culture and early ripening of the
currant-grape, although in this respect parts of Cephalonia are said to be even superior. The breadth of
ground under cultivation in Zante is, however, much
greater in proportion to the size of the island, and the

cultivation itself is careful and systematic, and very successful.

The currant vine differs essentially in its habits as well as in the time of ripening its fruit from the grape vine, and as it is more carefully and systematically managed in Zante than elsewhere, the present is the fittest place to describe its culture. Only having visited the islands during the spring, my account must be for the most part derived from others ; but I believe it will be found substantially correct.

The soil required for this vine is richer and more open, and the situation more sheltered than is the case with the grape vine. The gypseous marls, both in Zante and Cephalonia, are considered preferable to limestone, as they admit of the roots penetrating to a greater depth. Calcareous marls containing a little gypsum are, however, almost as good. Low situations, where water can be introduced, are desirable, for, without water, the tree does not flourish, and most of the plantations are encircled by ditches and mounds of earth, the ditches having rough sluices to retain the water when needed. The heavy rains generally fall in October and November after the crop is removed, and thus immediately after the harvest the field work begins, by putting in order these provisions for irrigation. In some places the mounds are planted with aloe, and this makes an excellent fence; but fences are not very common.

The vines are planted regularly, in rows about three or four feet apart. They are propagated either from

shoots obtained after the vine has been cut away
below the ground, or else by grafting currant vines
on the stock of a grape vine. In the former case the
shoots spring up from the old tree very vigorously
and rapidly, and in December are cut off, covered
up, and kept till spring for planting. They do not
bear before about six years. The grafts come more
rapidly into bearing, being ready in three years,
and, where possible, are preferred. The grafting is
effected in spring on the trunk of the old vine, a foot
below the surface of the ground, to which depth the
vine is amputated. " Two or three perpendicular
incisions are made in the stalk with a chisel near
the bark, into which the last year shoots of the currant vine are inserted, of such a length as to have
two or three eyes, or buds, above the surface: then
some moist marl is applied to the engrafted part, it
is wrapped in leaves and bound with rushes, and
the earth is thrown into the pit."

The pruning is done at intervals, and is a delicate
operation, requiring judgment. In December the
trees are cleaned, the dead, weak, and unpromising
branches are removed, and a few vigorous branches
of the last season are selected for the coming season,
attention being paid to their relative position so as
not to crowd the tree, as well as to the strength of
the shoots and their buds. Towards the end of
February the remaining branches are cut further
back to ensure active vegetation. Every bud, or eye,
is said to throw out three branches, one large middle
fruit-bearing branch and two lateral ones which are

barren, unless the middle branch is removed. Not more branches are left than about three or four, which are considered as many as the roots can nourish. The cuttings are profitable, being sold for fire-wood, and the quantity is so large that they are said to pay the expense of pruning.

The irrigation of the currant grounds takes place from the end of October to the end of December. After that it is only necessary to keep the ground moist.

When the second pruning takes place in February, the ground is moved about the roots of the vine, being taken away from the roots and [heaped round so that each tree is in a small basin. This is the usual method, but under certain circumstances the reverse is done; the ground is heaped round the trunk, and pits are left between the vines. In either case the watering the roots and the exposure of the soil to the air, are the objects. In April, the ground is turned up deeply and manured if necessary. It is then levelled.

When once the growth has commenced, it is very rapid, and as soon as the young shoots appear, the vineyards are closed, and great care is taken that the ends of the shoots and the buds should not be injured. The leaf is hardly fully out till the middle of April, and in July the first fruit is ripe enough for the table. It is then described as very luscious, highly-flavoured, and a delicious fruit; but it is soon cloying to the taste. From this time to the middle of August, when the vintage takes place, the greatest

possible interest is felt in the plantations. Rain at
this time is especially dangerous. The plantations
are watched, both by help of dogs who give notice
of the approach of every one, and by armed men
from look-outs constructed for the purpose. The
crop is of great value, and is necessarily much exposed, as the fences are very imperfect.

When ripe the fruit is black, and in that state it
is carried to the drying-ground, where it is exposed
to the sun and air, and frequently turned till dry.
In case of rain at this time, frames are provided to
protect the fruit on the ground. Being then separated from the stalk, it is put into bags and carried
into the city to the store houses of the merchants. It
is there closely packed in casks, and is fit for exportation. The plain or valley of Zante is chiefly under
currant cultivation.

Since the years when the attack of the _öidium_ proved
so nearly fatal to the hopes and prospects of the currant grower, as well as the cultivator of grapes for
wine, Zante has continued to suffer, and the disease
has rarely or never been quite absent from the island.
The only remedy applied, is to dust the growing and
ripening fruit with a certain quantity of brimstone.
The brimstone is ground in mills to the finest powder,
and by contrivances, invented for the purpose, is blown
upon the fruit. Much judgment is said to be required
in the application; and after all, there is a general
impression that the fruit never attains the purity of
flavour it used to possess. The crops of the last season
(1862) were, however, both large and of excellent
quality.

Owing to the competition that has arisen on the main land of Greece, and especially in the neighbourhood of Patras, the currant trade is not so profitable to the islands as it used to be; and the rather heavy export duty to which it is subjected, both encourages smuggling and bears heavily on the grower. The price of currants in the foreign market is not, however, likely to be reduced, so far as to interfere with the cultivation. The consumption seems to increase; and there is always at hand the means of utilising the crop by the manufacture of wine, to which the currant-grape is well adapted. The quality of the wine thus made is peculiar, and is, beyond a doubt, capable of improvement; and there is ample demand for any quantity.

The grape vine is little cultivated in Zante, having given place to the currant in most properties. It yields a rich, luscious, and strong wine, which, when carefully made, has an excellent flavour and bears keeping. A remarkable Muscat wine is made in small quantities. This is quite equal to the finest Lunel.

The olive is rather extensively cultivated in Zante, and is treated much more in Italian than Greek fashion. It is pollarded, and kept down to a convenient height. The ground is carefully manured. The fruit is beaten off the trees while green, and then salted. It is carefully handled; but the result is a kind of oil of only middling quality.

The common fruits of the table are both excellent and very abundant in Zante. There is a kind of sweet orange cultivated there and in some of the Greek islands, but not elsewhere in the Ionian group. The summer and autumn fruits are said to be delicious. The island is celebrated, even to a proverb, for its flowers, which are certainly extremely beautiful and varied.

From Zante, pleasant excursions may be made in various directions. The ascent of Scopos is one of these, and occupies a day very pleasantly. There is much to see on the slope, and something on the rocks beyond the hill. The height of Scopos is about 1500 feet. It is reached by following a pleasant path along the sea side for two or three miles, and then making a steady and steep ascent through brushwood and rocks, presenting a variety of beautiful views, to a platform near the summit, which has been levelled in a series of terraces, and is well cultivated. On this upper terrace is a picturesque monastery, charmingly placed among trees and shrubs, and in the midst of gardens and fields. Beyond the monastery is a huge boss, looking like a gigantic boulder, though apparently a projecting mass of conglomerate, from which softer shales have been washed away. It is the summit of the mountain and the real *look out* which gives its name to the whole.

Scopos is one of those isolated, well shaped, and picturesque elevations, that are rarely seen, and that cannot easily be mistaken or forgotten. There is nothing near it. It rises from the sea on three sides, and from a swamp scarcely above the sea on the fourth side. It is composed of limestone and gypsum, with a certain proportion of marl, and thus is kept permanently of the peculiar pyramidal form, which is the result of weathering on its material. The rock of which it is chiefly formed is stratified and highly inclined. The conglomerate, forming the odd, grotesque summit, consists of pebbles of limestone and a kind of marble, and angular flints. As it has been suggested that the mountain is of volcanic origin, I may say, that I did not discover the smallest trace of anything that could justify such an assumption. It is part of a mass of aqueous rock that has been elevated and water or weather-worn during and after elevation. It owes its pyramidal form to the general softness of its material, and its grotesque summit to the accident of a small local deposit, cemented into a hard conglomerate,—probably owing to some spring or the infiltration of water under peculiar circumstances, and only partially removed during the weathering.

The view from Scopos in clear weather must certainly be very fine,—including the whole of the lower land of Zante, reaching to Cephalonia and the islands adjacent, and also including the greater part of the Morea. Looking down on the town of Zante and its castle hill behind, and carrying the eye along the cliff to Acroteria, the whole of the bay of Zante is displayed; and beyond this first low range are the other low hills of the east of the island, crowned with small villages or isolated buildings. These strike the eye, and contrast with the garden-like appearance of the plain and hill sides, thus adding much to the beauty. Most of the houses being whitewashed, they are very prominent, even at the distance of many miles.

At the back of Scopos are bituminous shales, and

deposits of sulphur among the gypsum. These have never been utilised; nor are their conditions very strictly determined. My own stay in the island was too short to allow of my examining them in detail.

The general aspect of Zante, so far as the great plains are concerned, is very uniform. The whole is under similar and complete cultivation; the soil is rich and abundant; there is little water; and the roads are excellent. But the moment we pass from the main lines of road the case is very different. In order to reach a house near one of the small villages in the middle of the hill district on the west, I was taken in his own carriage by my kind friend, the Count Nicolo Lunzi, across a series of ploughed fields and through narrow lanes, scarcely wide enough to allow our conveyance to pass. Arrived at the house, we found that friendly reception which I have nowhere seen more charmingly illustrated than in the Ionian islands. It is indeed worth a visit to the islands to be thrown into a society so primitive, and exercising so unreservedly the ancient rites of hospitality on the largest scale. In this case we had the guidance of a member of the family. The house was one of those common enough in the country,—the residence of a family long settled in the island, and always cultivating the hereditary estates. Parts of several generations were here to be found. The old, old grandfather and his older sister, who rarely went out of the one room in which they lived—the not very young members of the next group, who managed the household—the active but almost middle aged third series—and the children of all ages of the fourth. The house was moderately large, with many rooms, chiefly on the upper floor. The rooms were small, except a sort of upper hall or gallery, occupying the middle of the house, and to which the stairs opened. All the wood work was black with age. It might have been oak or olive, but the grain was not to be seen. The sitting room was very small indeed, and rather crowded with furniture, including a kind of escritoire and a sofa. Two bed rooms, of larger size, opened out of it. Both in this room and in the hall were suspended a number of pictures, evidently of Italian schools, and some of them certainly very superior to anything one would expect to find under such circumstances. It was curious enough to see classical subjects, treated possibly by pupils of Titian, suspended on the walls of a house in the interior of a Greek island, and representing the old Greek mythology. Besides the stories of Danae and Europa, there were also illustrations of sacred history, and one or two portraits. I noticed especially the portrait of an old woman, coarsely but powerfully painted. As I had nowhere else in the islands seen Venetian pictures among the household furniture, I was the more struck with it here. It is, doubtless, the remains of the property of the former proprietors, perhaps the ancestors of these very people; and I think it worth while to make especial mention of this collection of art treasures.

The female members of this family struck me as being more handsome than any I had seen elsewhere; and I believe this is a characteristic of Zante; but the style of beauty is not in the slightest degree classical. The younger women were of moderate height, and had pleasant, oval faces, with tolerable features and dark eyes. The older women seemed short, and were less horribly ugly than is usual. The men were good look-ing and pleasing to a remarkable degree, but not with the finer and high kind of male beauty that I noticed in Santa Maura.

As usual, my companion and I were no sooner seated than slight refreshments were served, consisting of coffee, biscuit, and sweetmeat. The biscuits, by the way, are incorrectly named; for they are only once baked, but they are then kept dry till they become like chips. In this state they are kept a long time, and are pleasant enough to soak in coffee.

As soon as we could escape from this hospitality, we (Count Lunzi and I, with two guides) started on the object of our expedition, which was to see some rocks that are quarried in a village among the moun-tains. As the road was up hill and I was rather tired, they provided me with a mule, and certainly she gave me the roughest ride I remember to have had. We proceeded along a narrow path, worn into a deep ra-vine by the feet of thousands of mules for centuries, who had in time worked holes large and deep enough to bury a child in. Just now these holes were full of mud; and my animal, which was large and powerful, and left to exercise its own judgment, stumbled and floundered on to my infinite disgust. Seated high on a pillow, and utterly unable to do more than hold on, I must have looked ridiculous enough; but I preferred

it to the tiresome and rough walk, and reached at
length the edge of a steep, narrow gorge, looking
down sixty or eighty feet to the bed of stream tumbling
over the white slate, partly laid bare by the stream,
partly quarried at the bottom. Opposite, and rising
vertically from the stream, was another broken cliff,
with tufts of vegetation jutting from it, and with trees
here and there rising from the smallest ledge of rock.
Overhanging the cliff was the straggling but not inconsiderable village of Langadachia. I do not doubt
that, like many other very picturesque places, this
village looked much prettier than it would have been
found comfortable; but it was certainly an object for
the artist, and gave a high idea of the general character
of the mountain scenery of Zante. The quarries I
had gone to see were of a peculiar, easily-splitting,
white stone, apparently tender and soft, but answering
admirably for ovens, inasmuch as they seem capable of
resisting entirely the action of heat. The picturesque
features of the district are greatly assisted by the presence of a conglomerate, consisting of rolled fragments
of limestone and flint cemented together. This conglomerate forms a capping of much softer rock, easily
undermined. As the lower rock is removed, the conglomerate falls, leaving always a precipitous face and
a large quantity of loose, hard rock, in the lower
ground.

The view of Zante towards sunset, from this part
of the island, is far more beautiful than any views
obtained from near the east coast. The warm tints
of evening lighting up the houses and small villages,

falling on the low but pretty hills, and marking the varieties of outline, give quite a different idea of the country than those obtained from the Castle Hill or Mount Scopos. There is no time of the day when the country towards the west and north-west looks really well from these points; for, during the afternoon, the sun completely dazzles the eye and renders it impossible to see anything; and in the early morning, when the sun is in the east, the lights are thrown unfavourably, and the much greater elevation of the land behind prevents the smaller elevations from being appreciated.

The mountain districts of Zante, towards the north and west, are little visited. They contain several monasteries, situated for the most part in sheltered nooks among the mountains, in parts where there is little vegetation, except the arbutus, the myrtle, the heath, and abundance of wild thyme. A little arable land and a large space of feeding ground for goats is almost all that belongs to these establishments; but the monks are hospitable and their habitations pleasant. Here and there, there are vineyards in terraces, the soil being kept up by the stone walls, but there are few houses, and those that are there seem merely stone huts to shelter cattle.

A few small villages are, however, to be found in this out-of-the-way part of the island, and near some of these it is said gold was formerly found. The scenery towards the sea is very fine, and in the cliffs are some caverns of great beauty.

In this part of the island is the mountain of Vrachiona, the most elevated mountain peak. It resembles San Salvador in Corfu, in having two principal summits, but they are not connected by a ridge. The ascent is easy, and the view from the summit pleasing but not striking.

Behind the village of Langadakia, already described, is one of those singular, closed valleys, of which mention has been made in describing Corfu and Santa Maura. It is about a mile long and nearly a quarter of a mile wide, in its widest part, and the greater part is cultivated and arable land. In winter it is converted into a lake, but in the dry season the water evaporates, leaving only the contents of a number of cisterns, sunk nearly in the middle of the plain to about twenty feet deep. It has been remarked, with regard to this valley, that the temperature is remarkably low there throughout the year. No doubt, the great amount of evaporation from its surface may account for this; and some of the adjacent valleys are also said to have ice every winter, probably for the same reason. The whole of the hill country on the west side of Zante is cool, and the change of climate, from the intense heat of the plains, is felt immediately on ascending. The absolute height is not very great; but the valleys are sheltered from the south-west and west, and thus lose the influence of the sun before its rays have obtained their greatest power.

Zante, in ancient times, was celebrated for its wood :— "Nemorosa Zacynthus." Even now, the eastern shores of the island are fringed with a certain amount of tree vegetation, almost entirely olive groves; but the ancient forests, if they existed, as they probably did, have long been destroyed. So far as the plains are concerned, the change is profitable; but on the western hills and valleys there is room for a large quantity of timber, which would doubtless improve the climate of the island for certain purposes. Whether it would make it more fit for the cultivation of the currant, is, however, more than doubtful.

As, in describing Corfu, I introduced the account of a native—the Baron Theotoki—whose imagination being more vigorous and cultivated than my own, has seen parts of his native island with eyes that pierce below the surface, and discover excellences not manifest to every one; so here, I may fitly conclude my account of Zante—the garden and flower of the Levant —by quoting a Sicilian author, who wrote at the close of the last century. He says :—:

" Ecco l' amena, la ridente valle del Zante, o a meglio dir' tutto il Zante. O detto che gareggerebbe con quello di Tempe, se non che vi manea un fiume cheto, che lento vi scorra, e la rinfreschi. Le zampogne de' pastori per animarla, ed i muggiti amorosi delle giovenche, e de' tori, un verde più costante e più vario, che non e quello degli ulivi e delle viti, lo smalto de' fiori, il canto degli uccelli, vi manea in fine il riso, il piacere, la cortesia de villani : le grazie delle conta· dine. Questa può dunque dirsi ricca, ma non bella: in effetto il sentimento ch' essa vi desta al primo aspetto svanice in un momento colla sorpresa che lo produce, eppure questo momento e così sensibile che merita bene un viaggio per provarlo."—*Viaggio di Scrofani in Grecia.*

There are no rivers worth speaking of in Zante. The bed of a torrent, which is dry in summer, conveys water through the middle of the plain, and empties it during and after the rainy season into the sea, a little to the south of the city. The stream crosses the road leading to Mount Scopos, where a single arch is thrown over it.

Zante is almost without any remains of antiquity. One of the small island chapels at Melinado, about six or seven miles from the town, is built on the site of an ancient temple, dedicated to Diana, and exhibits some shafts and bases of Ionic columns, and an inscription of little importance. With this exception, hardly anything has been found. Zante is, perhaps, of all the islands, the least interesting in its historical associations.

CERIGO.

This island is situated considerably to the south of Zante, and close to the main land of the Morea. Even now, with all the advantages of steam, it is not very accessible, as the town is on a precipitous rock, and there is no good harbour in the island. Moreover, the best harbour is not near the town, and the steamers appointed to touch there, only engage to do so if the weather is favourable.

Those acquainted by experience with Cape Matapan, and its frequent winds, are best aware how often the

steamer must pass by without landing its mails or
taking off any stray passenger who may be desiring to
leave his prison. So bad was the communication
formerly, however, that it is recorded of a certain
Resident who gave himself a holiday in England for
six months without asking leave, that he would have
returned without being found out, had not despatches
requiring attention arrived about a fortnight before he
did, and found no representative of the government
authorised to receive and reply to them. A general
order was, upon that experience, issued by the Foreign
Office, that if any Resident shall absent himself forty-
eight hours from the seat of his government without
permission from the Lord High Commissioner, he is
held *ipso facto* to have resigned his appointment.

Like Corfu and Ithaca, Cerigo is full of historic
and mythological interest. More than either does it
belong to the realms of romantic poetry. It is indeed
the ancient Cythera.

> " 'Twas on these shores as ancient poets sing,
>   What time light zephyrs woo'd the infant spring,
>   Immortal Venus rose in glowing pride,
>   Bright as the day-star from the swelling tide."

But whatever its mythological history, and the importance of a number of small rocky harbours for boat
navigation in classical times, the poet is fully justified
in addressing it now.

> " Forsaken isle, around thy barren shore
>   Wild tempests howl and wintry surges roar."

It is, indeed, very rarely visited, and, except a couple

of caverns, and a curious breccia of bones contained in one of them, it seems chiefly remarkable for its honey, which is said to be excellent. The modern name, *Cerigo*, is of doubtful origin. The island is said to be rocky, mountainous, and mostly uncultivated. It is about twenty miles in length from north to south, and twelve miles across in the widest part. The people are industrious and frugal, and there is a certain amount of successful cultivation of corn and oil.

Two natural caverns in Cerigo have been described as particularly interesting. One is on the cliff, at the opening of a beautiful glen, through which a stream runs, working a few corn mills. The other is in a valley, about two hours' ride from the little town of Kapsáli, the capital of the island. Both contain stalactites, and one of them abounds with fossil bones, buried under stalagmite. The capital stands on a narrow ridge in the south of the island, acessible only by a narrow path, steep and winding, and commanded by a conical mound.

CERIGOTTO is a small island to the south-east of Cerigo, and part of the same government. It lies half way between Cerigo and Crete, being about twenty miles from either. It produces wheat for exportation.

CHAPTER XV.

THERE is frequent communication between Zante and
Corfu, most of the steamers touching at Argostoli,
where they remain some hours. When the weather
is favourable, the whole journey is extremely interesting, though unfortunately the night is preferred to the
day for the latter part of the passage. Zante, always
beautiful, and deserving its name as the flower of the
Levant, melts gradually into the horizon as we advance
northwards; while the gloomy mass of the Cephalonian
Black Mountain seems to rise higher and higher, and

closes the view towards the north. Except for this commanding elevation, the scenery of Cephalonia is less fine and less beautiful than that of Corfu, Santa Maura, Ithaca and Zante.

From Argostoli, with the wind in certain directions, it is not only possible but advantageous to pass between Cephalonia and Ithaca on the way to Corfu. Much more frequently, however, the outer course is taken; and the steamer passes to the west of the Cephalonian and Santa Maura shores, at too great a distance to enable the traveller to judge of the country. Even Sappho's Leap is left far away; and only a confused line of hill and mountain marks the picturesque cliffs of the south west of Santa Maura, the noble mountain of Stavrota, and the lower hills towards the north. After Santa Maura, we come in sight of Paxos, passing first its small dependency, Antipaxos; and soon the white cliffs of the south of Corfu are approached. Passing Lefkimo and the low hills of the south east coast, and leaving Santi Deca grouped with the other mountains in the middle of the island, we soon enter the harbour of Corfu.

The voyage from Corfu to Ancona is one which, under favourable circumstances, is performed in about forty hours. The Adriatic, however, is a treacherous sea, and even in fine weather is subject to an uneasy and restless swell—the result of storm in other parts of the Mediterranean. This swell is not only uncomfortable, but may greatly check progress. Leaving Corfu on the afternoon of a lovely April day, and steaming through the narrow channel between the

northern end of the island and Butrinto, nothing can
be imagined more beautiful, and no water can be more
calm.   We had brought fine weather with us, coming
from Zante, and there had been no change; but still,
when we had once lost the shelter of the island, our
vessel commenced those peculiar movements that are
too apt to cause unpleasant results to passengers, and
there was reason to believe that more than one of my
companions was soon paying his tribute to the ocean
god.   There was nothing, however, to try the temper
of old travellers; and the evening was lovely, so
that we could watch the sun set, gilding the snowy
caps of the Albanian mountains, until the moon rose
and tinted them with her silvery beams.   During the
night the sea continued troublesome, but next day it
gradually calmed, and we had a very favourable passage.   The course lies across the Adriatic, avoiding
all the islands on the Dalmatian shores; and there
was no incident till we could see the low, dark hills of
the Italian coast, contrasting with the much more distant but snowy mountain tops opposite.   These latter
were gradually lost, and Italy rose upon the horizon.

The accommodation on board the Austrian Lloyd's
steamer to Ancona I found excellent in every respect,
and the ship (the Europa) scrupulously clean.   The
cuisine did great credit to all concerned.   Like most
of the company's ships, the Europa was commanded,
and indeed manned, by the inhabitants of the Dalmatian towns, of which Ragusa seems that which gives
most of its sailors to Austria.

On first approaching Ancona from the sea, we come

rather suddenly on high land, which projects and forms a large bay to the south. Passing along close to the steep, white cliffs, streaked with marks of stratification and covered partially with brown vegetation, the much smaller open bay which forms the harbour of Ancona comes into view. The view of the town, built on rapidly rising ground, with two large forts, one to the north and the other to the south—two moles— a small but beautifully proportioned triumphal arch, erected by Trajan—the long line of quays, and the business and bustle of an important commercial port— all attract attention. The effect is very good from the sea; nor does the result of further and more intimate acquaintance greatly diminish the early impression. Without being large, or handsome, or grand— without strikingly good streets, public buildings, or houses—there is still an air of importance due to its position, and an appearance of life and growth, no doubt contrasting very strongly with its appearance under its late masters. Ancona is, perhaps, one of the cities of Italy that has most of all benefited by throwing off the Papal government, and getting rid of the protecting power of Austria. The rapid rate at which building is going on in all directions—the comfortable look and decent dress of the people— and the crowded state of the streets,—are all facts that help to prove this.

While, however, Ancona is well fitted to interest the traveller, let him take care of his own private affairs, as he will run the risk of emerging from the bustle with dissatisfaction. On landing, a score of lazy fellows seize hold of his luggage, each taking some one thing, and if possible loading a truck with a single portmanteau. For carrying a little luggage about fifty yards past the custom house to the nearest hotel, the *Hotel del Pace*, these good people had the conscience to ask eight francs of a small party of gentlemen travelling together. They received five, and were dissatisfied, though the whole luggage might well have been put on a small truck and carried up in five minutes by one, or at most two men.

We were rather surprised at the great leniency of the examination on entering the town, little aware that a much more serious and annoying operation of the same nature awaited us before leaving it by rail. Rarely have I seen so vexatious and needless a search. The contents of the smallest bag were turned out, and the long delay almost caused the whole party in the omnibus that conveyed us from the hotel to lose the train, and be detained another day in the town. It occurred to me, when too late, that the officers might have belonged to the old *régime*, and had recollections of the time when every traveller was expected to attend on such occasions with a couple of zwanzigers in his hand. The disappointment at not receiving this, which now, in most parts of free Italy, one really does not think of offering, was probably the reason of the unusual strictness towards all the party with whom I was travelling. However this may be, Ancona can never take up its due position among the sea ports of Italy, so long as this annoying and useless arrangement is continued. That in coming out of a town to proceed

by train, every carriage and every traveller is liable to
be made to lose the train, because he does not choose
to satisfy the rapacity of some harpies of the custom-
house, or even that every conveyance must be delayed
till proper examination has been made of all the personal luggage of the traveller, is so outrageous, that one
would suppose it needs only to be pointed out to be
corrected. It is also strange that no notice of this
important proceeding is given in the railway guide, nor
are passengers advised, as they ought to be, not to trust
to the diligence, but to take a carriage for themselves,
and allow an hour for the transit from the town to
the station to make sure of their places.*

The streets of Ancona are tolerably wide, and well
paved. The shops are well supplied, and the open
part of the town is clean. The less frequented streets
are indeed miserable enough; but this is perhaps to
be expected in a place that has so recently emerged
from Austrian despotism, acting in the name of the
Pope. It is pleasant enough to see the Italian uniform in every direction, and, though from want of
time and trouble to obtain an order from the Commandant, we could not be allowed to visit the castle,
yet the polite and regretful way in which the officer

* It is right to mention, that at the present time all the railway
arrangements at Ancona are abominable. There is only one person at
the ticket station, and he has no objection to cheat and worry travellers
in all sorts of petty ways. Merely that a number of persons behind
me might not lose the train, I was myself the subject of this piece of
rascality. I ought also to remark, that the Hotel del Pace was quite
as remarkable for extravagant charges and petty cheating as for the
goodness of its accommodation. It is, however, the best in the place.

of the guard on duty excused himself for not being able to admit us without, fully made up for the disappointment. The views from the fort, and generally from the hills around the town, are superb, both towards land and sea. The forts themselves are very large, and are no doubt strong.

The journey from Ancona to Bologna is both tedious and expensive for a railway trip. Every train stops a long while at every station, and the price is nearly equal to the average of the fast trains in England. Where there is any competition in England, the prices are in fact much lower with us than on this Italian line. Nearly seven hours and a-half are occupied in a journey of one hundred and twenty-six miles. Allowing the most reasonable modicum of luggage, the first class fare amounts to twenty shillings, and as in the German lines the fare is not more than two-thirds, and the rate of speed nearly double, while the French are also both much cheaper and much faster, the unreasonableness of the arrangements will be evident. It is to be hoped things will improve; but at present the line cannot be recommended.

From Ancona to Rimini the road, except for a short interval, skirts the coast. It then begins to cross Italy towards the north-west. The country passed is undulating, pleasing, and well cultivated, and affords a pleasant contrast to the severe and hard outlines of the hills and mountains in the Ionian Islands, and the gloomy foliage of the olive. Every thing looked lively, cheerful, and happy; and as one passes on through Bologna to Modena, and thence to Piacenza, and so on by Alessandria to Turin, one is inclined to look favourably on everything, and believe that the glory of Italy is on the return, and that the united country may long remain in peace under one constitutional government. The railway management is on a more satisfactory footing in the great plains of Lombardy than in the old papal states; but this is probably a natural and inevitable consequence of the much longer familiarity many of its people have had with the blessings of liberty.

One cannot help making a mental comparison between the Italians and the Greeks in traversing the former country, after having seen something of the latter. The national character handed down from old times is, perhaps, not so much altered as one would expect it to be, considering the extent to which the existing population of both countries is derived from a very mixed source. Of pure Greek blood in Ionia, as of the pure blood of old Rome in Italy, few, if any, can boast. Perhaps, if the actual ethnological history could be traced, there is more of it in both cases in a mixed state than one might at first suppose, but there cannot be a doubt that the overrunning of both countries by northern barbarians has penetrated deeply into every part of each. Still, some of the characteristics remain, and we may recognise them under various forms almost everywhere. And thus the Greek and Latin citizens, as each exhibits some of the strength and much of the weakness of his great ancestors, are to a certain extent comparable as their

forefathers were. The relative difference now traceable between the two is perhaps smaller than the absolute difference that has taken place in the case of either.
The Greek is the navigator; and, when convenient,
the smuggler, or even the pirate. The Roman both
cultivates the soil, and when he associates and lives in
towns, he organises and improves. The Greek assumes
the eastern, the Roman the western form of civilisation. Each of them loves liberty; but the Greek has
not yet advanced so far as the Italian in comprehending
its true nature in modern times, and perhaps is not
likely to do so. The cultivation everywhere, as well
as the style of the villages and smaller towns in the two
countries, and the appearance of the population, clearly
show how very far the Italian is in all respects the
more practical and accomplished citizen. As the Italian
becomes happier, he not only cultivates better and
earns more, but he evidently spends more, and enjoys
himself more openly. No longer now cowed and
melancholy, hoarding his little gains, and hardly
thinking it worth while to make a profit in any other
way than begging and cheating, even the lowest and
the poorest are more independent and more hopeful.
They also enjoy more luxuries.

It will always be a question how far the inhabitants
of the Ionian Islands and, indeed, of the Morea and
Epirus can properly be regarded as descendants of the
ancient Greeks. That Zante, Cephalonia, and Ithaca
were absolutely left without a single inhabitant by
the Turks, that most parts of Corfu and Santa Maura
were in like manner rendered desolate, and that the

old Greek element, if it exists at all, is in Leucadia, there is perhaps little doubt. But still, in the face of all that may be argued, it seems impossible that all the traditions and the language of an extinct people should be taken possession of by a mixed race who must have had some language of their own and some nationality of which to be proud. The inhabitants of Greece and the islands have long fully believed themselves to be Greeks. They are convinced that they retain some of the blood of that mighty people, few in number, but mighty in intellect, in their sense of freedom, and in arts:—that people who have been the heroes of all nations from the earliest history of civilization. Inferior they may be and are to their great ancestors in much that is essential, but the mass of the people are still not without many virtues, and the mode in which the Greeks of Greece long bore with the tyranny of their Bavarian king, and, having thrown it off, waited in patient resignation till their kingdom could be fully organised, must always be reckoned to their great credit. Few, if any people, who had been crushed under a government at once despotic, venal, and contemptible, for thirty years, and had by a sudden effort thrown off the incubus, could remain calm and expectant not only for weeks but months, while the great powers of Europe were shaping their future destiny. Greece and the Greek kingdom of the middle ages was hardly a reality, and could not stand; but an union of the peoples speaking the Greek language, holding the faith of the Greek Church, and imbued with the spirit of liberty, all

willing to combine, and anxious to become one strong
nation, is an idea that cannot be despised, and ought
not to be impossible.

It is not a pleasant reflection that what England
has done for and in the Ionian islands during the
half century they have been under her protection,
has not tended to bring out much of the better part
of the national character of the people. This may
be owing to the misgovernment that long left the
whole management of affairs in the hands of the
old oligarchy; and in this England has not done
its duty. In every island I was told that during
this period there had been little justice and no real
protection. The lower classes—the labourers and
the useful workers—were left to the cruel tender
mercies of those whose firm determination it was
to absorb everything. Perhaps it is for this reason
that even now the customs are so little changed; the
dress is so bad, the evidences of material comfort
so small, and the feeling with regard to the benefits
derived from English association so grudgingly admitted. And the people of the Ionian islands, unlike the people of Italy, have not been taught. Certainly, the latter are not yet thoroughly instructed,
although knowledge of every kind is advancing rapidly;
but there are many reasons why the Italians should
have been behind hand in this respect, and none why
the Ionians should. It is clear, that had the islands
been fairly and reasonably governed from the beginning
of our rule, they could not now, after so many years,
exhibit so small a result. A sound and regular system,

if established and adhered to, would doubtless by this time have grown to be a part of themselves. So far, then, the comparison of Ionia with modern Italy is painful and discreditable to the English as a people, and the uncomfortable feeling that this is the case, produces an impression not easily shaken off.

But is it not the case, that the natives of the Ionian Islands, whatever admixture of Greek and Albanian and Venetian they may consist of, are unteachable, unreasonable and ungrateful? I do not think so. That they are for the most part untaught is certain, and that they are thus unable to see even the tendency of what has been done for them that is really good, is also true. Not seeing that they have gained much, they are not very likely to be grateful, or to desire a continuance of the same kind of protecting government. Whether, having been longer in a slavish condition, oppressed by all the hordes, civilised and uncivilised, that have poured over and occupied Europe for two thousand five hundred years, they are more crushed— the iron has more deeply entered their soul—than is the case with the Italians, may be a point worth considering. They have certainly seemed more difficult to lift up, and being formed into a people, they show fewer elements of self-management and the power to govern themselves wisely and well. It is a very serious and interesting question, whether, under these circumstances, the people of the main land of Greece having effected their freedom from the Turks, and then having fallen under a hardly less mischievous

G G

and demoralising oppression under their late king, are now really in a state to benefit by and benefit the inhabitants of the Ionian Islands, who are children in self-government, and who yet by their position, and by the handling and treatment of England, have become rich, and, in a material sense, flourishing. Will the Islands retain their wealth-producing powers? Will the government of Athens keep in check the troublesome orators who have brought about the union? Will the mass of the people, left to the old oligarchy, long endure oppression without resistance? These are the questions to be solved. They are practical questions of no small importance. On their solution must depend the justification of the proposed immediate surrender of the Islands, to form part of a well-governed country, whose capital is Athens.

What have the English Governments done, and what have they left undone in the Ionian Islands during the term of their Protectorate? No doubt much might be said truly and effectively on both sides; but, without going into details, there are some facts that it is right to bear in mind. They have made roads, which the natives hardly seem inclined to keep in repair. They have supplied the towns with water, and they have greatly improved the streets, the public buildings, the harbours, and the defences. They have latterly taught the people to respect and understand justice. They have, as a government, dealt with perfect fairness to all classes; and they have done much to check both lawless violence and that perpetual litigation, which is so common in the south of Europe generally. In all these respects they have attended to the material wants of the people, and deserve credit accordingly.

On the other hand, they have not, till lately, so encouraged general education among all classes as to strengthen the intellectual character of the people. They have, in fact, kept all classes in the condition of children, so that they are not much more fitted to conduct their own affairs than they were half a century ago. By too soon granting them the power to do themselves harm and by checking useful measures, they have altogether stopped the progress that would by this time have altered the whole state of society, and more than ten years were absolutely wasted, owing to the incompetency of Lord High Commissioners appointed to superintend the affairs of the country. The islands were, and are, much more fit to be governed by a dictator, than by a constitution such as they now possess; but had they been brought by degrees to enjoy the freedom granted to them in 1848, it is quite possible that they might by this time have been fitted for it.

The great fault of the people now is the pertinacity with which they give up every other employment, if they can only obtain a place under government, however small. For the chance of doing this, they will sacrifice anything. They are also extremely fond of political influence, and have been known to spend large sums in many of the islands to ensure their return to the Assembly. This kind of bribery might be effectually knocked on the head by dissolving the Assembly, and proceeding to a re-election, at intervals not very distant. It is thought, that if it were not for votes purchased by the agitators, the character of the Assembly would be very different from what it is, and greatly improved. Numerous anecdotes were told me that support this view.

The probable result of annexation with Greece, is a question that cannot be passed over in considering the future of the Ionian Islands. To understand it, a short account of the different classes of society, and their relations to each other, is essential to the English reader who has not visited the islands; and, although something of this has been given here and there in several previous chapters, we may now with advantage consider the whole subject. When the general vote shall be taken of the whole population of the islands, it will be almost unanimous in favour of annexation. It is equally certain, that a very large majority of the votes of the intelligent and instructed persons dwelling in the towns, will be the result of a sort of nervous fear of being suspected of want of patriotism, combined with a sense that if the thing is to be it ought to be accepted willingly. On the other hand, a large majority of the lower classes will certainly vote in total ignorance of the meaning of the withdrawal of British protection, thinking that much of their poor condition must arise from political causes, though it is clearly traceable to causes altogether local. Of course, there are a number of demagogues, and a proportionate number of idle persons who are excited by foolish talking. The demagogues will influence the towns, and mere love of change will have much the same effect in the villages; for there, as well as in towns, there are always more talkers than doers.   There is, however, and this ought not to be overlooked, a national party of instructed and well-informed Greeks, who really and honestly feel that their path in the future lies in union with a country, of which they form a part by language, religion and feeling.

When we come to divide the population of the town of Corfu, we find not more than a third to be composed of Greeks, and of them, only a small number of families are educated and well provided for.   Most of these are remarkably pleasant and open in their manners, and are perhaps among the best specimens of Greeks that could be found.   With few exceptions, they would probably demur to immediate annexation; if asked privately their opinion by persons in whom they had confidence, but few, very few, would openly say so.   The great majority of the Greeks, guided partly by national feeling, and partly by the priests, who desire to be connected with their own people on the main land, will then really desire that the English should leave.

But one-third of the inhabitants are Jews, and have long been well treated, and allowed every liberty. These, if in Greece itself, would certainly not be able to retain their position, and may, perhaps, be subject to persecution, if left where they are under the new Greek government.   Aware of this, they would not of themselves desire a change, but timid by nature, they will hardly dare to oppose it.

The remaining third are foreigners.   Some of them may be expected to advocate change, for the love of change, but they would certainly suffer by the transfer of the island. The large sums annually spent in the islands, especially in Corfu, by the army and navy departments, are supplemented by the private expenses of officers and their families, by the outlay of those numerous English gentlemen who bring their yachts into the Mediterranean, and by the trade arising exclusively from English occupation. At the time of my visit to Corfu, there were four large war ships, the Edgar (carrying the Admiral's flag), the Queen, the Shannon, and the Trafalgar, all in the harbour at the same time, and during my stay one was paid off. A sum of about £3,000 was thus set at the disposal of a parcel of men, most of whom would immediately go on shore and squander the greatest part of their wages. The English sailor has not altered much in this respect, and the importance of an event of this kind happening from time to time in a small town may be imagined. Everything at Corfu is unnaturally dear, a result also clearly traceable to British occupation.

The condition of the villagers, and the method of managing landed property, must be taken into consideration, if we would understand the probable effect of annexation. The tenure of land is peculiarly unfavourable to the working classes, and is in so far unpopular. I speak now of Corfu. In this important island, which could well hold and feed a population of a quarter of a million (a thousand to the square mile), and which, according to historical accounts, has been peopled to this extent, the population, in 1861, excluding foreigners, was 64,220, and the foreigners (almost entirely confined to the town) amounted to an additional 6,500. The total population of the villages in 1860 was 45,214, including foreigners. The surface of the island cannot be estimated to contain less than 125,000 acres of available land, allowing about 20,000 for uncultivable and waste districts. With these figures, it may be thought that there is not sufficient strength for proper cultivation; but, owing to the fact that a very large proportion of the land is occupied by the olive, which is not in any way attended to, except when it becomes necessary to pick up the fallen fruit from the ground, there is really comparatively little done in the way of agriculture.

It is a remarkable fact in Corfu, that almost every grown male in the island has some land, or some rights over land. These consist partly in olive groves, and partly in cultivable lands, which again are either covered with old vines or are arable. There are, however, no divisions of land whatever in the olive groves, and the oldest inhabitant has to be referred to in the case of any doubt as to the proprietorship of particular trees. So much is this property divided, that I was informed by one of the most distinguished advocates of Corfu that in his own estate there were certain trees entirely surrounded by his property, that belonged to some small proprietors. Even the vineyards are not separated by fences, but they are generally small and distinguishable.

The descent of land is to the sons equally, the daughters being provided with a dower secured on the estate. This of itself insures the creation of very

complicated claims on the land.   These are multiplied
by the necessity that generally exists for the cultivator
to raise capital, by hypothecating a part or the whole
of his share.   Thus the land becomes overloaded
with burdens; and practically, in every village there
are a few monied men who hold possession of the land
by their claims arising from small loans.   The actual
cultivator is completely in the power of such men,
who are said to take undue advantage of their position,
and become the real masters and managers of everything.

Owing to the universal division of property, no one
in the island is without a resource.   Even those who
live entirely in the towns, and keep shops or carry on
the various professions, are all land owners, or hold
claims on land; and even the very poorest and most
miserable villager is provided for after a fashion, when
he has no means of obtaining work from without and
is not in the receipt of wages.   But these poor proprietors may be said to work with millstones round their
necks.   It cannot be supposed that they are very well
disposed towards those by whom they consider themselves aggrieved and persecuted.

Let us now consider the probable result of a sudden
change on this part of the population of Corfu.   The
protection being removed, and the country left to itself
for a time, the villagers will soon feel that the firm
hand they have long been accustomed to is no longer
there; and they will ask themselves, whether the time
has not come for them to look after their own interests.
There seems little doubt, that one of the early results

of this change of dynasty, if hastily made, may be a rising of the villagers against the small capitalists; and that in this way anarchy and the elements of a servile war may be introduced, and help to complicate the difficulties that will be felt in combining the Greek and island customs and institutions. ·

Another almost equally dangerous and troublesome result may probably follow, and may not be long in commencing. The warlike and half savage tribes on the opposite coast of Albania have always shown themselves ready to take advantage of circumstances, and will hardly let slip such an opportunity of booty as will be presented, if Corfu is left without British bayonets. In every age, from the earliest time to the present century, a change of dynasty in the islands has been marked by incursions of these neighbours. The distance is so small and the temptation so great, that the result is almost inevitable.

What I have here said with regard to Corfu will apply in some measure to the other islands. There is, perhaps, little or no danger of attack from without, so far as they are concerned; but the squabbles between the peasantry and the rich capitalists cannot be expected to terminate without much disturbance of the public peace. How far the formation of a national guard may keep down any tendency to riot on the part of the lower classes, remains to be seen. Cephalonia has generally proved the most permanently-troublesome and stubborn of the islands; and Zante that which most easily takes offence.

Such are among the reasons why, for the sake of

the Ionian people, and with the feeling that it is a duty imposed upon the English at the present time to judge and act for these people, at least to a certain extent, it would seem unfair and undesirable that the protection should too suddenly cease. There should be a very well established government at Athens, and a very clear understanding as to how the islands will be managed. A good and effective national guard should not only exist, but the people should have confidence in its strength before the exchange is made.

Another question remains to be considered:—how far it is for the interest of England that these islands, which have for fifty years been under her care, should cease to occupy her attention. Practically, the granting the constitution of 1848, by giving over the management of affairs to men, many of whom are mere political agitators, has greatly shaken the hold we had previously possessed. This measure also diminished greatly the power of the Lord High Commissioner. The roads, made under the rule of Sir Thomas Maitland, at a time when the Lord High Commissioner may be said to have been an absolute monarch, have hardly been kept even in decent repair since the new constitution; and although this year a sum has been granted to improve them, it has only been after a hard struggle.* The marshes, which might have been drained at a comparatively small expense, and with the greatest benefit to the health of the whole population, are now worse than ever; and in all other matters, the per-

---

* The last money voted for the roads was thrown away in open jobbing for election purposes.

mission and power to govern themselves has resulted in a falling off in the prosperity of the islands. It is to be hoped that the experience thus gained in self government may bear fruit when the people are united to Greece; but it is more to be hoped than expected, if one may judge by the recent behaviour of the Assembly.

As a military station, it has been said that Corfu, and the islands generally, are of great value. That Corfu is a valuable naval station, has never been doubted or denied; but that it is really wanted by or is necessary to England, has not been proved. Probably, one great reason of its importance to us, lies in the fact, that in the hands of an enemy it might be both troublesome and mischievous. If Greece is strong enough to keep up the fortifications and occupy the forts, it could not be in better hands than her's; but if Corfu, in the occupation of Greece, might become French or Russian at short notice, it would certainly be better that all the strong places should be dismantled and destroyed.

There is nothing in the other islands that affect England in a military or naval sense. With a few cruisers in the eastern Mediterannean, piracy is kept down and all the coast kept in order. There would seem to be nothing but Corfu worthy of consideration for purposes of offence or defence.

CHAPTER XVI.

I HAVE not given, in the preceding pages, any general account of the Ionian Islands as a group, because, although connected by government, they are singularly distinct in almost all points,—physical, historical, and political. They are not near each other; and though, with the exception of Cerigo, they seem to form an insular system belonging to the western shores of the Albanian and Grecian land, this system includes also, geographically, though not ethnologically, the Dalmatian islands to the head of the Adriatic.

But having described each island separately, I ought, perhaps, in a concluding chapter, to put together a few remarks that apply to all; and at the present moment, when the islands are about to transfer their allegiance and become an integral portion of a new Greek kingdom, this seems the more necessary.

I have said little of the mediæval and modern history of the islands, although, as the Venetian occupation and government have greatly influenced the population and habits of the people, the reader should be aware, to some extent, of the principal facts concerning that period. The modern history may be said to date in each island from a time when there was hardly any remaining population—the ancient inhabitants having been swept away, partly because of the Ottoman persecutions and partly because of the facilities for piracy the islands once afforded. The recent history is that of the last half century, since they have been under British protection. All these histories have been written; and the ancient history, though obscure, has not been neglected. It has too little to do with the present state of the islands to affect the present question, and where of special interest, it has already been alluded to in previous chapters.

The society of the islands, when they were first brought under English management, seems to have involved in each a separate oligarchy, consisting of the old Venetian families, and a *plebs*, made up of a mixed race of Albanians, Greeks from various islands, Sclaves from the east and Italians from the west coast of the Adriatic. All these were hardly so much mingled as discordantly placed together in the same locality. Villages rarely contained more than a few families.

Strangers in blood would hardly associate. Practically, law was neglected and set aside, if even it could be said to exist; and justice had little to do with law, which, if used at all, was a weapon in the hands of the rich to grind and destroy the poor. The whole of the power was in the hands of a few ruling families, and was jealously preserved by every means available.

It was no easy task that the first Lord High Commissioner found set before him, when he undertook to give a constitution to a people who did not connect with the idea of liberty one such practical notion as with us is considered essential to its very nature. Liberty to oppress and do wrong on the part of the upper classes—liberty to murder, and rob, and defame, on that of the lower. This was all that was understood by the sacred word. What Sir Thomas Maitland did was probably the best that could be done. He sketched out a system capable of being worked at the time, and likely to elevate the tone of the masses and curb the greediness of the ruling families. A certain amount of education he secured for all classes; he gave a certain appearance of power, hardly admitting of much wrong being done; and above all, he insisted on strict justice, at least in the higher courts. These matters once secured, the people, he thought, would soon become fit for free institutions. So long as this scheme was properly administered it answered its purpose thoroughly; and though not without errors, it at any rate worked well. But it was not always properly administered; for some commissioners were careless and some were crotchetty. At last came the revolutionary fever of 1848; and, to a people barely rising into an appreciation of the nature of law and right, it was then thought fit to entrust the task of governing themselves. , That this was an error, has since been generally admitted; but it was not seen till too late. There is little wonder that the civilisation of the islands was thus thrown back a quarter of a century, and that the original system, badly carried out as it was, made way for one theoretically superior, but practically very inferior.

Unfortunate as the change was, the evil was greatly increased by the speedy removal of its promoter, Lord Seaton, who, being an able and a firm man, might in time have guided the weak and trembling hands of the Republic in the right way. The appointment of a new Lord High Commissioner, little accustomed to govern, but especially unacquainted with this people and their history, resulted in the commission of a series of political blunders, which greatly interfered with the material progress of the islands, and even threatened to destroy the very foundations of society. It has taken some years to put matters once more in a fair course; and perhaps, after another generation, had the British rule continued, provided always that it had been administered judiciously, the people might reasonably and hopefully have been left to themselves.

The nature of the British rule, and the constitution under which the islands is now governed, is very peculiar, and appears highly complex. Under ordinary circumstances it works better than theoretically could be thought possible; but still it is both complex and

cumbrous.   It consists of a separate municipal government for each island, the head of the municipality representing the whole body, and controlled by an official
representative of the Lord High Commissioner, who
is called the Resident.   Without the sanction of the
Resident, the acts of the municipal council are absolutely void and of no force.

In each island the government is local; but there is
a control in all matters of expenditure and general
policy, exercised by the 'General Assembly,' which
consists of representatives of all the islands, elected from
time to time, according to the constitution.   This also
is controlled by the Lord High Commissioner, who, in
addition to his higher position as Commissioner, is also
the head of the local government, or Resident of
Corfu.   The position of the Lord High Commissioner
is one of great dignity and power; but the power is of
a restrictive rather than active kind.   He can do much
by withholding his assent to measures he considers undesirable; but he can hardly insist on the carrying out
of any measure for the general good.   The voting of
the public money, and the system of general taxation,
are matters concerning which he may suggest, but can
do nothing.   He has the appointment of those of the
law officers, including judges, who are natives of the
islands, but there are also two judges appointed from
England, and these, of course, are quite independent.
He does not interfere with military matters, there
being always an officer of high standing in command
of the army stationed in the islands; and, although the
General Assembly can do nothing without him, and he

has great power in many ways in the central government, there is yet a President of the Republic, elected for a term of years, and occupying a high and independent position.

It will be evident, then, that with so many independent heads, it is sometimes difficult to know where the power really resides. The Parliament is sufficiently free to allow of its members to abuse the whole world, and England in particular ; it can also interfere with and put a total stop to all public business of every kind, and render the whole population of the islands dissatisfied. Its power to do mischief is checked by the Lord High Commissioner's veto, which is absolute, and affects all acts passed and votes agreed to. In this way some of the worst mischief—that which is positive—can be prevented. Still, the presence of three kings, under such circumstances, in one small country, partakes rather of the complications of some of the eastern governments than the simplicity found convenient in Western Europe; and it seems by no means unlikely, as it has been found not uncommon, that affairs should be sometimes brought to a dead lock, and require the interference of the *Deus ex machinâ.*

One thing is clear, that the Lord High Commissioner, to carry on at all a government so complicated, must combine much firmness, temper and knowledge of human nature. Each of the seven separate republics represented in the General Assembly, has its own municipal council and system of local government, which must be superintended from head quarters; and thus, in addition to his duties in Corfu, the chief civil officer has to keep himself perfectly acquainted with what is going on every where around, and to see that in no case is the general system interfered with. This is managed by a method not less peculiar and anomalous than that adopted in Corfu for the general government. Each island has its Resident, its commanding officer, and its Regent—nominally the heads of the political, military and civil department; but really by no means so simple, and, in fact, affording a close parallel to the central system. Corfu has, indeed, its Regent as well as the President of the republic, and the functions and duties are altogether distinct; but, in the other islands, the Regent may be said to represent the President.

The position of the Residents in the islands is one of responsibility and power. It is true, that like the Lord High Commissioner himself, they are unable to force the people under their rule to do what is right, but they can altogether stop any commencement of wrong; and, by taking advantage of the times, when prudent, sensible and right meaning men occupy the higher posts in the various municipalities, they can bring on and carry the measures they think advisable. They may acquire extreme influence; and, of course, on the other hand, if unpopular, or inattentive to the peculiar character of the people, they may be unable to move. They not only possess an absolute veto on every measure, but the *procès-verbal* of each day's proceedings of the municipality must be signed by the Resident within the day in order that it should become valid. By merely delaying this signature, therefore, the acts of the municipality for the day are annulled. It is evident, that constant and extreme watchfulness on the part of the functionary are necessary, and that no opportunity should be lost. There is, as might be expected, an inveterate tendency to jobbing in all corporate matters, for in this way alone many people understand the advantage of possessing official appointments. This is the case, not only in the Ionian Islands, but in much larger and more important communities. It is a tendency, which, if checked at an early stage, does no harm; but, as it crops out on every occasion, the work of the Resident, who must look forward and see the probable consequences of every move, is certainly no sinecure. On the other hand, when he is firm and kind, the respect of the people has no bounds. All classes are quite clever enough to see what goes on, but few of them would have firmness to act in the right way; and there is fear, that when the change of government is effected, and Greeks occupy the highest and most influential posts, the result will at first be very unsatisfactory.

The Residents take rank immediately after the Lord Commissioner, and possess also local military rank, as Lieutenant-generals. They wear an official dress on state occasions, and occasionally hold levees.

The police system of the islands, as at present established, is simple, and very efficacious. By its agency, all brigandage, and almost all crimes of any magnitude, are completely held in check, and apparently without exciting invidious feelings among the lower classes.

Each village, from a very ancient period, has been accustomed to admit the authority of a Chief, who, under various names in different languages and dialects, is to a certain extent responsible for the good conduct of the whole community. This chief is now appointed from head quarters in each island, and is the most respectable and often the most wealthy person of the village. He has the right to carry arms, and is generally seen with a large knife in his belt. He is even allowed a gun, which for excellent reasons is refused to the common people. Formerly he had pistols, but this is no longer permitted. Under this Chief, or *Primate*, who does little, and receives no pay, beyond a few fees on the transfer of property, there is a Captain of fifty, who is the practical head of whatever police force may be needed. This officer is often not a native of the village; and, in case of need, his services are at the command of government. Under him again are sergeants—*Dec-archs*—or commanders of ten, of whom as many are appointed as each village may require, and the ten men are the common policemen. They are not always needed, or drawn out, but they are always understood to be available. The sergeant is paid according to his duty. He has to escort prisoners, and see to the effective working of the system.

Practically, the number of police is small, but theoretically there are means at hand for the establishment of a very complete system, which could be organised with rapidity. The regular police constables wear a uniform, and are drilled as soldiers. They are considered to form a trustworthy force, available for any public disturbances, and are believed to be perfectly well affected to the protecting government.

Before the establishment of this police system, the islands were almost always in a state of disturbance and misrule. Under it, they have been quiet and orderly.

The passport system and the system of police-passes in the Ionian Islands is peculiar and very troublesome, especially in these days when passports are being everywhere else abolished. It is too bad, that a British officer, stationed at Corfu, cannot leave the island to go to England, *viâ* Italy, where no passport is required, without obtaining a passport, for which he is charged heavily, and then obtaining the *visa* of the Italian consul and the police authorities, who also claim their fees. Certainly, the Italian consul should either not be allowed to grant *visas* or should be refused the power of charging half a dollar for this utterly useless and unmeaning form. It is easily understood, that for Austria, where the system still remains, though greatly simplified, certain formalities should be necessary; but why the owners of the Austrian steamers should be so particular in this respect, it is not easy to say. Practically, the whole affair is a complete farce, as far as any security is concerned. The passport is not given up to the steward of the steamer till after the passenger is on board and at sea, and is returned without being opened or looked at by the health officer, who first comes on board at Ancona. It is purely a fiction, carried on for the benefit of the consuls and police officers, and encouraged by the steamboat authorities. It is not less clearly a scheme well adapted to disgust and annoy travellers, and prevent them from taking the Ancona route.

The system of police-passes adopted in the islands is discreditable to all concerned. By them, difficulties are thrown in the way of intercommunication amongst the islands, which cannot but be injurious. That the traveller should not be able to go freely and without inquiry from one part of a small group of islands to another, all being under the same general government, is so unreasonable, that no rational account or explanation of it can be looked for. It is eminently discreditable to the British government and to the senate that such a state of things should have gone on so long without inquiry. The press is free. Any one may, in a public newspaper, make any statement he thinks fit; but the traveller is not free; and every person, whether merely a traveller for pleasure or engaged in any inquiry or business, becomes very sensible to the annoyance hence arising.

It is a characteristic of the islanders that they will not, if they can possibly avoid it, pay any direct tax. The tax gatherer is unknown; and it has always been found almost impossible even to collect the rents of property belonging to the State. The charge made for the supply of water by the Aqueduct in Corfu can scarcely be collected, except from the garrison and a few public institutions; and the same is the case throughout. The people have never been accustomed to direct taxation—even for lighting the streets, maintenance of roads, or other purposes of public utility.

The revenue of the islands for the twenty years has

averaged about £172,000, and almost the whole burden is thrown on the agricultural interests. Thus,
the export duty on oil and currants alone has averaged
upwards of £60,000. The remaining revenue, except
£5,000 obtained from the fees of the health officer, is
chiefly raised by the monopoly of salt and gunpowder,
the sale of stamps, and various import duties. The
post office establishment and the port dues must also
be added.

The revenue has been for many years somewhat
smaller than the expenditure; and a total debt exists
of about £300,000. Of this, however, one third, being
arrears of military contribution to the protecting power,
pays no interest; and a sum, at least as large as the
balance, is owing by individuals to the Government,
though it is not perhaps very likely to be paid. Owing
to the variable yield of the crops the revenue is subject to a corresponding change. Thus, an extraordinary crop in 1858 enabled the Government to pay off
£30,000 of debt.

The following are the principal branches of public
revenue and expenditure for the year 1860, a year
in which the income was considerably below the
average, owing to the smallness of the oil and currant
crops. Import duties:—grain £23,218, general mer-
chandise £30,993, total £60,838. Export duties:
—oil £27,578, currants £27,078, wine £995, total
£55,651. Of other duties the stamps yielded £11,806,
and sundries £12,560. The whole revenue was
£140,855. Of the expenditure the civil establishment, including interest of debt, cost £62,470, the
judicial establishments, courts of justice, police, and

gaols £25,042, education £12,880, and public works
£2,671. The annual charge for military expenditure
is £25,000. The total expenditure of the year was
£151,187, showing a deficiency of more than £10,000.
In the same year the municipal revenue was £15,837
and the expenditure 9,980.

The following statement of the various imports from
England into the Ionian Islands, in the year 1861,
will be useful, as indicating the nature of the trade,
and in some measure the wants of the islanders.

	Declared value.
Apparel	£18,087
Coals	16,324
Cottons and cotton yarn . .	188,760
Linen goods	2,901
Woollen goods . . .	17,794
Hardware	4,906
Iron of all kinds . . .	3,154
Soda	2,417
Sugar	9,190
Stationery	2,116
All other goods . . .	30,921
	£296,570

On the other hand, the trade of the islands with England exhibits a large but not equal value of exports.
The annexed statement of the exports and their value,
for the five years ending 1861, will be of interest for
comparison, and is instructive, as showing the extreme
changes that occur from year to year.

Tabular Statement of Articles Exported from the Ionian Islands to England from the Years 1857 to 1861, both inclusive.

Articles.		Quantities.					Computed Value.				
		1857.	1858.	1859.	1860.	1861.	1857.	1858.	1859.	1860.	1861.
Corn (Maize)	Qrs.	17,649	31,211	3,635	6,639	2,938	£31,427	50,319	£5,159	£11,508	£4,705
Currants	Cwt.	82,863	89,458	106,385	158,378	156,993	153,715	114,862	150,961	182,392	164,284
Olive Oil	Tuns	185	3,489	869	1,214	695	9,688	151,676	39,458	68,297	38,620
Fustic	Tons	31	13	41	37	34	186	66	562	325	248
Valonia	Tons	—	—	—	—	80	—	—	—	—	1,020
All other Articles .		.	.	.	.	.	13,555	5,666	3,500	5,209	4,280
							£208,571	£322,589	£199,640	£267,731	£213,157

NOTE.—Besides the quantity of currants exported to England there is about an equal quantity sent to the United States, and a large supply to Germany. Very much is also smuggled out of the islands. The oil goes chiefly to the East. Much of it is also smuggled out of the country. The large export duty is evidently the cause of this and much other smuggling.

TABULAR STATEMENT OF THE PRINCIPAL STATISTICS OF THE IONIAN ISLANDS, FOR THE YEAR 1860.

	Area in Square Miles.	Total Population.	Maritime Traffic.			Produce.						Live Stock.§			
			Vessels.		Tons.	Corn in Bushels.*	Oil in Barrls.†	Currants in lbs.	Wine in Barrels.	Flax in lbs.	Salt‡ in lbs.	Horses.	Horned Cattle.	Sheep.	Goats.
CORFU . . .	227	69,414	Entered 1,103	Cleared 1,110	350,965 / 353,275	83,609	12,254	—	33,875	23,230	8,748	3,609	4,652	20,959	27,739
SANTA MAURA . .	156	20,672	Entered 120	Cleared 121	7,178 / 7,294	105,500	3,030	70,000	56,060	11,000	—	1,690	1,620	32,000	23,600
ITHACA . . .	44	11,756	Entered 74	Cleared 88	7,995 / 9,614	15,520	3,220	697	6,350	14,000	—	320	210	6,365	7,510
CEPHALONIA . .	311	73,404	Entered 1,408	Cleared 1,461	61,866 / 64,736	89,480	12,980	16,180,000	41,180	25,940	200	3,310	1,760	53,980	33,400
ZANTE . . .	161	38,438	Entered 651	Cleared 657	81,124 / 82,389	32,868	31,560	14,000,000	10,374	4,745	60,000	3,084	1,232	13,430	16,708
CERIGO . . .	116	13,742	Entered 193	Cleared 194	2,831 / 3,093	77,000	3,000	200	500	5,000	2,000	1,150	900	1,950	3,000

NOTES.

* Chiefly Indian corn.　† The yield of oil varies so greatly in different years, that this must not be looked on as at all an average. I have no means of obtaining better information. Paxo in 1860 yielded 3,509 barrels.　‡ The return of salt made in Santa Maura is not given. It is, however, I believe, much larger than in Zante.　§ There is no return of the number of swine in the islands.

N.B. The following are the average prices of the principal products, &c. Wheat, 7s. to 7s. 6d. per bushel. Indian corn, 3s. 3d. to 5s. Oats, 2s. 4d. to 3s. Currants, 10¼s. to 140s. per 1,000 lbs. weight. Oil, 43s. to 50s. per barrel. Wine, 10s. to 20s. per barrel. Salt, 6d. to 1s. per bushel. Horned cattle, £10 each. Horses, £7. Sheep, 30s. Goats, 15s. Swine, 50s.

The import duties on cotton and woollen goods are 8 per cent. ad valorem to unprivileged, and 7 per cent. to privileged flags. The export duty on oil and currants is 18 per cent., and on wine 6 per cent. There are also small additional export and import duties for special purposes.

The value of money in the Ionian Islands is very high. Eight per cent. is the lowest rate of interest under the most favourable circumstances; and even small loans are not made on these terms, without many qualifications and the best security to double the amount. But this is nothing, compared to the extent of the usury that goes on in the country, and especially in the smaller islands. One per cent. per week is not at all unusual; and one per cent. per day is a rate that has very often been charged and paid. It is clear, that so long as this is the case, no healthy investment can succeed. Those who have money and can obtain these rates will lend money in other ways, where the return, however promising, is not only less certain but less considerable. It is easy to understand how these usurious rates are obtained. A small cultivator comes to the monied man with a cargo of oil in prospect. He must sell; and the other makes a bid. In the course of a very short time the crop will be got in and the oil sold; but it is rare that so much as five dollars are offered for what will probably fetch ten—and four, or even three, are much more usual.

It has long been desired to introduce a Government system of banking, to enable the lower classes to obtain advances on their crops at something like reasonable terms. It would be desirable, but probably involve difficulties; and the difficulty is partly, though not entirely, met by the Ionian Bank. By this institution, which has a branch in each of the islands, loans are made on profitable, but not usurious terms; but they hardly seem to reach the small proprietor, whose knowledge of business is very small.

Census of the Population of the Ionian Islands taken in the Year 1857.

Islands.		Females.		Males.		Foreigners.		Total.	Total of each Island.
CORFU	Town	5,711		5,718		4,492		15,921	
	Suburbs	3,567		3,211		881		7,659	
	Country	22,376		19,434		766		42,576	
	Islets	865	32,519	890	29,253	19	6,158	1,774	67,930
CEPHALONIA	Argostoli	4,388		3,657		1,226		9,271	
	Lixuri	3,610		3,195		90		6,895	
	Country	30,662	38,660	24,414	31,266	694	2,010	55,770	71,936
ZANTE	Town	7,098		6,656		272		14,026	
	Country	12,690	19,788	10,361	17,017	76	348	23,127	37,153
SANTA MAURA	Town	2,337		2,197		45		4,579	
	Suburbs	833		724		,,		1,557	
	Country	7,523	10,693	6,668	9,589	,,	45	14,191	20,327
ITHACA	Town and Suburbs	2,349		2,014		6		4,369	
	Country	3,635	5,984	3,476	5,490	,,	6	7,111	11,480
CERIGO	Town	705		676		12		1,393	
	Country	6,414	7,119	5,415	6,091	34	46	11,863	13,256
PAXO	Town	217		187		24		404	
	Country	2,151		2,056		,,		4,231	
	Antipaxo	57	2,425	50	2,293	,,	24	107	4,742
			117,188		100,999		8,637		226,824

Of the population of the Ionian Islands, the annexed table will give an idea at the time of the last complete census in 1857. Since that time there has been but little movement, and the facts of the case, together with a statement of some of the probable causes, will be found in the body·of the work, in speaking of the condition of the principal islands. I append, however, a statement with regard to the population of Corfu in successive years, for which I am indebted to the Secretary to the Government; but it must be understood that the means of obtaining an accurate result are not very satisfactory.

NATIVE POPULATION OF CORFU.*

	Males.	Females.	Births.	Deaths.
1857—Census . . .	32,755	29,490	1,957	1,484
1858 . ·	33,034	29,769	1,894	1,336
1859	33,473	30,208	2,140	1,262
1860—Census . . .	33,520	30,129	1,963	1,402
1861	33,805	30,415	1,854	1,295

The population of the other islands is, perhaps, increasing more rapidly than that of Corfu, but it is certainly not moving as it ought. There are many reasons for this, physical, social and political, most

* The population returns for the years 1858, 1859, and 1861, are rather estimates than proper census returns. The return for 1860 was also imperfect, but more complete than the others.

of which have already been alluded to in the accounts given of the various islands. It is not likely that the islands will ever again be crowded, as they appear to have been in the early days of European civilization; but there is no reason why their population should not be multiplied many times under a good government, and with a rich and contented people.

With these remarks I conclude. It is evident that the islands are rich in natural advantages. They have a soil that appears, indeed, rocky and barren, but a sky, under which the vine will bear abundant fruit when planted even in loose stones—where the smallest amount of labour is repaid a hundred fold, and whose ground is covered with trees which yield a profitable crop without labour. With corn and wine and oil in abundance, growing a fruit also, of which they almost possess a monopoly, having a coast indented with innumerable little bays and creeks, situated in the great highway of the European nations, having a population wealthy and intelligent, these islands cannot fail to exercise a considerable influence on Greece and the Greeks, when forming part of the United Kingdom.

That this influence may be for the benefit of both— that Greece, following the example set in the islands, may construct roads, spend public money on public improvements, administer equal justice to all, and encourage those means by which the islands have grown rich and intelligent under English auspices—that the good that is in each may favourably react on the other, and such evil and weakness as interferes with progress

may be avoided, will be the anxious desire of all Eng-
lishmen, who will long continue to watch the new
kingdom with eyes of affection, enhanced by those ties
of blood that already unite the crown of Greece with
the dearest hopes of England.

Note on a Leucadian Coin.

In the island of Santa Maura, among a few
other coins and objects of antiquity I was enabled to
collect, there is one coin of considerable interest. I
am indebted to my friend, the Rev. Churchill Babington, for the following *interim* account:—

" The coin is of considerable interest, and not yet
published. It reads—

Obv.—AVT. K. M. ANT. ΓΟΡΔΙΑΝΟC. Head of Gordian III., laureated to right.

Rev.—OKOKΛΙΕΩΝ. Fortune standing, holding a
rudder in her right hand, and a cornucopiæ in her left.—
Æ., size 6 of Mionnet's scale.

Mionnet (vol. iv. p. 864) has a coin with the same
legend of the reverse, but with Cybele for type; also
of Gordian III. On this he remarks—'Cette médaille
est bien conservée, cependant on ne trouve aucuns vestiges de la lettre M qui devrait être l'initiale de la
legende.' He refers it to Mococlia, in Phrygia, and
describes from Vaillant's Numismata Græca, a coin of
Gordian III., having for the legend of the reverse
MONOKΛΙΕΩΝ, and Cybele for type.

It seems to me almost certain that Vaillant's legend is wrongly read, and that there was no M. As Ilium is the substantive from 'Ιλιέων, so I should suppose that Ococlium is the name of the city which struck the coin. Its existence appears to be unknown, except from the coins, and its position is consequently very doubtful."

Mr. Churchill Babington has since discovered that Mr. Borrell has a paper in the Numismatic Chronicle on the coins inscribed OKOKΛIEΩN, and that the coin in question is described among them from an original in the British Museum. The specimens have not yet been compared; but as that now obtained is exceedingly perfect, it may help to throw light on the question involved.

THE END.

LEWIS AND SON, PRINTERS, SWAN BUILDINGS, MOORGATE STREET.

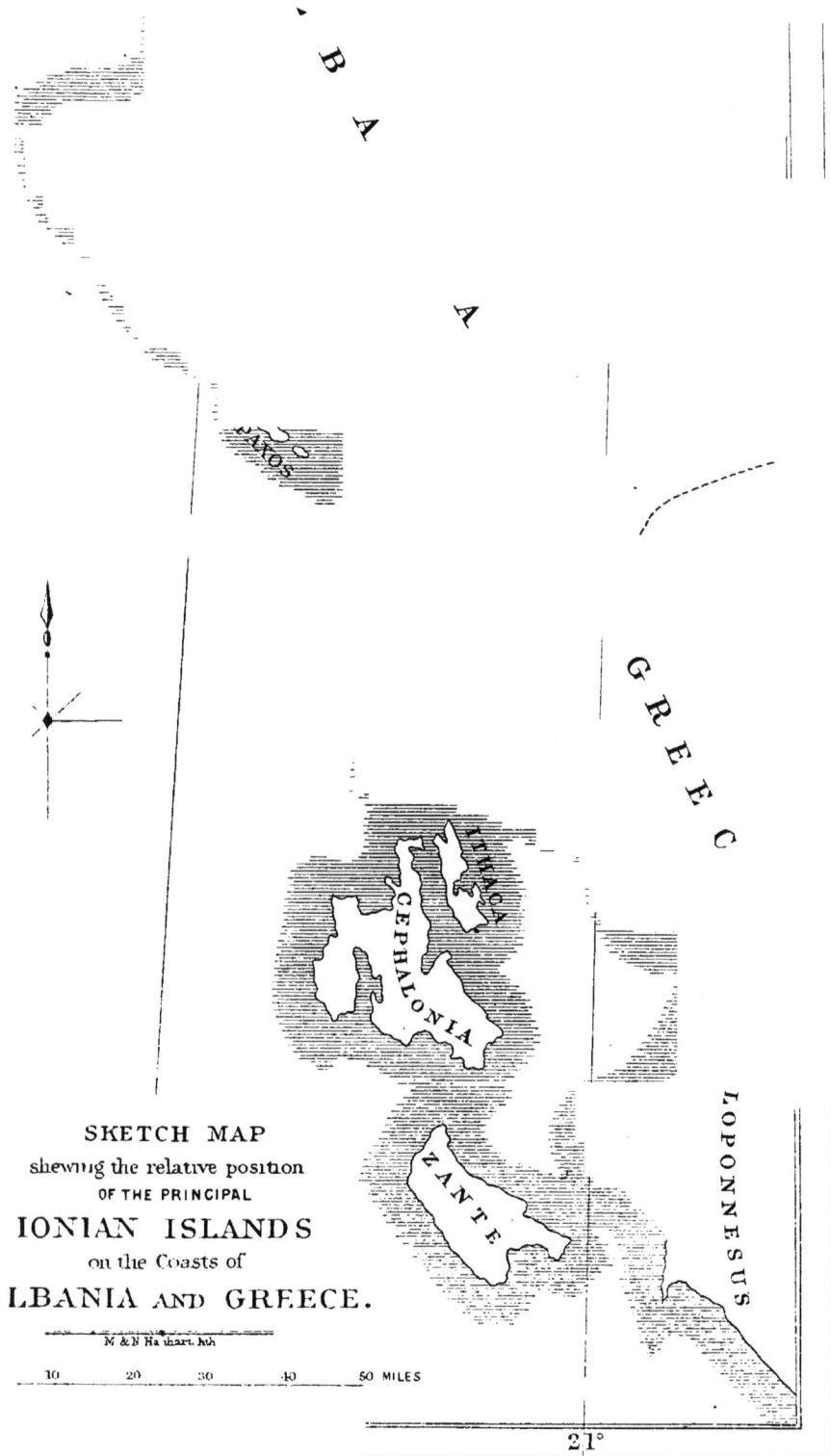

SKETCH MAP
shewing the relative position
OF THE PRINCIPAL
IONIAN ISLANDS
on the Coasts of
LBANIA AND GREECE.

M & N Hanhart. lith

10   20   30   40   50 MILES

Lightning Source UK Ltd.
Milton Keynes UK
UKHW010842021118
331644UK00014B/383/P

9 781331 985549